Uma Swaminathan became an expert on herbs and spices while growing up in a south Indian family and then later studying about the medicinal use of plants in ancient cultures for her degree in cultural anthropolgy at Rutgers University, New Jersey.

Her father was a research scientist and biologist who taught Uma the healing properties of plants from a scientific perspective. On the other hand, Uma's mother passed down an ancient tradition from her forebears on the art of preparing medicinal and healthy recipes.

At the age of 16, Uma learned to fly monoplanes and got her private pilot's license. She studied classical Indian dances and is a prolific painter. She had the opportunity to perform Indian dance all over the world and was honored by Princess Hitachi in Japan.

HEALING WITH
Herbs

Ancient Ayurvedic Wisdom for Health and Longevity

Uma Swaminathan

JAICO PUBLISHING HOUSE

Ahmedabad Bangalore Bhopal Bhubaneswar Chennai
Delhi Hyderabad Kolkata Lucknow Mumbai

Disclaimer:
This book is not intended to provide medical advice, diagnosis or treatment. What the author gives you is her life's experience of an ancient way of living with herbs, spices and medicinal recipes. The reader is advised to check with a certified physician before starting any new program.

Photography: Uma Swaminathan
Following photos courtesy of George E. Mathew: p. 104, p. 212, p. 220
Photography: Sreedevi Kashi

Published by Jaico Publishing House
A-2 Jash Chambers, 7-A Sir Phirozshah Mehta Road
Fort, Mumbai - 400 001
jaicopub@jaicobooks.com
www.jaicobooks.com

© Uma Swaminathan

HEALING WITH HERBS
ISBN 978-81-8495-822-5

First Jaico Impression: 2016
Second Jaico Impression: 2017

No part of this book may be reproduced or utilized in any form or by any means, electronic or mechanical including photocopying, recording or by any information storage and retrieval system, without permission in writing from the publishers.

Printed by
SRG Traders Pvt. Ltd.
B-41, Sector 67, Noida 201301, U.P.

Because my daughter asked me...

She presented me with a notebook so that I may write down my ancient recipes and stories. This book was originally intended for her. But she was so excited by what I had written, she insisted that I publish this book for all of you. To an imaginative and talented cook, baker, yoga practitioner and marathon runner, I am proud to dedicate this book to my daughter Sreedevi.

Contents

Introduction 13

I.
An Exploration into Ancient Traditions 17
Ayurveda, Siddha, Ancient Practices, Ancient Practices of Purification, Yoga, Life Stages, Kolam.

II.
The Transforming Herbs 35
Almond, Aloe Vera, Asafoetida, Bermuda Grass, Black Nightshade, Black Pepper, Long Pepper, Long Pepper Root, Camphor, Cardamom, Carom, Red Chillies, Cinnamon, Clove, Coconut, Coriander, Cumin, Curry Leaf, Edible Stemmed Vine, Eucalyptus, Fennel, Fenugreek, Galangal, Garlic, Ginger, Holy Basil, Indian Gooseberry, Indian Pennywort, Lemon, Lemongrass, Mustard, Neem, Nutmeg, Palm, Prickly Nightshade, Saffron, Sesame, Stone Apple, Tamarind, Triphala, Turmeric, Vetiver, Water Hyssop, Winter Cherry.

III.
The Power of Scent 129
Jasmine, Lotus, Fragrant Screwpine, Persian Violet, Rose, Bulletwood, Manoranjitham.

IV.
Recipes that Rejuvenate and Make You Radiant 135
Water Hyssop, Henna, Hibiscus, False Daisy, Shangupushpam, Eye Makeup, Eye Mask, Cleansing Scrubs, Shikakai, Face Masks, Depilatory, Oils for Massage.

V.
Energizing Food Enhancers

Cooking Oils 143

Honey 147

Sugar 149

Salt 153

Grains 155
Rice, Wheat, Oats, Barley.

Millets 159
Finger Millet, Foxtail Millet, Pearl Millet, Barnyard Millet, Kodo, Little Millet, Sorghum.

Legumes 163
Red Gram Lentil, Black Gram, Mung Bean, Bengal Gram, Peanut, Kidney Bean, Chickpea.

Tropical Fruits 167
Mango, Banana, Guava, Papaya, Sapodilla, Jackfruit, Pomegranate, Pineapple, Soursop.

Tropical Vegetables 177
Ash Gourd, Snake Gourd, Pumpkin, Bitter Gourd, Ridge Gourd, Okra, Eggplant, Beans.

Root Vegetables 183
Colocasia, Elephant Yam.

Tropical Greens 184
Drumstick Green, Spinach, Amaranth, *Aathi Keerai, Molai Keerai, Arai Keerai, Siru Keerai*.

VI.
Classic Recipes for Vitality and Health 187

Drinks 188
Asafoetida Buttermilk Drink, Ginger Buttermilk, Bermuda Grass Drink, Cardamom Drink, Cardamom Holy Basil Tea, Clove Cinnamon Tomato Drink, Edible Stemmed Vine Drink, Galangal Drink, Sweet Ginger Drink, Ginger Clove Drink, Lemongrass Ginger Tea, Lemongrass Drink, Cumin Tamarind Drink, Coconut Lemongrass Drink, Cumin Drink, Tamarind Drink, Tamarind Sweet Drink, Carom Betel Drink, Carom Neem Drink, Carom Drink, Almond Milk, Turmeric Milk with Black Pepper, Turmeric Cardamom Drink.

Payasam and Sweets 197
Milk *Payasam*, Camphor *Payasam*, Mango *Payasam*, Oats *Payasam*, Almond *Halwa*, Sesame *Ladoos*, Ginger Honey Candy, Foxtail Millet Sweet *Pongal*, Finger Millet *Halwa*.

Legiyam 201
Black Pepper *Legiyam*, Cumin *Legiyam*.

Main Dishes 203
Idli, Dosai, Rice *Adai*, Legume *Adai*, Yogurt Rice, Lemon Rice, Pearl Millet *Kanjee*, Pearl Millet *Adai*, Little Millet *Pongal*, Oats *Kanjee*.

Sundal 209
Black-eyed Bean *Sundal*, Sweet *Sundal*.

Sambar varieties 213
Sambar Powder, Daily *Sambar*, Ground Masala *Sambar*, Prickly Nightshade - Fenugreek *Sambar* (*Sundakkai Mendiya Kuzhambu*), Pepper *Sambar*

(*Milagu Kuzhambu*), Concentrated *Sambar* (*Vetha Kuzhambu*), Pitlai *Sambar*, Buttermilk *Sambar*, Mango Buttermilk *Sambar*.

Rasam varieties   221
Rasam Powder
Black Pepper *Rasam*
Split Red Gram *Rasam*
Long Pepper *Rasam*/*Kandathipili Rasam*
Cumin *Rasam*/*Jeera Rasam*
Lemon *Rasam*/*Elimichampazham Rasam*
Lemon *Rasam* with Ginger
Neem Flower *Rasam*/*Vepampoo Rasam*

Pachidi and Kosamalli Salad   227
Tomato *Pachidi*, Cucumber *Pachidi*, Gooseberry *Pachidi*, Stone Apple *Pachidi*, Mango *Pachidi*, Carrot or Cucumber *Kosamalli*, Banana Stem *Kosamalli*.

Side Dishes   230
Black Nightshade Greens, Lentil *Usli*, Banana Flower *Usli*, Banana Stem *Kari*, Plantain *Kari*, Jackfruit *Kari*, Snake Gourd *Kari*, Sauteed Bitter Gourd *Kari*, Eggplant *Kari*, Broad Beans *Kari*, String Beans *Kari*, Colocasia *Kari*, Ash Gourd *Kootu*, Snake Gourd *Kootu*, Seven Vegetable *Kootu*, *Avial*, Lime Leaf and Curry Leaf Mix, Curry Leaf Chutney, Edible Stemmed Vine Chutney, Eggplant Chutney, Coconut Chutney, Tamarind Mint Chutney, Bermuda Grass Fritters, Ginger Pickle.

Postpartum recipes   242
Barley Water, Betel Leaves Juice, Garlic Milk, Almond Drink, Coconut Water, Dry Ginger Tea, Curry Leaf Mix, Black Pepper Stew, Garlic *Rasam*, Dried Black Nightshade, Post Delivery Tonic, Cumin Asafoetida Powder, Garlic *Legiyam*, Curry Leaf Powder.

Bibliography and Notes   249
Glossary   250
Closing   252

Acknowledgements

I am honored to be blessed by the world renowned His Holiness Sri Sri Ravishankar Guru*ji* of The Art of Living Ashram, Bangalore, India. I thank him from deep inside my heart for his approbation.

I am also honored to be blessed and for the encouragement given by His Holiness Swami Dayananda Saraswati*ji* of Annakati, Tamil Nadu. I am deeply touched by his warmth, affection and kind words that kept me on track with this project.

I am very grateful to Suzanna Al-Said, Her Royal Highness of Oman, who kept asking me if I was done with the project and giving me constant push to complete this book. She took me to the Sri Sri Ravishankar Ashram herb garden where the Ayurvedic doctors gave us a personal tour of the premises. I was able to take some valuable pictures and notes.

I would like to thank Mr. D. K. Hari and Hema Hari, authors of many books, including *2012 The Real Story*, for being supportive and for providing resources, guidance and encouragement to complete my project. Their in-depth knowledge of history, of the Vedas and the immense amount of research they have done is an inspiration to me.

I thank Mr. Raman*ji* of the Arsha Vidya Ashram of His Holiness Swami Dayananda Saraswati*ji*, who provided unconditional devotion to my project. He gave me a tour of his herb garden and allowed me to take pictures and reinforced my understanding with explanation of each herb and its benefits.

I am indebted to my brother-in-law, Mr. Venkat Chary, for his devotion to the project and providing space and resource in his quiet office in Mumbai for my work.

I am very grateful to Dr. Thirunarayanan, a Siddha doctor from Chennai, for always being there for any query I had on herbs and spices. His guidance was very valuable.

I adore Kalpana Premkumar, a simple, god fearing woman, who loves to grow medicinal plants, who had inherited the Siddha home recipes from her ancestors, and who was more than willing to share her knowledge and recipes of the ancient Siddha medicine folklore.

There are no words to thank the beautiful Sheela and Ravi; they are awesome for allowing me to crash at their place every time I went to Bangalore for research. This helpful couple would always send me back with a plant that grows in their yard. Sheela would treat me to papayas, bananas and guavas from their own garden, and Ravi would gladly pour a glass at the end of the day to relax and enjoy.

I sincerely thank Latha Anantharaman for the initial edits of the book and George P. Mathew for the initial formatting of this book.

I would also like to thank Vetri of Bharathi Discovery Designs, Chennai, Tamil Nadu for the initial digital layout and design assistance.

Thank you, my dear Jasdeep Kaur, for modeling for the *nethi* and yoga photos on pages 20 and 30.

I would also like to acknowledge and thank my son Koshek (www.subversivereality.com) for organizing and putting together the website, online and offline marketing and promotion campaigns for this book. I was happy when he turned out to be just the copywriter I needed.

And the final credit goes to Cate, the person who did the painstaking work of refining the layout and text of the recipe section and bringing the book to life. I thank her deep from my heart.

Lastly, I want to acknowledge my daughter, Sreedevi, for her selfless help with the project.

I have so many beautiful people around me who have been an inspiration, and I extend my gratitude to all who have aided this project in many ways, including Stevie Lischin, Frankie Hutton, Nathan Jagan, Vinatha Kumar and Gita Iyer, one of my dearest friends who I have known since I first came to the U.S. I would also like to acknowledge my sons Karthik and Ashvin for moral support.

I am ever grateful and thankful to the supreme source for providing the beauty and abundance in nature for us to cherish and preserve.

Introduction

As a child, I loved to watch the butterflies as they danced gently in the air above me. My father was stationed at a veterinary research institute in the hill station of Mukteshwar in the Himalayan mountains and our family would have our occasional picnics among the backdrops of snow crested peaks and rolling green valleys.

On a makeshift outdoor stove of hot coals there was a clay cooking pot filled with water and the herbs we picked from the shrubs around us. Among the ingredients were the petals of the nasturtium and rose, which grew plentiful in our garden and were the main attraction for butterflies.

"See these beautiful butterflies? You too will transform yourself into beautiful people just as the caterpillar becomes a butterfly, when you sip and eat the elixirs of these plants," my father told us.

With this we would gleefully have our herbal soup in anticipation of our beautiful transformation in the near future.

I also would like to give you a transformation through this book. I want to transform the way you think about food and to expand your mind to see possibilities in the culinary experience that go far beyond the sense of taste.

I will show you that foods are actually doorways to various states of consciousness. Change the foods you eat and you will change the doorways and the experiences you have in life.

Another Way to View Food

There is a saying in India:

Eat one serving, you are a yogi or divine person.
Eat two servings, you are a bhogi, or one who gratifies his tastes.
Eat three servings, you are a rogi, or one who carries a negative aura or disease.

My father would say that our stomachs were not garbage containers to be filled, but rather, temples that ought to be respected and offered pure food.

Food is sacred; eat what is good, and eat the right amount at the right time, he would often remind us children.

When I was a child, the sweets and snacks in our house were always locked up in the larder and meted out as occasional treats. Our first major meal of the day, served before ten in the morning, was comprised of *sambar*, a green vegetable, a grain, ghee, *rasam* and yogurt. Dinner was usually light and early. Special meals were prepared during festivals for those who observed a fast and for pre-natal and post-natal women.

In our modern world, we have extended the life of human beings at a cost. While science and medicine are increasing our understanding of how the body and mind functions, the assortment of foods available today are poisoning our system and decreasing the quality of life.

We want quantity and quality, but our modern lifestyle has left us lacking. Food is used as a quick fix to enhance our mood with high sugar, high protein and high caffeine, and then we rely on allopathic medicine as a quick fix to extend our lives.

A long life must also include an abundance of life force. The world should be as vivid and colorful as a butterfly is to a child. Our brains should be fully aware and our bodies should feel as light as butterfly feathers.

But what we are left with is a life lacking in sensitivity and vitality. A long life in a dimmed state of consciousness cannot be an extension of life, but rather an extension of pain and suffering. What kind of longevity is that?

People today are looking for alternatives. The great news is that an alternative exists in our kitchens and in our ethnic grocery stores. There is an ancient tradition that has been time-tested through generations where food and herbs have been used as medicine, beauty tonics and life enhancers.

And what is wonderful is that you can also have an amazing culinary experience that will not only stimulate your tongue and your body, but your entire consciousness.

Yes, we do have the power to transform our bodies, minds and consciousness through the foods and herbs that we consume — just as the caterpillar, when consuming the right leaves, can transform itself into a beautiful butterfly.

An Ancient Tradition

I grew up in a liberal and modern south Indian family. But like many things in India, where the new and the old live side by side, an ancient tradition of herbal medicine and cooking recipes have been passed down to me. This book started out as a notebook through which I intended to pass down the recipes to my daughter.

Many of these recipes are more than a thousand years old. Some may even go back to the early days of civilization. References can be found in the ancient Vedas that may go back more than 5000 years.

Unlike north India, south Indian culture has remained unchanged and consistent for thousands of years. It may be the longest surviving ancient culture in existence. It is definitely the longest surviving living tradition in the world. While north India has had many invaders, and every ancient culture the world over has been overthrown with change, south India has remained almost the same.

This is why when an anthropologist wants to study the original culture and practices of the ancient world, she will want to study the living Vedic practices of the Iyer community in south India.

The Iyers have been known to pass down ancient traditions and secrets for generations. They have been known to memorize entire volumes of the Vedas and recite the magical incantations forwards and backwards with perfection. The Vedas that are published as books are really just an outline of the true Vedas which can only be passed down orally.

Just like the Iyers, other south Indian communities have preserved ancient knowledge too. There is a preserved Vedic tradition that is incredibly potent, yet held quietly among groups of people and families. And as these communities are increasingly being oppressed, more and more of this ancient knowledge is being buried in secrecy, or worse, re-packaged in half understood psuedo-Hinduism for western audiences who do not know the difference.

Yet, the tradition quietly survives among Iyer families. I am from this Iyer community. This is my family tradition. And now with the publication of this book, I am going to reveal them to you.

A Whole New World Awaits You

I am opening a door to another world. Please enter and look around. Use the recipes and observe how you feel. Add the herbs to your own foods and notice how they change the flavor and benefits of your own recipes. Above all, learn the secrets of an ancient tradition that will bring benefits into your life. Having grown up in this tradition, I personally saw what it did for people. I have seen family members and members of my community get healed and live extremely long lives without the use of modern medicine. I have seen many men and women with a glow on their faces, what in India we call *tejas* (fire), brimming with health and vitality.

I have seen elderly people into their 90s that had sparkles in their eyes, elderly people who had energy to walk miles and miles on foot to make pilgrimages to temples all over India.

I have seen amazing miracles among the Iyer community of India and I hope I can also bring such miracles to you.

I will show you how to combine herbs with other complimentary foods to nourish your body, mind and spiritual soul. You will learn how to make herbal transformations that you can integrate into your lifestyle to boost your health, vitality, happiness, quality as well as quantity of life.

Now, these herbs and traditional recipes are not magic pills — nothing in life is. But a diet plan based on the principles outlined in this book will put you on the path to health and longevity. What I give you here is my life's experience of an ancient way of living as prescribed by *siddhars* and rishis that has been collectively time tested.

I am absolutely certain that this book will transform your life. I am eager to hear from you and how you have benefited by this book. Please contact me at **dansingnatural@gmail.com**

May you be like the butterfly!

PS: In addition, as a free gift to you, I want to give you as much value for purchasing this book as I can possibly give beyond the constraints of a printed book. Please visit my website at **www.herbaltranformations.net**. I will be adding free extra chapters, special tips, and recipes just for you. Please look for a special section of the website titled "Bonus Chapters and Extras" and use the secret password found in this book, which I will reveal to you on the website.

Right: Festivals and ceremonies begin with Kolam, a symbolic representation of the universe where the gifts of nature abound.

Thiruvannamalai Temple

Ancient Art of Yoga with Music and Dance

I. An Exploration into Ancient Traditions

For as long as we know, humans have been studying cultures and asking: why do we do what we do, and how does that affect our daily lives? Here, I will show how certain practices of a culture had been used to preserve eternal youthfulness to help one maintain a healthy mind, body and soul.

This tradition includes the practice of yoga, the use of ayurvedic herbs, Siddha medicine, cleansing rituals, art and meditation in a combined daily routine that heightened the perceptions of the people who lived that tradition. A main part of that daily routine was cooking and eating food. As a matter of fact, rituals, art and spiritual practices would revolve around the cooking and eating of food.

For over 3500 years, India has supplied spices to the world. Indian medicine is ancient. The earliest practices are mentioned in the Vedas, possibly dating back to the 3rd millennium BCE. The *Rig Veda,* dated in its written form by most scholars from 1500 BCE to 3000 BCE, is the world's oldest written record of botanical preparations and treatments. The medicinal use of herbs and spices is acknowledged in these writings. The *Charaka Samhita* and *Sushruta Samhita,* the oldest written records on Ayurveda dating from 1000 BCE, describe thousands of plant remedies, including, for example, the Indian Snakeroot known as *Rauwolfia,* from which is derived the drug Reserpine now prescribed for high blood pressure.

What is Ayurveda?

The word "Ayurveda" means the science of life. Knowledge of Ayurveda is not just aiming to cure illness but rather a holistic understanding of physical and mental well-being. Practitioners believe Ayurveda combines the knowledge found in the four Vedas or scriptures.

Ayurveda stresses the distinction between cooling and heat producing foods. Heat producing foods, when eaten in abundance, could cause skin problems and digestive irregularities. Foods need to be balanced according to the season and the body type. Ayurveda determines the root cause of health problems through the individual's characteristics rather than focusing on symptoms.

The individual's body corresponds to the universe. Just as there are five elements in the universe, the five vital breaths of the body are water, earth, fire, space and air. The body is said to contain three *doshas* that include the five vital breaths. *Pitta* is fire and water, *vata* is space and air, and *kapha* is water and earth.

Our body is made up of mostly water, as is the earth. The seasons and cosmos affect us in terms of what we eat that is produced by earth. The vast space in which the stars and galaxies exist correspond to the spaces within our body, the lungs and stomach, that are vital to our survival. Fire or energy is what determines the metabolism of our body, which converts food and creates heat in the body. The air we inhale supports the functioning of all organs.

In each person, one or more *doshas* will be predominant. Each kind of body is susceptible to certain diseases. Since *vata* is wind, it is related to movement. The qualities of *vata* people are dry and cold. People with too much *vata* may build up gas in the body and experience arthritic pains. *Pitta* is characterized by heat energy in the body that controls digestion and metabolism. Too much *pitta* could lead to acidity in the body. *Kapha* is characterized as moist, dull, sticky and static. *Kapha* people are prone to chest congestion, cough and cold.

The foods that you eat, according to practitioners of Ayurveda, affect the characteristics of your body. Foods are described as *sattvic*, *tamasic* or *rajasic*. *Sattvic* foods keep the *doshas* in balance. *Tamasic* foods can create an imbalance and *rajasic* foods can get the doshas out of control.

What is Siddha?

The Siddha system is based on the premise that only a healthy body can help develop a healthy soul. Ancient practitioners regulated their life with intense yogic exercises, fasting and meditation. In the process, they are said to have achieved even curative powers. "Secrets" of Siddha medicine were passed down orally as well as written on palm leaf manuscripts, from which the system developed as it is practiced in India today.

Siddha medicine is mainly practiced in Tamil Nadu. However, some practitioners say there is a north Indian school of Siddha medicine that developed in the Himalayan region. Those who developed it, the *siddhars*, are considered saints with spiritual powers. They are reputed to have received knowledge from harnessing the universal energy source that is Shiva, through intense meditation and fasting. Evolved practitioners could tell which disease had possessed a person simply by looking at their eyes, the color of their nails and lips, observing the condition of the hair and scalp, and by feeling the *nadi*, a nerve channel.

Indian scriptures say there were 18 main *siddhars*. The father of Siddha medicine was Agasthiyar. Siddhar Konganar specialized in alchemy and employing the elixir of life, known as *muppu*. *Muppu* is a mix of three ancient salts that is supposed to create miracles in healing and rejuvenation, but its method of use is still held secret. *Kayakalpa* treatment was developed by sages thousands of years ago and introduced by Siddhar Edaikkadar for prevention of aging and even to defy death. *Kayakalpa* was also practiced to attain mystical powers. It was a system of intense internal cleansing, yoga, exercise and meditation.

Ancient Practices

Ancient Indian medicine covers all sorts of ailments and consists of mainly vegetable drugs, all of which are from indigenous plants. Minerals such as gold, silver, copper, sulfur, lead and sulfate were also used.

The physicians collected and prepared their own drugs. And so did the people. Even to this day, most households in south India still prepare their own drugs. Homemade recipes are commonly followed to create tonics to treat cough, chest congestion, skin irritations, common cold, stomach cramps and diarrhea.

A strict diet was followed with only two meals a day and even the amount of water to be taken before and after the meal was prescribed in the *Charaka Samhita*.

Almost every tree, bush, weed or herb has some spiritual significance. This culture did not practice "a religion", but the practice can be described as a way of life, the practice of the art of living. Spirituality is intertwined with food, medicine and hygiene. Food was prepared with care according to the season, the time of day, the movement of the moon and the planets.

Washing away the toxins from the body was considered a precursor to good health and so was fasting. Detoxification and cleansing of the organs became part of a daily ritual. One such ritual was *nethi* or nostril cleansing. The nose is the passage to the pineal gland and the brain. Oxygen inhaled is converted to life force that cleanses the brain first and spreads throughout the body. So, in this method, lightly salted water is poured through one nostril and drained through the other. This was believed to ensure a healthy mind, free of the effects of aging. Detoxification with purgatives was also practiced. Herbal decoctions were administered for such purposes.

Fasting, which is associated with the moon cycle, was of vital importance. According to the ancient treatises on Ayurveda and Siddha, the gravitational force of the moon and the planets affect the emotional patterns and physiology of the body. The moon attracts water, creating high tide and low tide. This has a bearing on the human body, which contains mostly water. Therefore, a day-long fast with liquid intake was recommended on the full and new moon days to detoxify the body.

The *nethi* pot is used to irrigate the nasal passageways, clearing the path to the third eye. It is important to use clean filtered water for this with a tincture of sea salt or Himalayan rock salt. Pour the water down one nostril and allow it to flow out the other.

It clears acidity and stabilizes the mind. Many Hindus observe a fast on the 11th day after the full moon, or *ekadasi*, a day dedicated to Lord Vishnu, the preserver and sustainer of life.

Breaking the fast was equally important. Special food is eaten at dusk and the next day, a light diet consisting of leafy vegetables, *nellikai* (Indian gooseberry) and medicinal herbs is taken. This is to ensure that a hitherto empty stomach gets the food that balances the *doshas*. I feel so fortunate to have grown up in a family that followed these ancient practices. I have enjoyed immensely the healthy foods that were prepared by my mother and grandmother in their fasting rituals. Naturally, they would ask us to go on a fast also, for *ekadasi* day is auspicious and according to tradition all our sins would "gallop away".

Hindu texts emphasize eating the right kind of food, since food is the main source of energy for the physical body. In the *Taittriya Upanishad*, the physical body is described in relation to food: "All beings that exist on earth are born of food. Therefore, they live by food. Again, they go back to earth and merge with it to become food."

Food occupies an important part in the religious life of Hindus. It is offered to the gods and ancestors during rituals, served to the poor, and offered to animals and birds. A baby is introduced to solid food in a ritual called *Annaprasana*, literally the intake of grain. During funerals and annual death rituals, special food is offered to the departed souls and ancestors. The devout say a prayer and sprinkle water around the plate or banana leaf in which food is served. This is to purify the food and make it worthy of consuming. Food is then offered to the five vital breaths.

In his book titled *Hinduism*, V. Jayaram gives a holistic description of food: "*Annam* means food. Food is in truth the Lord of Creation. From food seed is produced and from this beings are born." He says Hindu texts refer to the physical body as *annamaya kosha* or "food body" because it is produced by food. It is the outermost of our five sheaths. The remaining four are the breath body, mental body, intelligent body and the bliss body, which surrounds the inmost *atman* or the soul.

Ancient Practices of Purification

Ancients and traditional families carried on age-old practices of personal hygiene, bathing and skin care. Bathing before sunrise was essential for purity of mind, body and soul. They believed that one should bathe before eating, doing yogic exercises or engaging in rituals associated with spirituality and tradition. People bathed with oils and then scrubbed themselves with herbal powders, turmeric and sandalwood. Herbal eye washes were and still are very important.

Teeth were cleaned with twigs from *neem*, *peepal* or banyan trees, or with charcoal. The ends of the twig were chewed into a brush and the medicinal qualities of these twigs kept the gums healthy.

Karuvelam pattai powder (*Acacia* nilotica) was also used to brush the teeth. Until a few decades ago, many people used a mix of charcoal and salt sold under the name Monkey Brand, which is even found in some American health food stores.

In *Sanatana Dharma*, God resides within you. The deities that are created are concepts of our own selves. If one notes the careful bathing habits that are observed by the Iyers, one can see that these reflect the ancient rituals they follow when bathing the gods — whether it is a priest bathing a large image in a temple, a householder bathing the small deities enshrined in the home, and even how they bathe themselves and their offsprings. It is not just superficial washing but rather a cleansing both internally and externally. It is cleansing of the space and removal of negativity. Natural ingredients are used for this purpose that have specific healing and rejuvenating qualities: milk, honey, yogurt, fruit juices, sandalwood paste, turmeric water, sesame oil and ghee. It is inevitable that people would look to those same ingredients to preserve their own youthfulness.

Hygiene in the home was codified into rules of purity that were strictly adhered to. Footwear was always removed before entering the house to keep out the street germs. I remember my grandmother watching like a hawk to remind us to remove our shoes and wash ourselves as soon as we came home from school. Cow dung, a disinfectant, was used to clean the entrance of the house and also to clean the floor after a meal was eaten. Women who were menstruating stayed out of the kitchen.

Hygiene in the kitchen was of huge importance. Fresh water was stored in earthen pots to keep it cool and a sprig of holy basil dropped into it to remove contaminants such as fluoride. Fluoride can discolor and crumble the teeth, cause bone cancer and Alzheimer's disease as it calcifies the pineal gland. Traditional people kept cooked food away from milk products so that bacteria from one would not

accidentally contaminate the other. These practices were essential before the days of refrigeration. Today, very few families observe them.

Before preparing the sacred meal known as *madi samayal*, women wore washed clothes which were not touched by anyone else. The pots and pans were cleaned and kept in the sun to be sterilized. No one was allowed to touch them including family members until they had bathed and worn clean clothes. The meals were cooked in earthenware or stoneware and served on silver plates. When a disposable plate was needed, banana leaves, lotus leaves or almond leaves were used. Since food is known to absorb elements of the container, it was especially important to use the right kind of leaf, metal or stone. A far cry from the plastic and styrofoam that we eat out of today.

Even the daily meal was considered sacred. Cooked food was first offered to the elements of the universe, and then a handful was placed outside for the birds, especially the crow. Only then did the families sit to eat. Brahmin men saluted the sun and sprinkled water clockwise three times around their food to energize it and purify the space. Then they touched water to their mouth, eyes and other parts of the body to invoke speech, sight, energy and strength. Water is the essence of life, therefore drinking lots of water and eating on time was an integral part of the tradition. The orthodox never touched their lips to their drinking tumbler. Even in a healthy person, saliva carries plenty of germs, so these precautions were strictly observed. The concept of *yechal* (saliva) was so important that it became a cultural taboo. That

Uma Swaminathan | 23

meant not tasting any food while cooking and never eating from another's plate.

One of the most widely known practices of the indigenous people is the smudging of sacred symbols on their bodies and on the spot associated with the third eye or the pineal gland. Many men wear a smudge or three stripes of *vibhuti*, the sacred ash of cow dung, on their arms, chest and forehead. The ancients believed it would energize and strengthen their knowledge and memory. Women more commonly mark their foreheads with a powerful mix that contains turmeric, sandalwood powder, saffron and a calcium compound made from lime or seashells that empowered them. This is called *manjal kumkumam*. This is what the red dot on the forehead was meant for. Sadly, many have forgotten the real purpose of this mark and these people who do wear them consider them purely ornamental, using glue to adhere synthetic decorations to their forehead.

Life Stages

The key to longevity is intertwined with art, music, dance, rituals that celebrated puberty, pregnancy and the sacred thread ceremony.

Beginning at birth, the child is groomed to follow the path of eternal youth. Every aspect and juncture in life is replete with rituals that use herbs, fruits, flowers and grains that represent energy, strength and wisdom.

Our mother and father come before God, so say the ancients. The mother brings life into this world, provides nutrients to the unborn and the newborn, and nurtures the new creation. For all these reasons, rituals of care were prescribed for the mother-to-be that included medicinal foods, hygiene regimen and exercise. The foods for the mother provided energy and abundant flow of milk. Balanced nutrients ensured overall health for the mother and the baby.

A ritual known as *Seemandam* was performed on one of the odd months of pregnancy, such as the fifth, seventh or the ninth month. Ancients did this for the birth of every child. Nowadays it is performed only for the first-time mother. The pregnant woman's hair is parted at the center and turmeric is applied at the part to invoke the third eye, where Shakti resides. Shakti is power, strength and energy. Since the child's brain is known to start developing in the womb, soothing music is played during this ritual to help the child develop a calm and logical brain. A powerful Vedic mantra called *Udhagasanthi* is recited to empower the mother and the unborn.

The rishi Sushrut describes in his ancient Ayurvedic text *Sushruta Samhita* a powerful compound that is to be used during the *Seemandam*: "Having pounded milk with any of these herbs—*sulakshmana, batasurga, somalata, sahadevi* and *vishwadeva*—one should instill three or four drops of juice in the right nostril of the pregnant woman. She should not spit out the juice." Besides having immense medicinal value, this compound prevented miscarriage. Another traditional prenatal custom was that the expectant mother was forbidden to see an eclipse and was also admonished to avoid its attendant shadow as they believed that the radiation created during this lunar event would adversely affect the developing fetus.

When babies were delivered at home, the delivery room was carefully prepared. Using *Vastu Shastra*, the elders decided the direction of delivery. It is also believed that the placement of the stars and constellations affect the baby at the time of birth.

Next, the room was cleaned. A lit lamp or fire, water, grains and mustard seeds were kept there. The newborn was welcomed to the world with ghee and honey placed on the tip of his or her tongue to develop memory and immunity.

Traditionally, for 10 days after delivery, the mother and the baby were kept in isolation. No one other than the person caring for them was allowed in the room. This had to do with keeping the mother and the baby free of infection. The mother's stomach was bound for those 10 days. My twins were born in New Jersey. I had just turned 21 and was left to fend for myself, in a new country with a new culture and no pampering from my mother. In the 1960's, it was not even a phone culture but a postal mail culture. Being oceans away, my parents could not help me much, so I used Dr. Spock's book, *Baby and Child Care,* as my Bible. Although it was difficult being far from my mother at this time, one fortuitus outcome of this separation was the collection of handwritten recipes my mother sent to me by post.

In many Indian families, these special medicinal foods are still made for the new mother. The diet known as *pathiya samayal,* a prescription for 40 days after delivery, includes foods with garlic, black pepper and ghee. The food is medicinal, nutritious and well balanced, helping to heal and rejuvenate the new mother, that in turn makes the newborn healthy, happy and smart. The particular ingredients in *pathiya samayal* help increase the blood supply and milk production. Among them are betel leaves, lime, fennel, barley water and a homemade compound of herbs and spices called *pillai-petha marundu* or "childbirth medicine."

From the first day, the baby is bathed in hot water with herbal oils to strengthen the muscles and bones and then the oil washed off with mung flour. After the bath, *sambrani*, a benzoin resin extracted from the bark of several trees of the genus *Styrax*, is lit so that its smoke disinfects the room and also dries the baby. The mother is encouraged to breastfeed the baby. The isolation ends on the 10th day with the naming ceremony, a happy occasion with music and sumptuous food when relatives and friends can come and see the mother and the baby.

Among Brahmins, young boys, charged with carrying on religious knowledge, are initiated into adulthood in the *Upanayanam* or sacred thread ceremony. A mantra known as the *Gayatri Mantra* is whispered into their ears during this ceremony. It is true that the mantra is now freely chanted everywhere, but its secret transmission in the ritual acknowledges the need for the initiate to be particularly attuned to it so that his mental channels are open to absorb the universal energy of the mantra. Males and females recited mantras that were in reality affirmations to empower the body, mind and soul. Dr. Usui of Japan who promoted Reiki, the universal life force energy, studied the ancient art of yoga and meditation in

Photos, from top:: 1. *Upanayanam*. 2. Nine grains, symbolic of fertility.

India. He learned the power of the *Gayatri Mantra* and how it was passed on through the initiation process. Using this knowledge, he said that anyone practicing Reiki had to be attuned to open the channel and absorb the universal energy.

In the ancient stories, the goddesses also went through initiation ceremonies. These have survived as coming of age rituals for young women, celebrated with music and dance and mantras that initiated them into womanhood. One can still see in some villages young girls perform the *pinnal kolatam*, in which they braid colorful ropes while dancing, the *kolatam* or stick dance, and *kummi* with its coordinated clapping.

Yoga

Yoga is said to have originated in India five thousand years ago. The discovery of the Indus Valley Civilization in the 1920s unearthed evidence of yoga practices in the art and figurines that were excavated. We also know that yoga was practiced by rishis and *siddhars* long before this discovery.

Yoga means union or one-pointed awareness. It has two components: one is union with the physical body and the other is union with the supreme reality. Therefore, physical exercise including dance, yogic exercises, sports and mental exercise in the form of meditation, chants and music were all part of yoga that helped keep the person in balance and in good health, leading to longevity.

Yoga was practiced in many ways. *Surya namaskar*, the powerful salutation to the sun, was used by the ancients and is still widely taught. Many of the old texts suggest that women also performed yoga and meditation and attained great powers. From later history and literature we know that women meditated and practiced Bhakti Yoga which is also known as the yoga of complete devotion. It is goddess Parvati who is credited with passing on the knowledge of ancient medicine to *siddhars*. Lakshmi, the consort of Lord Vishnu, is the emblem of wealth and prosperity and Saraswati, the consort of Lord Brahma, is the goddess of all the arts and knowledge. To Brahma, Vishnu and Shiva are attributed the powers of creation, preservation and destruction. They attained their powers through intense meditation and yoga.

My father often told us to look within and pray for the well-being of every part of our body so that we could attain the power to control ourselves. Our everyday postures all contributed to our practice of yoga: squatting, sitting cross-legged, prostrating before our parents, elders and deities. Elders blessed the children with the palm of their right hand to pass energy. A special kind of ritual exercise was *thopikarnam*, crossing one's arms to hold the opposite earlobes while squatting down and standing up seven to fourteen times. This was believed to improve the brain function and enhance memory. It was frequently performed as an offering to God and far more often as a punishment in school!

Yoga has become very popular in the West. But what most people learn as yoga is really only a small branch of the yoga system practiced in India. The physical yoga postures are called *asanas* and are part of a branch called Hatha Yoga. Yoga itself is the process of joining the lower physical being with a higher spiritual being. For this connection to be made, the body and the consciousness must be able to grasp subtle things by developing an acute sensitivity.

Modern yoga teachers rarely teach students how to develop the necessary sensitivity of the mind or how students can improve their meditation practices through diet and simple thought management. For instance, foods are classified by three *gunas* that can affect the mind.

The first guna is called *tamas*. Tamas is all foods that dull the mind and make it weak. A weak mind is unable to grasp deep conceptual thoughts or use the imagination. *Tamas* weakens the muscle of the will so there is also a lack of self control. The mind is easily moved around by external forces. Foods that are considered *tamasic* include onions, garlic, meat, lard, old food, left overs, foods preserved artificially in a freezer or by preservatives.

The second guna is called *rajas*. Rajas is all foods that excite the mind and make it unfocused. A scattered mind is unable to rationally use concepts or hold an image in the imagination for any great length of time. The mind is easily affected by emotion, passion and anger. Food that is considered *rajasic* include lean meats, coffee, tea, chillies, peppers, refined sugar and salt.

The third guna is *satvas*. Satvas is all foods that sharpen the sensitivity of the mind and the heart. The imagination is vivid and powerful. The sensitivity is strong and subtle. The awareness is expanded. Using ones willpower is as easy as lifting a feather. *Sattvic* foods include fruits and vegetables as well as milk and natural foods grown in healthy environments.

The *gunas* also classify three types of thoughts. *Tamasic* thoughts are thoughts of resentment and bitterness. *Rajasic* thoughts are those that are power hungry and possessive. *Sattvic* thoughts are those that are unconditionally loving and forgiving.

An important *sattvic* practice is *ahimsa* or harmlessness. This is the intentional practice of not harming anyone or causing any pain or suffering to anyone or anything. Just meditating on this intention can cause immense peace in the mind and flood it with incredible spiritual energy.

Many people practice yoga for years without understanding the importance of developing *sattvic* thoughts and eating *sattvic* foods and wonder why they are not developing higher states of consciousness or better self control. Yet there are entire states of consciousness that are ready to be experienced for those who purify their minds with love and blessings for the world around them. When that subtle sensitivity occurs, the feeling is so brilliant that there is no turning back.

Thopikarnam is an ancient yoga practice. One starts in a standing position, crossing the hands and pinching the opposite earlobes with the thumb and forefinger. From here, with feet anchored flat on the ground, you bend at the knees down to a full squatting position while taking a deep breath and then exhale upon rising back up.

Pinching of the earlobes provides acupressure that stimulates the neuro pathways and helps balance the left and the right brain. This activation of brain cells and neurons help to enhance memory and clarity of thinking.

At the temple, devotees do *thopikarnam* as a divine offering to Lord Ganesha.

Kolam

Among the essential arts for girls in every traditional household is the drawing of *kolam*. Young girls gather together to challenge each other with skills learned from their elders. A *kolam* is a design drawn on the ground in front of the house to purify the space, energize it and welcome wealth and prosperity into the home. Whether it is the daily drawing on the threshold or the larger and more elaborate art that sets the tone for a celebration, the *kolam* is inspired by the sacred geometry of the ancients.

Kolam is drawn every morning before the sun rises. The area in front of the house is washed with cow dung mixed water to sterilize it and make it smooth. For a dry *kolam*, women drizzle rice powder evenly between their first finger and thumb. For a more durable wet *kolam*, women use a piece of muslin soaked in a thin rice batter and squeeze it steadily between their fingers. With practice comes precision and control, and by the time the sun comes up, one can see marvels of grids, dots and loops in front of every house. *Kolam* is also drawn in front of the family altar and on the front steps.

Kolams are also drawn to invoke the blessings of the nine planets. For each planet, on its dedicated day of the week, a special *kolam* is drawn to invoke peace and prosperity, or to fend off anger and inauspicious vibes. The special geometrical drawings for sacred ceremonies are in the form of *yantra*, a symbolic representation of the universe. This art was an integral part of life for the ancients.

It reminded them every day of the power of the universe and its influence on their well being. It reminded them that the universe is the eternal *Brahman*, which is the eternal self, to preserve and cherish. When I was young, my parents encouraged me to draw many kolam designs because, they told me, it was good for my mind. I remember how womenfolk who drew *kolam* daily seemed to be mentally very sharp.

Another important goal of *kolam* art is to subtly affect ones' state of mind, for it is believed that the thoughts of the cook will affect the cooking. Much like an athlete gets into a peak state before a big game, a cook that goes into a positive state of mind will cook with a better feel for the subtleties of the cuisine.

KOLAM ART

Shown here are the sacred art of *Navagraha Kolams*. These are *yantras* drawn to propitiate and invoke the blessings of the nine astral bodies. The nine planets are ascribed attributes which are represented by deities. The *kolam* that is associated with each corresponding planet invokes those attribute qualities or feelings within the ritual performer. The food we prepare is energized by harnessing the power of the patterns of the *kolam*. Below are the steps to draw the *kolam* starting with dots.

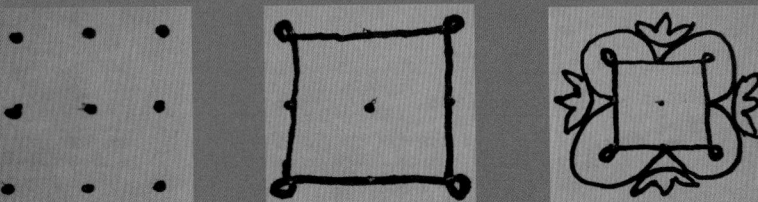

Monday *kolam* is for the water god Varuna who is associated with the Moon. Offerings are made of white flowers, stone apple leaves, silver and grains.

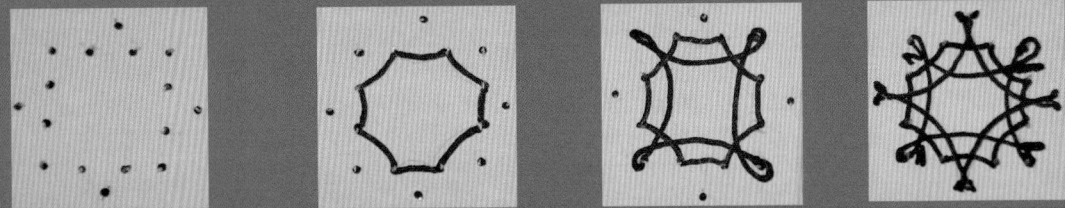

Tuesday *kolam* is for Karthikeya, who is associated with Mars and fire and represents our burning desire for knowledge. Wheat, jaggery and red flowers are the offerings.

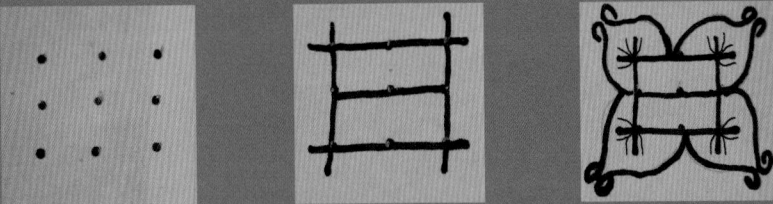

Wednesday *kolam* is for Lord Vishnu who represents Mercury and is also associated with the color green. Yogurt, ghee and mung dal are given as offerings.

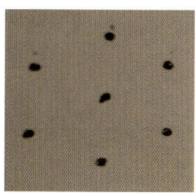 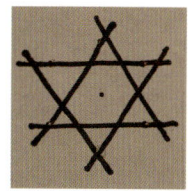 

Thursday is for the rain god Indra who is important to farmers for the sustenance of their crops. Offerings are in the form of milk, ghee and Bengal gram.

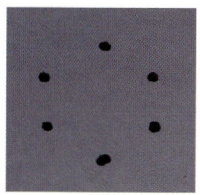  

Friday *kolam* is for Indrani and goddess Laxmi, who are associated with Venus. Laxmi represents wealth and prosperity. Flowers of the day are white and yellow.

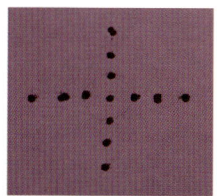 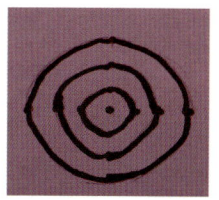 

Saturday *kolam* is represented by Sani, who is associated with Saturn and includes the twin planets, Rahu and Kethu. The *kolam* on this day has the effect of deflecting negativity, unhappiness and adversity.

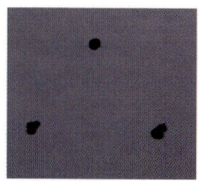  

Sunday is for Surya, the sun god. This is an auspicious day for weddings and represents prosperity and happiness. On this day offerings are made of sweets and red flowers.

Uma Swaminathan | 33

II. The Transforming Herbs

In the great epic Ramayana, there is an episode where Rama's brother Laxmana is fatally wounded in battle, having succumbed to the arrow fired by Meghnad, son of the demon king Ravana. Hanuman, the monkey god (shown left), in his attempt to save Laxmana, approaches the Lankan royal physician Sushena for help. Sushena advises Hanuman to make haste towards the Dronagiri Hills and retrieve four plants: Mruthasanjeevani (restorer of life), Vishalyakarani (eliminator of arrows), Sandhanakarani (rejuvenator of skin), and Savarnyakarani (refresher of complexion). Hanuman, unable to suss the four plants from the scores of foliage, hauls the entire medicine mountain on his shoulders and returns with it. It is from this cocktail of potent herbal remedies that Laxmana was finally revived.

Almond | Badam Paruppu

Prunus amygdalus
Boosts energy and alertness

Almond

Almond is called *badam paruppu* or *vaadumai* in Tamil and *badam* in Hindi. The ornamental ancient Indian species seen alongside the streets of southern India grows wild throughout the region. The almonds we get in the markets are the kernels from a modified variety grown by commercial farmers.

Almond is a drupe; a fleshy fruit with a central hard, stone-like seed within which is the almond seed. There are two varieties of almonds. The bitter variety known as *amara* has hydrocyanic acid and is used as a sedative. The sweet almond known as *dulcis* is a demulcent, relieving irritation of the mucous membranes of the mouth. It is also highly nutritive.

Many families in south India eat almonds every morning to boost energy and alertness. This is best done if the almonds are soaked overnight and then peeled. Soaking almonds helps neutralize the enzyme inhibitors on the almond skin, removes tannins, and also allows the seeds to start sprouting. This process is beneficial for the almond as it increases the vitamin and nutrient content that will help the body rejuvenate, thereby increasing longevity. My father was such a drama king! He would enjoy and dramatize whatever he did — whether it was reciting a verse from Shakespeare or simply cooking a meal. We loved watching him. He would peel the almonds and look at it with such love to see if he could find the sprout. Then he would make us close our eyes and open our mouths. Finally, he would drop an almond in and ask if we could feel the energy.

Almond is also used as a base ingredient in many curry dishes to enhance the flavor, give body, and to provide nutrition. Almonds are made into drinks and sweets.

Almonds contain omega-3 and omega-6 fatty acids and are rich in minerals such as manganese, copper, potassium, phosphorus and magnesium. They are also rich in antioxidants and vitamins. Cholesterol-free, almonds are abundant in monounsaturated fats and low in saturated fats.

In Ayurveda, almonds are prescribed to control diabetes and boost memory. My father always said, eating a mere six almonds a day would keep a person healthy and mentally sharp. Almonds and raisins in combination is a favorite offering to the gods. High in protein and iron, it is an energy food that is eaten as *prasadam* blessed by God. Almond calms the nerves and is said to be an aphrodisiac. One can make a drink with almond, honey and saffron to increase the libido.

The oil of sweet almond has an abundance of vitamin E. Regular use of almond oil can remove the wrinkles on the face. Almonds are used with yogurt in a face pack to rejuvenate the skin.

Aloe Vera | Katrazhai

Aloe barbadensis
Plant of immortality

Aloe Vera

Aloe is called *gheekumari* in Hindi and *katrazhai* in Tamil. A beauty secret of Cleopatra's, aloe is a lovely plant that has been in use since ancient times. The Egyptians call it a plant of immortality and in Ayurveda it is known as a miracle plant.

Aloe vera is easy to grow both indoors and outdoors. Every household should have a few aloe plants on a windowsill, because fresh aloe is more effective than processed aloe for its many uses.

Aloe has antifungal, antibacterial and antiviral properties. It stimulates the development of collagen, which keeps the skin youthful. The clear gel is used as a skin rejuvenator and as an anti-inflammatory agent. It helps heal minor burns, cuts, insect bites, skin rash, sunburn and irritation from poison ivy. Aloe is useful in healing areas of skin with nerve cell damage.

If you have fresh aloe, just pick a stem, remove the gel from inside, blend into a paste and store in a jar. Use it fresh on your face or any place on your body that needs healing. Once applied, the slimy gel evaporates and leaves a smooth skin. Fresh gel can be stored for a week.

Aloe juice is highly cooling and reduces fever. Taken internally, aloe vera can enhance the rate of cellular regeneration and recovery. Aloe vera is a natural immune booster and is beneficial in fighting cancer cells and tumors. Studies confirm similar findings in animal research showing the application of Aloe vera gel onto the skin significantly inhibits the progression of skin cancer. They have also found that aloe stimulates the production of melanin which protects the skin from radiation and the progression of tumorous cells. Aloe also helps to strengthen the liver.

For stomach ulcers and the white discharge in women, take some fresh aloe and mix it with cumin and palm sugar. Make a puree using a blender and drink raw. Fresh aloe gel can be eaten raw in salads or mixed with juices.

Aloe contains aloe gel and latex. The latex looks slightly yellow in color and lies beneath the aloe skin. Always remove the outer green fibrous skin. The inner lining of this skin is generally used as a laxative.

Aloe can be used as an underarm deodorant. Use fresh aloe gel everyday after shower or bath under your arms as this is what the ancients did for good hygiene and to improve the skin.

Asafoetida | Perungayam

Ferula asafoetida
Stimulates digestion

Asafoetida

Asafoetida is called *perungayam* in Tamil and *hing* in Hindi. It is obtained from a perennial plant that grows in temperate climates. The plant grows up to six feet in height with clusters of yellow flowers. A fully mature plant produces gum resin, which is collected and dried for use. The resin has a strong, foul and even repulsive smell, but when used in dishes, it is absolutely divine.

Even though asafoetida is native to the Middle East, it is found in the spice racks of most households in India. It is used in daily cooking, pickles and soothing tamarind and yogurt drinks.

The pure resin, which looks like brown crystal chunks, is better than the powder, which usually contains additives. The resin can be roasted in a pan, crushed, saved and used as needed. Roasting allows the resin to puff and become crisp, which makes it easy to crush and store. Asafoetida must always be stored in an airtight container as the smell can permeate other products.

One can safely use a pinch of asafoetida in soups, soothing cold drinks, steamed or sautéed vegetables, fish, poultry and meat. All the dishes of a typical south Indian morning meal contain asafoetida.

My grandmother used to soak small chunks of asafoetida in a jar containing ¼ cup water. Soaking softens asafoetida. After the dish is prepared, she would drop a spoonful of this water into the dish to give it a fresh aroma.

Asafoetida has many medical properties. It is extremely heat-producing when it is raw but when toasted or fried, it loses its heat-producing qualities. It is a carminative. Asafoetida reduces flatulence, stimulates digestion, and works as an intestinal antiseptic. Asafoetida is often combined with other carminatives such as ginger, cumin seeds and black salt when used medicinally. It is also an effective emmenagogue, helping free flow of menstruation. It is used in heavy doses in the villages of India as an abortifacient along with papaya fruit.

According to Ayurveda, asafoetida excites sexual hormones and is considered to be an aphrodisiac.

Asafoetida is used in almost all savory dishes.

Bermuda Grass | Arugampul

Cynodon dactylon
King of all grasses

Bermuda Grass

The trailing bermuda grass, known as *arugampul* in Tamil and *durva* in Hindi, has been in use in Ayurveda and Siddha medicine since ancient times for its many medicinal properties. It is known as the king of all grasses.

Bermuda grass contains high amounts of chlorophyll and its molecular structure is similar to the red blood cells in our bodies. It is an alkaline herb that controls acidity. It is also an antioxidant. According to ancient medicine, it is used in treatment of asthma and bronchitis. It is also a cooling agent and helps keep skin, eyes and vision healthy. It is used to stop nosebleeds and to control excess bleeding during menstruation.

Bermuda grass blended with palm sugar into a morning drink is said to have a detoxifying and rejuvenating effect. A little of the grass can be mixed in any hair oil for a cooling effect and to remove dandruff. A paste of arugampul with turmeric and lime can be applied to relieve skin irritations.

I recall my mother giving bermuda grass juice to my sister during her post-natal days. This wonder grass helps increase the flow of breast milk and adds to the nutritional value of the mother's milk, thereby passing on immunity to the baby. It helps to regulate metabolism, allowing nutrients to be absorbed. It eliminates toxins which helps the new mother shed the weight gained during her pregnancy. *Siddha* specialist Kalpana Premkumar notes that the properties of bermuda grass heal the uterus post-delivery, help the brain function more alertly, while also protecting the body against diabetes and obesity.

Wheat grass juice, which has a similar taste and health benefits, is popular everywhere now.

In south India, this divine herb is offered to Lord Ganesha so that one's path is free of obstacles. Ketu, one of the twin planets, resides on the left leg of Lord Ganesha at a shrine in Kalahasthi in southern India and is adorned with garlands of bermuda grass. According to belief, a garland so offered, when brought into the house, helps ward off infections and diseases.

For skin diseases, make a paste with bermuda grass, turmeric and lime and apply it.

Drink half of a glass of plain bermuda grass juice every morning for weight reduction and general good health.

Black Nightshade | Manathakali

Solanum nigrum
Fights ulcers and cancer

Black Nightshade

Black nightshade is called *makoy* in Hindi. A common plant in south India, I notice that it pops up every spring even in odd places in my garden in New Jersey. Known as *manathakali* in Tamil, it belongs to the same family as brinjal, tomatoes and capsicum.

Every part of the plant is useful. Its leaves can be used as greens. Fresh leaves can be chewed to heal mouth sores and ulcers. They can be soaked in a jug of water for a few hours and used as a gargle. The leaves made into a paste with turmeric are used topically for skin irritations. Its twigs can be used in soups.

In southern India, the green leaves and ripe berries of black nightshade are eaten, though in America and Europe, the plant is considered poisonous. The ripe fruit can be eaten as berries and is quite delicious. I pick the stems and strip the leaves, flowers and green seeds, and cook them as a vegetable. Sautéed berries are also added to idli batter or to *kuzhambu* and *morkuzhambu* after these dishes are prepared.

The potent green berries are also prepared in a special way for a longer shelf-life. They are soaked overnight in salted buttermilk that has been tempered with ground fenugreek and turmeric. The next day, the berries are removed from the liquid and dried in the sun. The remaining buttermilk is saved to be used again, to continue the process for a few more days until all the buttermilk has been absorbed completely. These dried berries can be stored and used for up to a year. They are sautéed in ghee and eaten with rice to relieve stomach ailments.

The benefits of black nightshade are immeasurable. It has been used in folk medicine for treatment of various cancers, especially that of the mouth and stomach, and as an anti-inflammatory and liver-protective agent. It is used as both preventive and curative herb for ulcers.

Researchers at the Institute of Biochemistry and Biotechnology at Chun Shan Medical University in Taiwan investigated this plant's special action on liver cells and found that heavy doses of black nightshade killed cancer cells of the liver.

The plant contains iron, calcium, vitamin C and niacin and lots of vitamin B. It is used in the treatment of fevers, diarrhea, liver enlargement, piles, dysentery and gastric ulcers. It is an amazing healer of eye nerve problems. The seeds are very potent and cannot be eaten raw.

This ancient herb has been part of the diet of the indigenous culture since time immemorial.

Black Pepper | Milagu

Piper nigrum
Immunity builder

Black Pepper

For thousands of years, pepper was the most sought after spice. The Romans and other traders paid for it in gold. The British through the East India Company cornered the market for the most precious of all spices, the black pepper.

The pepper plant, called *milagu* in Tamil, is a parasitic vine. It climbs over 30 feet high by attaching itself to tree trunks. The peppercorns grow on a catkin three to five inches long and look like miniature brussels sprouts.

When tender, pepper can be pickled with lemon and salt. The mature pepper, when dried in the sun, shrivels and turns black.

Black pepper is used almost daily in south Indian cooking, especially in *rasam*, a clear soup. Pepper *rasam* was adapted by the British as Mulligatawny soup.

Pepper is also a common ingredient in household remedies. Hot milk boiled with a pinch of ground pepper and a pinch of turmeric is often taken to relieve cold and cough. The fire or heat in the pepper destroys toxins and relieves indigestion. Black pepper is used to treat fever and sore throat. It improves appetite, helps clear the respiratory system and improves blood circulation.

Pepper contains piperine, which helps prevent liver disorders. Recent research shows that combining turmeric and black pepper supports faster absorption of nutrients. This combination has been an age old recipe for healing and rejuvenating.

On the day of the festival of Diwali, it is customary to take an oil bath at dawn. The sesame oil is heated with crushed black peppercorns in it and used warm on the head before bathing. This ritual was practiced to protect the person from catching cold.

Pepper is also used in special diets, particularly for women. Many postpartum foods are made with black pepper and garlic. The combination helps the baby develop immunity through the mother's milk while improving the blood count of the mother.

Black pepper smoke revives unconscious patients affected by epilepsy seizures and fainting.

There is a Tamil saying: *"If you eat ten black peppers a day, you can even eat in an enemy's house all day."*

Long Pepper | Arisithippili

Piper longum
Powerful longevity herb

Long Pepper

Long pepper belongs to the pepper family. In ancient times the Greeks and the Romans traded gold and copper for long pepper. It is not as spicy as black pepper but has a strong pungent taste and therefore only four or five peppercorns are used at a time.

Long pepper, a miracle herb, is called *pippali* in Hindi and *arisithippili* in Tamil. It is used in south Indian cooking and in Ayurvedic medicines and as home remedy for respiratory diseases, coughs, cold, asthma and bronchitis. The roots, stem and peppercorns contain piperine. Piperine, also known as bioperine, helps in absorption of nutrients while eliminating toxins. Long pepper is credited with curing throat infections and insomnia. It is an antidepressant and antibacterial. With regular consumption, it removes discoloration of the skin.

It is a powerful *rasayana* herb in Ayurveda; that is, it is said to enhance longevity. It is a blood purifier, a carminative and a digestive aid. A common treatment for asthma is a peppercorn-size dose of long pepper powdered along with crown flower (*errukku* in Tamil, *Calotropis gigantia*) in equal parts, taken twice a day.

Long Pepper Stem

Called *kandathipili* in Tamil, is the stem of the long pepper plant. It is a great cure for colds, pneumonia and insomnia. With the slightest sneeze or cough, my mother used to make a delicious rasam with black pepper and long pepper stems. The combination relieves fever and body aches and pains. This combination is also given as postpartum food to improve the appetite and purify the blood.

A *rasam* made with black pepper, long pepper and long pepper stem relieves chest congestion and symptoms of pneumonia.

Camphor | Karpooram

Cinnamomum camphora
Wards off evil spirit and germs

Camphor

Camphor crystals are obtained from the camphor tree, which can live over a hundred years. Thin sheets of the wood and bark are soaked in water and then heated. The resin which floats on top is collected and cooled. The cooled resin forms crystals that resemble salt crystals. Its twigs and leaves are also used in medicine.

Most families in southern India have camphor in their homes. There are two kinds of camphor. One is poisonous if eaten and is burned as an offering to the gods at the end of a prayer. The edible kind, called *pachai karpooram* in Tamil, is also highly fragrant and is used in very small quantities to flavor sweets.

In Ayurveda, camphor has been used for over four thousand years as medicine. It kills germs and keeps diseases at bay. The drug is used as sedative and a narcotic. It stimulates the blood and the nervous system. If used in small doses, it acts as an aphrodisiac. It is used to treat coughs and colds as an expectorant.

Camphor oil is used as a rub for headaches and rheumatic pains. For a quick remedy, mix camphor with eucalyptus oil to rub the area to relieve pain. To get rid of chest congestion, put a little camphor in coconut oil and heat it. Then rub the oil on the chest. A formula that can be stored and used as needed contains camphor (4 small pieces) and carom or bishop's weed (4 tablespoons soaked and blended to make a paste). Heat ¼ cup of coconut oil, add bishop's weed paste and camphor. Cook until no trace of water remains. Remove, cool and store in a jar and use as a rub for pain in the body due to arthritis and tiredness.

Camphor is combined with eucalyptus and other herbs to make cough drops. It has a cooling effect and acts as a mild anesthetic. Camphor also repels bed bugs, flies and mosquitoes. It is used in aromatherapy to cool and calm the body.

Camphor is burned at the end of prayer in many households to "purify the surroundings" and is believed to ward off evil spirits or negative vibrations. The burning of camphor for this purpose is called *arathi* and it is the offering of fire, the energy source, to God in a clockwise movement accompanied by the ringing of bells or the blowing of a conch to invoke the mystical sounds of the universe. Camphor emits a calming fragrance. Since it is believed that God is within us, one imagines every aspect of the body and thought to be rejuvenated and free of negativity. Camphor, when fully dissolved in the flame, leaves no residue.

Cardamom | Elakkai

Elettaria cardamomum
Queen of aroma

Cardamom

Cardamom is called *ellakai* in Tamil and *elaichi* in Hindi. The plant is native to the Kerala region in southern India. The pods grow like an orchid at the base of the plant.

Cardamom has been a part of Indian cuisine and medicine for thousands of years. It is the queen of aroma in Indian sweets, puddings and drinks. In northern India, it is used in curries, tea, rice pulao, cooling drinks and sweets.

This aromatic spice stimulates digestion, relieves flatulence and contains antioxidants. Cardamom seeds are munched after supper, like an after-dinner mint, often along with fennel. Cardamom is also used to treat coughs and colds as due to its anti-inflammatory properties.

In Ayurveda, it is used as a potent mucus eliminator and to relieve muscle spasms, stomach and heart ailments. cardamom is also used along with honey to improve eyesight. Aromatherapy with cardamom is used to stimulate the brain. Powdered cardamom seeds are used to relieve mental depression. Newlywed couples are traditionally encouraged to drink milk laced with cardamom and saffron before going to bed as an aphrodisiac.

In temples, the holy water given to the devotees is made fragrant with camphor, cardamom, and holy basil.

Two varieties of cardamom are popularly used in India. Black cardamom, called *badi elaichi* in Hindi, is the large variety. It has an overpoweringly pungent, sweet smell and is commonly used in north Indian cuisine. It is also an important ingredient in Ayurveda. Black cardamom is considered a *tridoshic* herb since it balances all the three doshas: *vata*, *pitta* and *kapha*.

Sweet dishes that are offered to the deities always contain cardamom as it is the essence of life.

Carom | Omam

Trachyspermum ammi
An antacid

Carom

Carom, also known as Bishop's weed is called *omam* in Tamil and *ajwain* in Hindi. It is related to dill, coriander, caraway and cumin.

Carom grows wild in many parts of India and it is also cultivated. It is a small bush that looks like a parsley plant, with clusters of flowers that produce tiny yellowish-gray seeds that almost resemble caraway seeds. The seeds are bitter and have a pungent fragrance, somewhat like oregano.

It is a common ingredient in south Indian savories and snacks.

Carom is also an important spice in traditional medicine. Carom oil has thymol, a powerful antiseptic, antibacterial and antifungal agent. Thymol is used in herbal toothpastes.

The seeds are rich in vitamins, antioxidants and minerals. They are said to purify the blood and improve appetite. Carom is given in combination with other herbs and spices to lactating mothers. My mother always had powdered carom seeds ready at hand. She would lightly roast a cup of carom seeds until the raw smell disappeared. She would then grind them and keep the powder in a jar to use in various recipes.

Used in combination with fennel and cumin in a decoction, carom can relieve gas and gas related pains. A drink made from carom can instantly relieve acidity. Carom tea with ginger after a meal is soothing to the stomach and aids digestion. My mother gave carom seed water to her grandbabies to cure indigestion and relieve colic pain. It eliminates gas and promotes healthy bacteria that soothe the baby's stomach. Carom seed with fennel is also good for colic. The seeds are boiled together, strained and served at room temperature with a little sugar. (I have two older sisters. Keeping with the tradition, they would come to their maternal home for delivery and post delivery care.)

It is believed that eating carom seeds regularly cures alcohol cravings.

My mother made delicious tea out of carom powder, ginger, lemon and honey. Sometimes she would add a little cardamom and raisins to it. She would give this to all of us as a tonic and digestive aid.

Red Chillies | Sigappu milagai

Capsicum minimum
Increases metabolism and helps to reduce weight

Red Chillies

Red chillies are called *sigappu milagai* in Tamil and *lal mirch* in Hindi. The people of southern India use two varieties: the long red chillies and the almost round ones that are a half inch to one inch in diameter.

The hot pungency of red chillies creates fire in your mouth. Those who have had red chillies in their diet cannot live without it. Dried red chillies are used in cooking, either whole or ground.

Red chillies are blessed with potassium, manganese, calcium and other minerals. It contains vitamins B, E, C and K. It helps to remove toxins, increase metabolism and promote weight loss by letting the body perspire. It also aids digestion, improves blood circulation, builds immunity and curbs inflammation. A popular weight loss recipe uses red chillies, lemon and maple syrup. Even though in Ayurveda chillies are used to promote weight loss, it is carefully combined with other foods to balance the *doshas*. People who traditionally cook with red chillies do not make special weight loss recipes but simply use it in their daily foods. When the metabolism is stimulated, one can lose weight in any case. It is also considered an aphrodisiac.

In Ayurveda, red chillies are prescribed for rheumatism and arthritis. It is a good remedy for nasal congestion. A warm tea infused with red chillies can do wonders. It also helps bring down the cholesterol level in the blood, thus helping eliminate heart problems. Postpartum food excludes red chillies for 40 days because they produce heat and could irritate the stomach of newborns who are on mother's milk.

A note of caution: Some people are allergic to the fumes released when red chillies are roasted. The fumes can cause severe cough, asthma or breathing problems. If you are allergic, keep the windows open and stay away from the fumes.

Red chillies are traditionally associated with anger in India. A dish spiced with red chillies is never served to friends or relatives without being accompanied by a sweet dish. If a neighbor wants to borrow some red chillies, they are always given with a little sugar. They are also used to ward off the evil eye. Many shops in India have a swag of red chillies hanging in front of their stores.

Cinnamon | Lavanga pattai

Cinnamomum zeylanicum
Blood purifier, good for diabetes

Cinnamon

Cinnamon is a tree native to India and Sri Lanka. The inner bark of the cinnamon tree is used as a spice. Whole cinnamon is available in the market in the form of pieces of rolled bark four or five inches long. A small piece of real cinnamon tastes sweet and spicy with a tinge of heat to it. Cinnamon is a spice widely used in north Indian cooking. It is called *lavanga pattai* in Tamil and *dalchini* in Hindi.

I do not recall my parents or grandmother using cinnamon as medicine. However, south Indians do use cinnamon in cooking and a very popular dish called *bissi bela bhath* has both cloves and cinnamon in it.

When the British came to India looking for spices, the aromatic, soothing effect of cinnamon was a sure win and today cinnamon tea has become widely popular. I love the aroma of hot apple cider with cinnamon prepared during Christmas. The whole house smells of cinnamon and apple and the fragrance is soothing to the body, mind and spirit. The drink calms your nerves and alleviates depression and anxiety, while building your immune system. It increases the heat in the body, so it relieves the symptoms of cough, cold and asthma and generally gets you through the winter in good health.

In Ayurveda, cinnamon plays an important role and has been in use for over four thousand years. It is highly revered in Chinese, Egyptian and Greek pharmacology. It controls the *kapha* and *vata* humors of the body.

Cinnamon contains antioxidants. It helps lower the cholesterol and triglyceride levels in the blood. It is anti-inflammatory and an antiseptic, useful in treating bee stings, skin infections, cuts and bruises.

Cinnamon sticks can be boiled in water, strained and stored in a spray bottle to treat infections and injuries. The spray also helps control itchiness caused by allergies.

Cinnamon powder and honey mix is a home remedy for pimples. Apply it overnight or during the day on affected areas. Honey-cinnamon jam can be used on bread, oatmeal and with apples.

A honey-cinnamon drink or tea can be taken daily to improve overall health, protect against heart diseases, improve the functioning of the colon, regulate sugar levels in the body, relieve menstruation discomfort, arthritis, nausea of pregnant women and bladder infections, while also helping the immune system, thus resulting in longevity.

Cloves | Grambu

Syzgium aromaticum
Natural anesthetic

Cloves

Cloves are called d*evapushpa* in Sanskrit which means *"flower of the gods"*. In Tamil, they are called *grambu* and in Hindi they are known as *lavang*. They have been in use since ancient times.

Clove is an evergreen tree native to Indonesia but widely prevalent in India. The flower buds that are picked when mature are what we use as the spice. Clove oil is extracted from the dried flower bud.

Clove, an integral part of Ayurveda and Indian cooking and used throughout the world, has a strong aroma and taste. Clove is added in *garam masala*, a curry mix in north Indian cooking, and in pulao, a rice dish. In the south, it is used in sweets and as medicine. I use cloves and cinnamon in tomato soup. It tastes delicious and is a healthy appetizer that perks you up.

Clove oil is sold as an oral anesthetic for toothaches and as an antiseptic. It is anti-inflammatory, anti-fungal and a mild antioxidant. It can be chewed for sore throat and cough and for any feeling of nausea. It is also used as a stimulant and an expectorant.

I used to carry cloves in my pocket when I went to teach in New Jersey. I would munch on one as a breath freshener or to alleviate a sore throat. Some of my students teased me saying, "Oh, Mrs. S. is doing drugs." Then, I showed them how the spice looked and educated them of its virtue. Later, I found many of them munching on cloves!

Clove enhances the action of white blood cells which fight diseases. A combination of clove oil, garlic and honey is used to relieve asthma and chest congestion. Boil 1 glass of water with 6 to 8 pieces of cloves and take a little at a time, 4 times a day, for asthma.

A paste of cloves and carom taken in equal measure with a little fenugreek powder can be applied on the face once a week to treat pimples.

Clove oil is also used as a rub for rheumatic pain and muscular cramps, headache, allergies and itching.

Clove tea is a stress reliever as it removes tiredness and fatigue, energizing the body. Pregnant women can take clove tea to relieve nausea and gas.

Clove leaves have spiritual significance too. They are used in tantric practices by some groups in south India.

Coconut | Thengai

Cocos nucifera
Natural electrolyte

Coconut

The coconut tree is a tall palm that grows widely in the tropics, particularly in the coastal areas. What one buys in the market is the hard brown nut that has been removed from the woody husk of the fruit. Coconut is called *thengai* in Tamil and the tree is called *thennamaram*. In Hindi, the fruit is called *nariyal*.

The indigenous communities consider it *kalpa vriksha* or the tree that provides all the necessities of life. The fruit is versatile, containing milk, water, pulp and oil. Its shell is used to make cups and the fronds are plaited to make walls and roofs. The coarse fibers are used to prepare a cleaning agent and to make ropes. The ribs from the leaflets are made into brooms. Coconut oil is used in cosmetics and soaps.

Coconut pulp and oil have been in use as food and medicine for thousands of years. Coconut water taken from young coconuts is a refreshing drink full of electrolytes. It has abundance of minerals such as magnesium, iron, calcium, zinc, phosphorous, sodium and nitrogen. It contains niacin, thiamin and riboflavin, all B-complex vitamins, and Vitamin C. Coconut water can rehydrate the body if a person has diarrhea. Coconut contains high levels of potassium, which is also good for energizing the body. Some drink coconut water during fasting.

But wait, the secret has yet to be revealed! The power of coconut water—the secret of eternal youth—contains *kinin*, a substance that has been proven to be an anti-aging agent. In addition, the triglycerides found in coconut fat enhances memory and cures Alzheimer's disease.

The tender pulp is sweet and full of nutrients. In the next stage of maturity, the flesh of the coconut is the most nutritious part. It boosts metabolism and builds immunity. It is in the third stage of maturity that the oil is derived.

Coconut balances the *pitta* and *vata* of the body. It is used in healing and detoxifying the body. It is a natural stress reliever and detoxifier. Eaten with poppy seeds and ghee, it helps insomnia and relieves hot flashes in menopausal women.

Coconut also produces an intoxicant. An alcoholic beverage known as toddy is made out of it. Small earthen pots are tied to the flower stem to extract the sap. The toddy, when fresh, contains B-complex, vitamins A and C, potash and minerals. At that stage, it has no alcohol content but within a couple of hours, it starts fermenting. Toddy is found only in special shops in the villages. I have not seen it sold commercially but the toddy farm is usually tied up with a local vendor with government permits to prevent contamination and illegal activity.

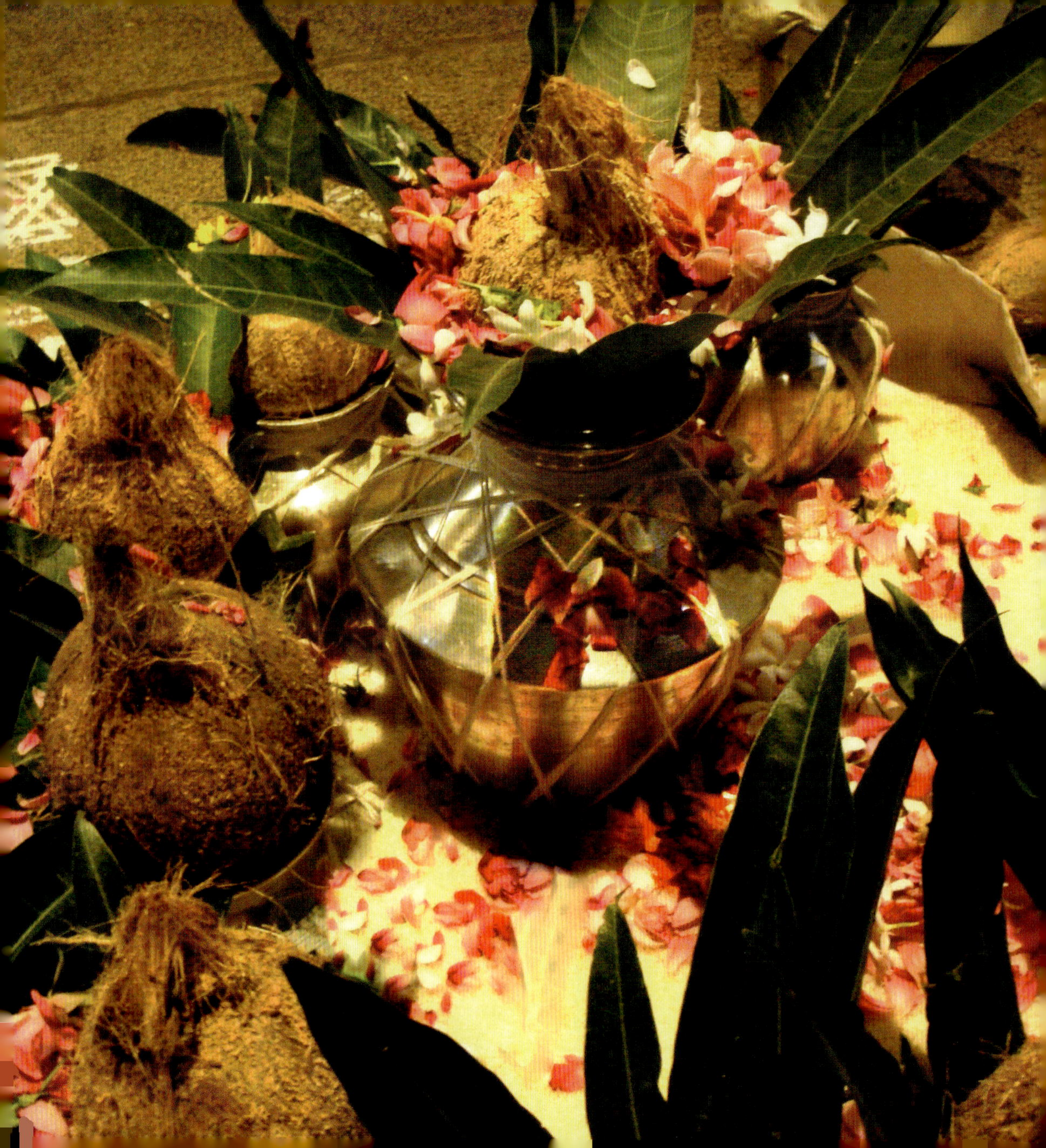

In India, the coconut palm is considered a divine tree. The coconut is revered from the time of the Rig Veda. It is also regarded as an elixir of life. Coconuts are considered the purest form of offering to God. The thick outer layer of the coconut is synonymous with the human ego. This ego has to be shed to reach the state of spiritual inquiry, so the worshipper breaks the shell and aspires to a higher consciousness. A coconut is broken before starting any new venture such as releasing a new film, driving a new car or building a new home for an auspicious beginning.

The importance of coconut is exemplified in Vedic rituals where a coconut is placed on the mouth of a metal pot known as the *kalasam*. The *kalasam* must be filled with water or grains and coins. A swag of mango leaves surrounds the coconut. The pot has now become a *purna-kalasam* symbolizing an abundance of food, health and wealth. In the *kalasam*, the coconut represents abundance, prosperity and strength. It also symbolizes fecundity. The water represents the source of life and the mango leaves represent fertility, regeneration and rejuvenation. The fragrant jasmine and rose flowers that decorate the *kalasam* stand for the beautiful aroma of life.

Hindu rituals surrounding the birth of a child, the naming ceremony, first birthday, puberty, initiation ceremonies, engagement, wedding, anniversaries and significant birthday celebrations, all call for the use of *kalasam*. In south Indian wedding rituals, the coconut stands for prosperity and fertility. A coconut with turmeric and betel leaves in a bag (like a party favor) is given to every female at the end of the wedding. The turmeric symbolizes freedom from sickness and the coconut eternal life.

Coriander | Kothamalli

Coriandrum sativum
Store house of Vitamin C

Coriander

Coriander, also known as cilantro in English, is called *kothamalli* in Tamil and *dhania* in Hindi. It is an annual herb cultivated in tropical and subtropical regions. It cannot withstand much heat, so it is grown in hilly regions. The plants grow six inches to one foot high. The flowers grow in tiny clusters and are whitish-purple in color.

It is easy to grow coriander in a pot. The seeds are rubbed with a flat object to split them so that they germinate faster. It is then sowed a quarter inch deep in the soil. Water regularly until they germinate. Allow them to grow three to four inches tall before you pick leaves to use as garnish.

The green leaves are used in chutneys, to flavor the food and as a garnish. The seeds are used as a spice. As one walks through the streets of south India, the morning air mesmerizes the senses with the aroma of roasted coriander seeds. The seeds are a key ingredient in south Indian *sambar* powder. While it cooks, the aroma of coriander refreshes and calms. Besides using the seeds, *sambar* and *rasam* are always garnished with fresh green coriander leaves.

A caffeine-free drink is made out of coriander seeds as a substitute for coffee. The seeds are fried dark brown and powdered and used to make coffee the same way the regular coffee is made.

Coriander has been a part of Ayurveda for thousands of years. Both the green herb and the seeds are used in medicine. It is a good source of phytonutrients, copper, iron, magnesium and calcium, The leaves are rich in Vitamin C. Coriander has been credited with many healing properties. The three-spice combination of fennel, cumin and coriander is a recipe from heaven. It helps with digestion and assimilation of nutrients.

Coriander reduces flatulence and acts as a stimulant and a blood purifier. It also has diuretic, anti-bilious and aphrodisiac properties. It is said to improve memory. It is used for healing urinary tract disorders. Coriander is a cooling herb.

The juice of coriander leaves is used in treating liver disorders, skin rashes and itchiness. According to *nattu vaidyam* (folk medicine), coriander controls blood pressure and cholesterol levels. The fresh leaves are washed and soaked in water overnight. This water is strained and taken in the morning as tea. Recent studies confirm what the ancients knew of this super herb and its healing qualities.

Cumin | Jeeragam

Cuminum cyminum
Eliminates gas and abdominal pain

Cumin

Cumin is cultivated as a winter crop in subtropical areas of India. It is an annual plant growing up to two feet high. The seeds look much like fennel seeds and the leaves are very similar to fennel as well.

Cumin belongs to the parsley family. It is known as *jeeragam* in Tamil and *jeera* in Hindi. The word *jeeragam* comes from *jeeranam*, meaning digestion. The ancients consider cumin as a medicine for digestion. Some interpret the word as 'seer' meaning vitalizing and 'agam' meaning the body. Cumin is said to vitalize the body.

In *Charaka Samhita* it is known as one of the herbs that aids digestion and relieves abdominal pain.

Cumin is a versatile spice and is used in many parts of the world. The Mexican chili and taco seasoning is made from cumin seeds. Indian cooking revels in the use of cumin. It is used in curries, *rasams* and many vegetable dishes and legumes.

Cumin for medicinal uses can be taken daily. It contains calcium, iron and vitamins that are good for the eye. According to Ayurveda, cumin stimulates the pancreatic enzymes, which in turn aids digestion and may also protect against cancer of the stomach and liver. It also contains antioxidants that protect the body from free radicals. It has minerals such as copper, iron and zinc.

Cumin relieves gripping pain in the intestines because of its carminative and stomachic properties. It also relieves bloating due to excessive gas in the stomach.

A simple cumin decoction is used to detect false labor. To make this, roast 2 teaspoons of cumin seeds in a pan till they are almost black, then add 2 cups of water. Bring to a boil and then simmer till it is reduced to half. Add 2 teaspoons of palm sugar and simmer for a minute longer. Strain and drink hot. Expectant mothers can drink a few ounces of this decoction, and if the pain is false labor, it will miraculously go away.

A similar decoction with lemon juice, known as *jeera kashayam*, is taken before food as an appetizer and to stimulate enzymes. To help digestion and keep the body cool, boil 1 teaspoon of cumin seeds in 1 cup of water, leave it overnight and drink it the next morning.

Ground cumin and turmeric tea is taken to treat kidney stones.

Curry Leaves | Kariveppilai

Murraya keonigi
Rich source of calcium

Curry Leaves

Curry leaf is a small tree that grows wild in south India. It is called *karivepilai* in Tamil and *kari patha* in Hindi.

When Westerners talk about Indian food, they think of "curry" as a spicy sauce. For a south Indian vegetarian, *kari* means a vegetable dish. The word comes from *karigai*, which in Tamil means vegetables. For meat eaters of the south, it means a meat dish. The British coined the word "curry" from the "kari-plant." The south Indians call the plant *karivepillai* sometimes spelled as *karuvepillai* The aroma of the *kari* leaves are like a mix of herbs and spices. So, historically, curry which the Indians know as "masala" was a mix of spices developed for the palate of maharajas of different regions of India. The spices included varied across regions. In the south Indian Brahmin cooking there was no such thing as a curry sauce. However, Madras curry powder, a modern concoction, is quite popular, curry leaf being one of the popular ingredients.

The breathtaking aroma surely grabs your attention when curry leaves are being sputtered in oil. When sputtered in coconut oil, it exudes a unique aroma that blends in with the dish. It is difficult to eat the leaf and generally it is removed from the food before serving. Some dishes call for ground curry leaves. Personally, I prefer this method as you get the benefit of all the nutrients in the leaves.

Curry leaf is used in Ayurveda for medicines and as a home remedy for various illnesses. The leaves are blessed with antioxidants, vitamins A and C, iron and folic acid. They are a rich source of calcium. According to Ayurveda, it also has cancer fighting properties because it contains valuable anti-carcinogenic chemical compounds. Curry leaves are included in the delicious dishes that are given as postpartum food. Drinking a leaf tonic can slow the progression of cataracts.

Curry leaves are beneficial in controlling diabetes. My father believed that eating five to ten leaves a day would keep sugar levels under control. The people of the south region love to drink buttermilk with curry leaves and asafoetida.

The leaves are also good for the hair. Throw in a few curry leaves in coconut oil, warm this oil and let it sit for several days. Use this oil to massage your scalp regularly. It helps to control premature graying and promotes healthy and shiny hair.

Edible Stemmed Vine | Perendai

Cissus quadrangularis
Miracle bone setter herb

Edible Stemmed Vine

Perandai is the Tamil name for the edible stemmed vine, also known as boneset. It grows wild throughout southern India. Sometimes, one can see this strange looking creeper on fences and along the roadside. It is easy to grow as a potted plant on a window sill.

In Ayurveda and *Siddha*, it is known as *asthisamharaka*, meaning that which heals and protects the bones. The bone-setters of south India are famous for using the stems and roots of the herb to heal and set broken bones and treat injuries of the muscles, cartilage, tendons and nerves. The vine is made into a paste and applied on the injured limbs. The oil extract which is available these days can be used for massage. The *perandai* powder, or in the juice form, is also administered internally as medicine.

It is used to treat muscular and arthritic pains and swellings. To get rid of arthritic pains, one must eat *perandai* consistently for a few days. This herb is also a remedy for osteoporosis. Osteoporosis can happen due to old age, in women after menopause and at any age due to Vitamin D3 deficiency. Vitamin D is essential for bone density. Even though the sunlight provides this vitamin, a good percentage of people in India are Vitamin D3 deficient. The symptoms are pain in joints and hips, difficulty in walking, and hairline fractures. Proper diet that includes *perandai*, milk and/or yogurt and lots of green vegetables and a little early morning sunlight can solve this problem.

Used as a treatment for obesity, this vine also aids digestion. The herb brings down the *kapha* and *vata doshas*.

Siddha expert Kalpana Premkumar says that *perandai* juice with honey is given to regulate menstruation. *Perandai* is anthelmintic, antibacterial, anti-inflammatory and an aphrodisiac.

Perandai is an ingredient in delicious recipes for chutneys, *kootu*, *vadai* and *perandai* juice is also added to *appalams (papad)*.

My father told us that this plant can be fed to cattle to cure many diseases.

A word of caution: This herb contains oxalic acid concentrated on the nodes of the vine and can cause an itchy sensation of the throat and the mouth. The nodes must be removed before preparing a poultice and or a dish. While cleaning *pierandai*, one may even feel the itch in the hands. Rubbing oil on hands before cutting *perandai* protects one from the itch. My mother would always add tamarind to any dish with *perandai* as it neutralizes the itchiness.

Eucalyptus | Nilgiri maram

Eucalyptus camaldulensis
Heals cold, cough, headaches and joint pains

Eucalyptus

Eucalyptus is called *nilgiri maram* in Tamil. It grows in abundance in the Nilgiri hills of southern India. Eucalyptus grows wild in many parts of India at higher elevations. In the United States, the California coast boasts an abundance of eucalyptus, although the tree is native to Australia, where the koala bear thrives on its leaves.

Eucalyptus leaves and the aromatic oil of the leaves and branches have a wide range of medical uses. Eucalyptus is used to treat cold, cough, headaches, fever and chest congestion. It is taken internally as tea, tincture or lozenges. Ayurvedic formulas are available, but one must be careful when making home remedies, especially if consuming internally. Always take the advice of a naturopath or an Ayurvedic doctor.

In Ayurveda, eucalyptus is used to treat infections and inflammations, body aches, tuberculosis, laryngitis and many other disorders. Eucalyptus is anti-inflammatory, decongestant, antibacterial and antispasmodic. The essential oil is beneficial in relieving asthma patients of the breathing discomfort. Gently rubbing the oil on the chest helps dilate the blood vessels allowing oxygen into the lungs.

If the leaves and bark are readily available, use them in steam baths and inhalation to relieve nasal congestion and headache, sinusitis, skin disorders and joint pains. Inhalation dissolves mucus from the lungs and removes bronchial infection from the respiratory tract.

Eucalyptus has an anaesthetic effect and therefore is useful in treating body pains, headache and toothache. It can be used in combination with clove oil to rub on affected areas. Take a small amount of the oil and briskly massage the area.

Fennel | Sombu

Foeniculum vulgare
For metabolism, digestion and an antidote for food poisoning

Fennel

Fennel, which is called *sombu* in Tamil and *saunf* in Hindi, is a perennial herb. I have seen fennel just popping up randomly along roadsides. The leaves and seeds are used in Ayurveda and in home remedies.

Fennel is aromatic, sweet tasting and cooling to the body. The seeds are chewed as a natural mouth freshener and digestive aid, sometimes in combination with betel leaves, *gulkhand* (rose jam) and betel nut. Fennel helps eliminate flatulence and metabolize food. It is a natural diuretic and eliminats toxins. Therefore, it is a natural weight loss agent. The leaves, roots and seeds are used in tonics or drinks to control weight.

The seeds and roots are used in helping the functions of the liver, spleen, kidneys and gallbladder. When my brother got jaundice, my mother made fennel tea every day for him so that the jaundice would not affect his liver. He was kept in isolation and lots of neem leaves were strewn around the room to ward off germs.

Fennel leaf and root juice is used as an antidote for food poisoning and insect bites. Fennel tea eye wash is soothing and clears painful infections of the eyes. It is also credited with enhancing vision. A combination of fennel, cumin and coriander calms the nerves, aids in digestion and is good for lactating mothers. Fennel tea induces labor, whereas cumin, which looks similar to fennel, relieves false labor pains.

Fennel seeds, anise and betel leaves are ingredients of a drink to relieve colic pain in babies. This is an age-old grandma recipe. During the colonial period, the British learned much about ancient medicines of India. In 1851 an Englishman with the surname Woodward formulated a mix known as gripe water which included fennel, dill, alcohol and sugar. He marketed this with the powerful phrase, "Granny told mother and mother told me." But of course, the real south Indian granny formula did not contain alcohol.

My grandmother used to make a face mask with fennel and turmeric. She applied this once a week and left it on for 15 to 20 minutes. At the time, I did not realize the significance of this ritual, but now I realize that this is why she always looked so young and beautiful!

Anise is similar to fennel in its healing properties. It is a digestive aid and usually eaten after a meal along with cardamom and fennel. It stimulates lactation in new mothers.

Fenugreek | Venthayam

Trigonella foenum - graecum
Cooling herb, stops diarrhea

Fenugreek

Fenugreek known as *venthayam* in Tamil and *methi* in Hindi is an annual plant that grows in cooler regions. It grows up to two feet tall and has trifoliate leaves. It bears yellowish-white flowers. The seeds have an interesting rectangular shape and produce a yellow-hued dye.

It is the favorite spice of the south. Both the leaves and the seeds are eaten. They have a strong fragrance and a slightly bitter taste that can be neutralized by adding any sour ingredient such as tamarind or tomato.

Fenugreek is used daily in south Indian cooking, especially in *sambar*. The leaves are used as greens and can be combined with *mung*, red gram or potatoes to make delicious dishes. Mango pickle is well preserved, aromatic and tasty because of the fenugreek and asafoetida in it. Sprouted fenugreek seeds are a delicacy in salads.

Highly valued for its medicinal properties, fenugreek is good for the eyes. It contains a compound similar to estrogen that helps neutralize premenstrual discomfort and problems associated with menopause.

Fenugreek has antibacterial properties and is used externally in poultices for boils, abscesses and inflammation. Internally, it is used to relieve diarrhea and soothe inflammation of the digestive tract. It is also used to control diabetes. It is an aphrodisiac, antidysenteric and a coolant.

Whenever we had an upset stomach with diarrhea, my mother would give us one teaspoon of fenugreek seeds with yogurt. We would gulp it down as though we were taking medicine. It would start working within minutes and after a few doses the diarrhea would stop. It is cooling and healing to the stomach. The probiotics in the yogurt also heals the stomach and controls diarrhea.

Tooth powder prepared with cardamom, *triphala* and fenugreek helps heal chronic gingivitis. Fenugreek, when soaked and blended, has a gooey and soapy consistency. Along with *shikakai* (soapnut) and other herbs, it is used as a cooling cleansing powder for body and scalp, especially after an oil massage.

Soak a teaspoon of fenugreek seeds in a cup of water. Leave it overnight and drink it along with the seeds in the morning. This is a good drink to prevent and or cure diabetes. Beware, you may also start looking more youthful!

Galangal | Chitharathai

Alpinia galanga
A sure remedy for cough and cold

Galangal

Galangal known as *chitharathai* in Tamil and *kulanjan* in Hindi is a plant of the ginger family. Its aromatic rhizomes are used in cooking and herbal medicine.

Galangal is used in combination with licorice (*Glycyrrhiza* glabra or *athi maduram* in Tamil) as a folk cure for colds and sore throats. It was a common medicine made in my house when we had coughs and colds. The taste is not bad either. One can drink it like a soup and feel the results right away. My grandmother used to make a *kashayam* with galangal, *sukku* (dried ginger), *kandathipili* (long pepper stems), dried raw dates, *athi maduram* and palmyra palm sugar. This recipe heals not only a cough and cold, but it also clears fevers and chest congestion.

The south Indians boil dried galangal root in water. This is called *sukku jalam*. Drinking this prevents respiratory ailments during the winter months. In Ayurveda, galangal is used as a poultice to cure pains related to the spinal column, especially the lower back. It is used for muscular pains of the body. It is carminative, stomachic and a stimulant. Galangal is used in treating cattle and horses as well.

In the Vedic tradition, the ancients believed that everything we have in nature, including flora and fauna, are gifts from the universal source energy that is God. Therefore, everything in nature is the "spice of life."

Hildegard of Bingen, a saint who lived in Germany during the middle ages, saw mystical visions and later wrote about them. She was a polymath—a music composer, prophet, scientist and herbalist and it is believed that she healed many influential people of her time with herbal remedies. She introduced the word *veriditas*, in this famous sentence, *"O Nobllissima Veriditas: O most noble greenness, you whose roots are in the sun and who shine in bright serenity in a wheel that no earthly eminence can comprehend."* She saw God in all of life. The plant world and every creature is an expression of divine power on earth and this is the vital energy or *veriditas*.

Hildegard of Bingen visited India to study the mystics and their healing powers. Dubbing galangal the "spice of life" in her book *Physica* now titled *Hildegard's Healing Plants*, she created galangal formulas for heart ailments, digestion, and for the rejuvenation of the senses of hearing and vision.

Garlic | Poondu

Allium sativum
Rejuvenates cells and purifies the blood

Garlic

Garlic is called *poondu* in Tamil and *lahsun* in Hindi. It belongs to the onion family.

Garlic is widely used in India in daily cooking as well as in pickles. Orthodox cooks avoid it because it is not considered *sattvic*: it is believed to produce heat and is known to be a *tamasic* herb. However, it is widely used even by the orthodox as a medicine and a tonic, especially for lactating mothers.

Garlic is an expectorant, carminative, antiseptic and a stimulant. New mothers are given garlic to rejuvenate the cells, strengthen the blood and produce breast milk.

Garlic has long been part of Ayurvedic and *Siddha* medicine. According to Ayurveda, it has five of the six tastes. The five tastes are sweet, bitter, pungent, salty and astringent. It does not have the sour taste.

Regular consumption of garlic reduces cholesterol and prevents blood clots since it is an anticoagulant, thus helping promote a healthy heart. It is a natural remedy for high blood pressure. It is used to treat tumors and ulcers. It is a folk medicine for snakebites. It is antifungal, antibacterial and antiviral. Besides being an aphrodisiac, garlic heals and strengthens the bones. Perhaps because it is said to kill bacteria and viruses in the body and in our environment, garlic is believed to ward off evil spirits.

The vegetables of the allium family can cause intestinal gas leading to irritable bowel syndrome (IBS). In general, when garlic is used in food, it is combined with ginger to counteract the IBS problem. Through time, this combination, along with onion, has become a gourmet masala that is also breathtaking.

Garlic contains essential oil with sulfides allyl propyl, disulfide, allicin and allisatin one and two that are cancer blocking agents. Besides, it also contains a flavanoid called quercetin which has anti-inflammatory and antioxidant properties that scavenge free radicals that harm the healthy cells, therefore inhibiting the growth of cancer cells.

In the *Siddha* folk medicine tradition, garlic is used to treat asthma, allergies and ear infections. They make a pickle out of garlic cloves which are then stored in a tight jar. Two bulbs of garlic taken every morning will help treat asthma. A spoon or two of fresh garlic juice is taken to cure an itchy throat.

Ginger | Inji

Zingiber officinale
Maha aushadi or the supreme medicine!

Ginger

Ginger is called *inji* in Tamil and *adarak* in Hindi. Ginger is cultivated in tropical regions. Growing well in hot climates and sandy soil, it is the rhizome growing in clusters at the base of the plant that is used in cooking and medicine.

Ginger is an important ingredient in south Indian cuisine. My mother used it in many traditional dishes. As a young person, I hated ginger, as did my siblings and friends. We disliked its intense aroma and spicy taste and we would pick out the pieces of ginger from our plates and discard them. Of course, we were yelled at for throwing away this mighty rhizome, a rejuvenator and killer of diseases. As a person matures, one starts enjoying that very aroma and taste that he or she so disliked.

Tender ginger is pickled and also added as a spice in daily cooking. Ginger tea and beverages can be made with fresh or dried ginger. Restaurants in south India serve a drink that combines ginger and lemon or lime as an appetizer and digestive aid.

For thousands of years, ginger has been used in traditional Indian medicine. It has magnesium, potassium and zinc, which are all good for health and balancing of the thyroid. It is used fresh and also in the dried form. The dried rhizome, known as *sukku* in Tamil, is used in medicine and is useful in relieving coughs, colds and chest congestion. It dilates the blood vessels, causes warmth, increases perspiration and brings down the fever stimulating blood circulation as well. It helps absorb nutrients into the body. Having anti-inflammatory properties, it helps to relieve and heal joint pains. The powdered ginger is used in making ginger tonics that help digestion. A quarter teaspoon in milk will improve the appetite. If you suck on a piece of *sukku*, it will relieve toothache. A decoction made of *sukku* will eliminate stomach pain, vomiting and stomach disorders. Chewing on a piece of ginger helps cure throat infections.

In India, ginger is an integral part of the spiritual tradition. During the harvest festival of *Pongal*, a ginger plant is tied along with the turmeric plant to the pots in which the new harvest of grains and legumes are cooked. The cooking area is cleaned and *kolam* is drawn around the cooking stove or fire. The fresh ginger and turmeric crops with rhizomes and leaves represent the eternal life force of nature. The sun provides us the bounty with which we prevent diseases, rejuvenate and heal ourselves. Therefore, during the *Pongal* celebration, the fresh harvest is first enclosed in the powerful geometrical symbols of *kolam* that represent the universe, then the cooked food is offered to the sun god or Surya before being eaten as *prasadam*.

Holy Basil | Tulsi

Ocimum sanctum
The incomparable one!

Holy Basil

Holy basil is the most sacred of all plants in India. It is called *tulsi* in Hindi and *tulasi* in Tamil. There are two varieties of this healing herb: *Krishna* and *Rama*. Krishna *tulasi* has small, purplish green leaves, while Rama *tulasi* has large green leaves.

In mythology, Krishna's mystical Vrindavan garden is full of *tulasi* plants because it is believed that the plants emit life. Those who walk in the garden feel energized and rejuvenated. Growing up in India, it seemed like the way of life to see my grandmother going clockwise around the sacred plant after lighting a lamp and then prostrating before it. She would call on us to join her. She would tell us that *tulasi* is a goddess, a life giver, supporting stamina and endurance, the protector, who will rejuvenate the whole body and give one a youthful look. *Tulasi* is the female who holds the family together. She is "the incomparable one," the queen of herbs and ancient wisdom.

Tulasi leaves are offered in temples, especially to Lord Vishnu, either loose or in garlands. The holy water given to devotees contain *tulasi*, saffron and camphor. Rosary beads are made from the woody stems. *Tulasi* has anti-inflammatory, antiseptic and antibacterial properties. It is used to treat coughs, colds and flu. This herb, full of antioxidants, is a stress reliever and a nerve tonic. It improves memory. When I was growing up, the earthen pot for drinking water had *tulasi* leaves. Our job was to gather the leaves for the pot. Our parents and grandparents repeatedly told us that it was good for the brain. And so it is. Recently, experiments have shown that it removes fluoride from water, which is harmful for the brain and pineal gland.

Tulasi promotes general good health and relieves gastric trouble, cold and cough. A warm *tulasi* tea with honey every morning boosts the immune system. It is heat producing and that effect can be counteracted with coconut water or yogurt in the diet. Take 2 teaspoons of *tulasi* juice to stop runny nose and fever. Tulasi, dry ginger and cloves ground together and applied to the forehead as a poultice that cures headache. To enhance immunity in children, give them warm milk with a few *tulasi* leaves.

A face wash or splash made with *tulasi* is an excellent remedy for pimples. Heat water, add the leaves and simmer for 15 minutes. Cool, strain and pour into a spray bottle and hydrate the face for bright and young looking skin. *Tulasi* leaves can also be added to any face pack. *Tulasi* makes a great chutney with coconut, betel leaves, tender mango leaves, tamarind and black gram with asafoetida and red or black pepper. However, its uses in daily cooking are limited. It is far more important for its ritual and medicinal uses.

Indian Gooseberry | Nellikai

Emblica officinalis
A wonder fruit more valued than gold!

Indian Gooseberry

The Indian gooseberry is a deciduous tree found only in the tropical regions of Southeast Asia. Its small, yellow-green fruits have a bitter-sour taste and one has to develop a liking for them. The tree is called *nelli* in Tamil and the fruit is *nellikai*. In Hindi it is called *amla*.

Fresh fruits are eaten raw. They can be preserved in brine and also eaten ground into chutneys and in *pachidis* (yogurt salad). My mother used to make *nellikai* pickles, sauces, jams and medicinal decoctions with them.

Nelli has many outstanding qualities and has been used in Indian pharmacology for many years. Eating the fruits in the natural form provides maximum benefits to health. Replete with antioxidants and concentrated vitamin C, they are also antiviral and antifungal. Eating *nellikai* helps control blood pressure, diabetes, gall-bladder infections, cholesterol and improves energy levels.

The seeds are used in Ayurvedic medicines to control diabetes. *Nellikai* improves the immune system. It controls vomiting and light-headedness. It also relieves tiredness and weakness. It clears toxins from the small and large intestines. It eliminates gas and urinary infections. It is good for the eyes, strengthens the bones and cools the body. A few drops of the juice can be poured into the nostrils to control nosebleeds. It promotes hair growth and curbs premature graying of hair. My mother used to prepare a shampoo with *nellikai* powder, *shikakai* and a little fenugreek. This natural cleanser leaves your hair fragrant, shiny and bouncy, while cooling the scalp. Now, you may wonder where you are going to find *nellikai*. Ayurvedic pharmacies incorporate the properties of the fruit into tablets and powders and many health food stores sell them.

Nelli often features in Indian legends. When Ayurveda and Siddha medicine were being developed thousands of years ago, the sages would go into the forests looking for newer herbs and plants. According to a legend, a sage named Chyawan Rishi created a secret recipe with a combination of herbs and fruits and the most important fruit he used was the Indian gooseberry, the wonder fruit. The name Chyawanprash, a popular *legiyam* in the markets now owes its origin to this sage and his creation.

A folktale tells of a person named Adiyaman who gave a *nellikai* to Avaiyar, a woman poet, saying, "*Vazhnalai needikum*," meaning, "*May it extend your life eternally.*" According to another legend, Adi Shankaracharya sang 21 songs in praise of Mahalakshmi, asking her to bestow good fortune on a poor woman who gave him a *nellikai* as she had nothing else to offer. The goddess is said to have showered golden *nellikais* through her roof.

Indian Pennywort | Vellarai

Centella asiatica
Fights ADD and ADHD

Indian Pennywort

A gift from heaven, *Indian pennywort*, called *vellarai* in Tamil and *gotu kola* in Hindi, is an annual herb that grows in tropical wetlands in many parts of the world. One can find *vellarai* growing wild near water sources, ditches and edges of lawns. It is also cultivated for its multiple uses in medicine.

Vellarai has been in use in Ayurveda for thousands of years. It contains phosphorus, calcium, magnesium, zinc and other minerals that are very important for menopausal women. It also contains vitamins. In Ayurveda, *vellarai* is considered an antiaging herb, providing strength, vigor, mental alertness and youthful energy. It is a brain and nerve tonic for the young and the old. It keeps body aches and pains away and improves eyesight. It is also good for the heart as it lowers blood pressure and for skin problems such as rash, itching, eczema and skin ulcers. It is known to improve the libido and stamina in men.

Vellarai tonic is used in dermal and nerve diseases. It is known to promote memory. The roots of the plant are used in medicine as it has antibacterial and antiviral properties. The leaves can be cooked as greens and eaten. Fresh leaves can be added to salad and eaten raw. It has a slight bitter taste that becomes neutralized with tomato.

It is heat producing and so must be neutralized with cooling foods. Clean the leaves and sauté them in ghee with ¼ teaspoon cumin and a few cloves of garlic and tomato to make a delicious side dish. Chutney or *thohayal* can also be made from it. Chutney is eaten with a snack and *thohayal* is eaten with rice.

I feel sad when I see young children suffering from stress, anxiety, attention deficit disorder and other mental ailments. These are further complicated by the use of dangerous medication such as Ritalin. Why could we not just make pennywort and other herbal supplements part of the diet and save the children? It is safe and nutritious.

The following text from the website www.ritalindeath.com illustrates the problem: *"Since the death of our 14-year-old son Matthew caused from the use of Ritalin prescribed for ADHD (Attention Deficit Hyperactivity Disorder) our family has been informing others world wide via the internet about ADHD and the dangers of psychotropic drugs in memory of our son and countless other children that have died over the years as a direct result of using psychotropic drugs. We wish to expose the health risks, dangers, deaths and suicides that are a direct result of administering Ritalin and other psychiatric drugs to children."*

Lemon | Elumichampazham

Citrus limon
Wards off evil eye

Lemon

Lemon is a versatile citrus tree. Its fruit is used throughout the world in foods, beverages, medicine and during rituals. It is called *elimichai* in Tamil. A larger variety known as bitter orange which is green in color is called *narthai* in Tamil and is used as medicine in the form of dried pickle in south India.

Lemon is a popular ingredient in Indian cooking. South Indian cuisine features lemon rice, lemon *rasam*, lemon *kosamalli* and a wide variety of salty and spicy pickles, including salted whole lemons in brine, salted sweet lemon jam and cut lemons in a spice mix. In our family, we never threw out the lemon peels. Even after it is squeezed, a little juice remains. We save these and make pickles out of them. Grate them, blend them or finely chop them, add salt, red chilli powder, roasted fenugreek, roasted asafoetida and turmeric. Saute all the above in sesame oil, add raw sugar or jaggery, saute again for a few minutes and you have a great pickle. We ate the pickles with yogurt rice or millets. Pickled lemon stimulates digestion besides being very tasty.

Lemons are full of minerals that are good for the heart, the nervous system and digestion. They contain potassium, magnesium and calcium as well as an abundance of vitamin C. They prevent rickets and lower blood pressure. Eating lemon helps the body absorb calcium and iron.

In Ayurveda, drinking warm lemon water in the morning is key to good health. This regulates the bowel movement. Once a year, my mother would go to an Ayurvedic center for a two-week treatment to detoxify. Her routine included drinking lemon water first thing in the morning, which eliminated uric acid. Too much uric acid in the blood causes joint pains. Eating excessive amounts of protein can also cause high amounts of uric acid in the blood. She returned from these treatments slimmer and absolutely beautiful with clear, shiny skin. That was our inspiration to follow healthful habits.

However, I must admit that, while in school and college, one tends to resist sound routines and can fall prey to unhealthy eating habits. I bet my mother also ate unhealthy foods when we were not looking—and that was why she had to go to this center once a year!

Lemon water aids in digestion; it strengthens and stimulates the liver. It has antiseptic properties, builds immunity, helps in weight loss and reduces cholesterol. Lemon is an effective remedy for allergies. Lemons contain pectin which provides energy and reduces craving for food. In American restaurants, one can request a wedge of lemon for the drinking water. I always squeeze the juice into the water. It is refreshing, nutritious and a healthy appetizer to have before the meal. The Japanese

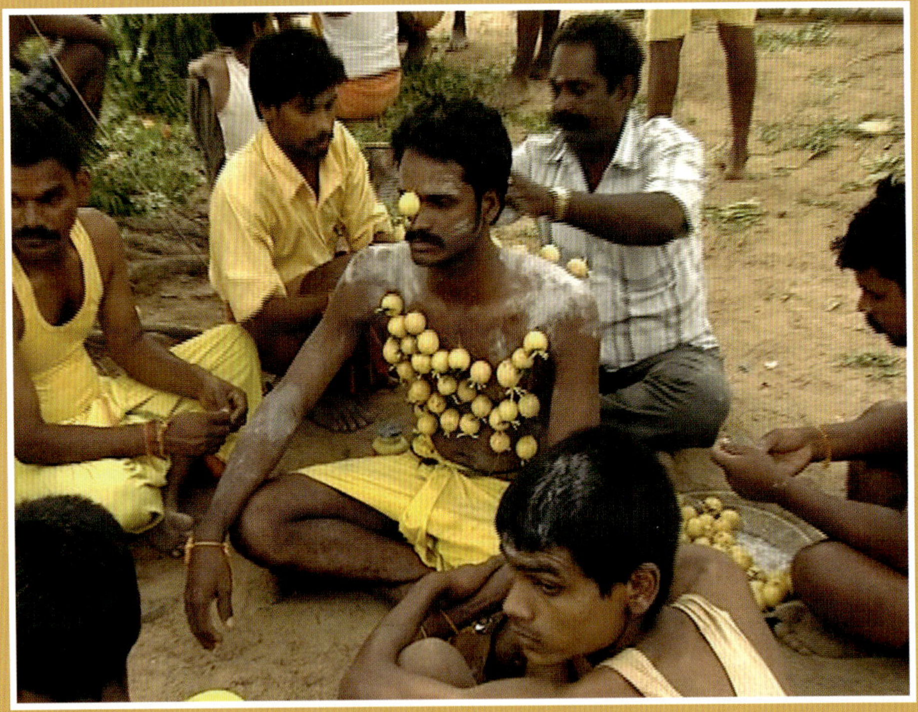

love to drink water with lemon and honey. It is sold in vending machines on practically every street corner in Tokyo.

Even though it is a source of citric acid, lemon is alkaline and some studies suggest that an alkaline environment inhibits the growth of cancer cells. All parts of the lemon plant are used in medicine. A popular herbal powder that is eaten with rice is made from lemon leaves. Fresh seeds of lemon are peeled and ground up and mixed with honey and taken as medicine to cure nausea and vomiting.

Lemons are also used in rituals throughout the world. I was intrigued by the use of lemons during the making of a documentary on the fire walking ritual. Some fire walkers had 20 to 50 lemons stitched on to their bodies. The person feels no pain and there is no wound or blood when the lemons are stitched on. The sacred cow dung ash known as *vibhudi* is used as an antibacterial agent. This is rubbed onto the skin before the piercing is done. The lemons are used to ward off evil spirits and to provide strength, courage and stamina to walk on the fire with bare feet.

As one walks along the streets in India, one can see red chillies and lemons tied in front of some of the stores. According to belief, this wards off the evil eye. When our gardener passed away, lemons were put at the doorway of the house to help his soul cross over peacefully.

Being alkaline, lemons are calming and therefore it is offered to goddess Kali who is also known as Parvati, the consort of Lord Shiva. In the form of Kali, the goddess becomes the destroyer of evil and she is depicted as being fierce. To calm her and receive her blessings, lemons are offered in the form of a garland. Lemons also remove negativity from the surroundings.

Lemons are plentiful and readily available to all, making it easy to incorporate their healthful benefits in your daily routine.

It is also a practice to light lemon lamps for Goddess Durga. The fragrance from these provides positive vibrations. It relieves stress and calms the mind. Does it not make sense that one would light lemon lamps at homes as well? Here is how you can make your own lemon lamps.

Cut a lemon into two halves. Squeeze out the juice, and remove all the fiber. Then turn the lemon inside out. Now add ghee or sesame oil and insert a wick and light the lamp. According to tradition, the juice is never consumed before an offering is made to the goddess.

The juice is first offered as *nevediam* (an offering), and then taken as *prasadam* (a blessed food) in the form of lemonade or any other dish. The tradition also says one must light odd numbers of the lemon candle such as 1, 3, 5 or 7.

Lemongrass | Karpurapul

Cymbopogon citratus
A diuretic, cooling herb

Lemongrass

Lemongrass is native to Asia and grows plentifully in south India. The Tamil name is *karpurapul* and it is sometimes known as *Cochin* grass or *Malabar* grass.

This incredible herb is bestowed with many healing properties besides containing vitamins and minerals. It has vitamins A,C, and B-complex. It is antifungal and antibacterial and it reduces levels of uric acid and cholesterol.

In Ayurveda, lemongrass is used as a sedative and antidepressant. It improves the functioning of the nervous system thus controlling anxiety, nervousness and tension. It helps stimulate blood circulation, alleviates fevers and aids digestion.

My mother used to make a drink with lemongrass and barley. Both are diuretics and eliminate toxins from the body. When taken as tonic or tea, it can reduce weight. Simply boil the two ingredients together in water and drink as tea. One can also boil a bunch of lemongrass in a quart of water and drink as tea, sipping slowly. It acts as a blood purifier and rejuvenator. The lemongrass aroma is somewhat lemony and is intoxicating when used in teas and in food preparations.

Lemongrass oil is made from the leaves and flowers. The oil, known as citral, is used in manufacturing cosmetics and perfumes. It functions as a fungicidal and antiseptic for healing wounds and bruises and fungus of the skin and nails.

Also used in aromatherapy for its calming effect, it is a cooling herb that can relieve headaches and stress.

Citronella and lemongrass are related to the species of grasses belonging to the genus Cymbopogon. Citronella, known as *Cymbopogon* nardus, is not edible. Citronella oil is used as an insecticide and to repel mosquitoes. It is used extensively in the cosmetic industry and in the manufacture of incense.

Mustard | Kadugu

Brassica juncia/nigra
Mustard oil cures arthritic pain

Mustard

Mustard is called *kadugu* in Tamil and *sarson* or *rai* in Hindi. It belongs to the family *Cruciferae*, which includes cabbage, broccoli and brussels sprouts. Mustard comes in many varieties and sizes. The white mustard seeds that are slightly yellow in hue are commonly used in Western countries to make the eponymously named condiment. In India, the more popular variety is dark brown in color.

The mustard seed has a pungent smell and a slightly bitter taste. The south Indians use mustard seed daily in almost every dish. Mustard seeds are popped in oil (as you would pop corn) and added as a garnish to dishes. You ask why? This is because mustard increases the *pitta* factor, and therefore is considered heat producing, but when popped, it loses its heat producing quality. Sometimes, the word sputter is used instead of pop, because the mustard makes a sputtering noise when popped. It releases a strong yet pleasing aroma that complements the dish. Secondly, it is high in selenium and has omega-3 and omega-6 fatty acids. It helps lower the blood pressure, boosts metabolism and acts as an anti-inflammatory agent.

Mustard oil is never used in daily south Indian cooking but it is used in mango pickles. Mustard seeds are also ground raw to be added to pickles as a preservative. The famous south Indian mango pickle known as *avaka manga urugai* is made with mustard seeds as the main spice.

The greens are a treasure of vitamins A, C and K, carotene and antioxidants. A favorite in the Punjab region where mustard grows in abundance, corn flatbread or roti and mustard greens are a very popular combination.

Mustard has been in use in Ayurvedic medicine for thousands of years. Both the seeds and leaves are used in food and medicine. Mustard is considered to have valuable antioxidants. It contains a good amount of magnesium, potassium, phosphorus and calcium.

Mustard oil is used in massages to relieve arthritis, rheumatism, aches and pains of the muscles and joints. It produces heat when used this way and sometimes even causes skin sores. Mustard greens have anthelmintic qualities. In Ayurveda it is used to cleanse the cranial cavity.

A word of caution: Overeating mustard greens could cause thyroid problems.

Neem | Vepamaram

Azadirachta indica
Anti-fungal and anti-bacterial

Neem

The Neem tree is also known as *margosa* in English. It is called *vembu* in Tamil, or more commonly *vepamaram*. The leaves are known as *veppa ellai* and the flowers are called *veppam poo*. The tree is native to southern India. It grows in the wild and is also cultivated in gardens.

The medicinal uses of neem are wide-ranging. Simply sitting under the shade of a neem tree or breathing in the breeze wafted through the branches is considered to have a healing effect.

All parts of the tree—the twigs, flowers, seeds and leaves—have been used for thousands of years as a natural healer, protector and insecticide. The flowers are dried and used in making *rasam*, chutney powders and *angaya powder* that are healing to the stomach and as postpartum food. Neem heals ulcers and removes intestinal worms. It is considered a blood purifier and when taken regularly is believed to improve eyesight.

Neem is a super beauty aid. A teaspoon of pure neem powder mixed in the bath water helps clear skin infections. Washing the face with neem water clears blackheads and pimples. Neem powder can be added to face packs.

My father and my uncles would chew on tender neem leaves all the time. It is a natural way to keep the heart healthy and sugar levels down. Neem is very bitter and as a child I would avoid it at all costs unless I could gulp it down in pill form.

The Tanjore district in the state of Tamil Nadu in southern India is a haven for many indigenous medicinal plants. As one travels through the region, one cannot help but notice the villagers tending and caring for their plants that, in turn, create a small income that enables their survival. It was exciting to walk through a village where everywhere you turned there were neem trees. I noticed that the seeds and flowers that fall from the trees are picked up by passers-by and street vendors alike. These are then cleaned and sold to the markets and wholesalers. While walking through a bamboo thicket in a village, at each clearing I saw small farms. Majestic neem trees stood with huts situated underneath them. People sat in the shade of the tree for healing and for its therapeutic value. I found neem seeds and other herbs drying in the sun in front of a hut. The woman sitting at the entrance told me that she makes neem oil and sells at the local market. This oil is medicinal and of great value. It is excellent for treating bronchitis and wheezing. Neem oil is an astringent. It is very potent and is used in combatting many types of fungus and skin diseases. Later, this woman very proudly showed me how to make a toothbrush out of a neem twig.

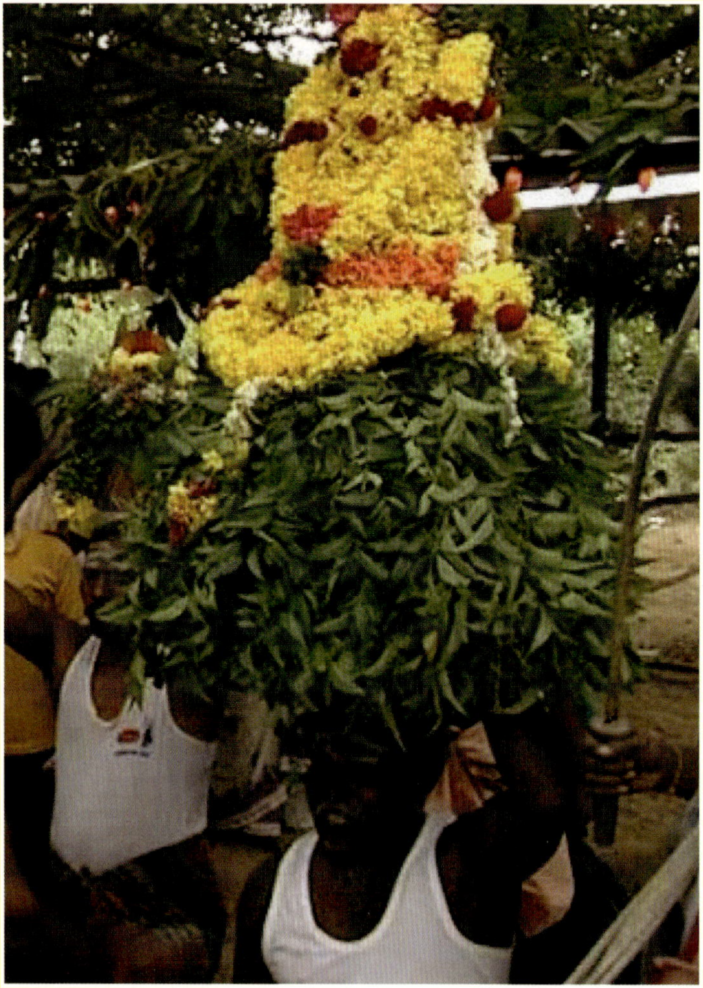

While chatting with her, I noticed that the entrance to her mud hut with thatched roof had a string of fresh neem leaves attached to the upper windowsill. This keeps mosquitos and flies at bay. Neem works as a natural insect repellent. Young neem leaves and twigs were also used as smoke stacks to repel flies and mosquitoes. My father incorporated crushed neem leaves, bark and sometimes the neem seed cake in the rose garden and vegetable gardens. Dried neem leaves are left in cupboards to protect clothes and books from insects.

The neem peat is the roughage left after extracting oil from the seeds. This is made into fertilizer and is called neem seed cake. Not only is it an organic fertilizer it also acts as a pesticide.

The leaves have antibacterial, antiseptic and antifungal properties. Neem leaves ground with yogurt are applied on burn scars to heal them. Neem leaves are commonly strewn in the sick room when someone has chickenpox or measles and sprigs of leaves are also used to fan the body to soothe the itch. Traditionally, a sprig of neem leaves was hung on the door of a sick person's house to warn people of contagion inside.

While filming a fire walking ritual, I observed that in order to show the fire walker's devotion to Shakthi, (the Power concept, also known as Kali), they would pierce their bodies and stitch lemons onto themselves as a way to build courage and strength. During this time, the devotees did not feel pain or burning sensations. Beforehand, they had applied neem, a variety of other herbs, and medicinal ash to their skin and this prevented them from getting infected and enabled them to sustain pain through the piercing process.

At the moment before fire walking, it is believed that evil spirits also lurk around them, stopping the person from devotion and accomplishment. Those who immerse themselves deeply in the rituals and meditation sometimes go into a trance.

Perhaps the participants are in a state of self-hypnosis, but the locals believe that they are possessed by evil spirits and use branches of neem leaves to thrash them out by means of waving, fanning and even hitting the fire walker with neem fronds.

Left: Neem leaves carried on man's head. Image from film, *Firewalkers of Tamil Nadu.*

Nutmeg | Jadipatri

Azadirachta indica
An aphrodisiac and rejuvenator of sexual organs

Nutmeg

Nutmeg is called *jaiphal* in Hindi and *jadipatri* in Tamil. Nutmeg has been in use since ancient times.

The tree is grown in the state of Kerala in southern India. It is an evergreen tree and two spices are produced from the pod: nutmeg and mace. Mace is the stringy outer shell and nutmeg is the kernel inside the seed. They smell about the same but each has its own distinct taste. Mace is milder whereas nutmeg is sweeter. Nutmeg is best grated from fresh kernels. Mace is always powdered.

Mace is used in small quantities to flavor food. Nutmeg is used as flavoring in certain Indian sweets and savory dishes.

In Ayurveda, nutmeg is known as a *rasayana* herb. The antioxidants in nutmeg improve the immune system. It stimulates and revitalizes the body thereby reversing the aging process.

Hot milk with nutmeg and honey is delicious, calming and relaxing. Taken before bedtime, it helps one sleep soundly. Nutmeg powder added to fresh Indian gooseberry juice (*nellikai*) can also be taken at bedtime to cure insomnia.

A remedy for rheumatism or sciatica pain is to massage the area with fried nutmeg powder in sesame oil. Fry ½ teaspoon of nutmeg in 1 tablespoon of sesame oil, cool and use when needed.

Nutmeg has antifungal, digestive and astringent properties. In Ayurveda it is used for digestive disorders, convulsions and for treating fever. It is also used for anxiety and depression. It contains hallucinogens and is an intoxicant. Nutmeg is used in many aphrodisiac tonics and for treatment of sexual disorders. Nutmeg extract has been used in Ayurveda to improve the libido, boost stamina, improve sexual health and enhance performance.

Nutmeg also has cosmetic uses. A paste of nutmeg made with sesame oil softens skin and removes wrinkles.

Palm | Nongu

Palmyrah palmate
Cooling electrolyte drink full of minerals

Palm

Palmyrah is called *nongu* in Tamil and *taad* in Hindi. The route from Chennai to Pondicherry and the vicinity are full of palm trees. Palmyrah looks quite different from the coconut palm. The leaves are more like fans and clustered. The fruit looks like a smaller version of coconut but more purple in color. When the hard covering is removed, the fruit inside looks like a clear jelly, round in shape but flat like a donut. This jelly is palatable and sweet with a seductive aroma. The fruit should be eaten when soft and tender. The mature fruit gets hard just like a coconut.

Along the way, street vendors sell this jelly fruit to travelers in the early summer season. On a hot day, it is refreshing and cool and I mean this literally—cool—as if it came out of a refrigerator. It is cooling to the body as well.

When I was young, vendors carrying baskets full of *nongu* on their heads would walk through the neighborhoods selling the sweet *nongu* palm. Sadly, I do not see them anymore.

Palm sugar is made out of this fruit. This sugar is cooling to the body and many medicinal recipes call for this sugar. Jaggery, a coarse dark sugar, is also made from this plant.

A special fermented alcoholic drink, known as "toddy" is extracted straight from the tree. Usually, small earthen pots are tied to the fruit to extract the sap. Within a couple of hours, the toddy starts fermenting. It is an intoxicating drink only found in special shops in the villages. I have not seen this sold commercially, but in the villages the locals make toddy wine. It can be taken before the fermentation process as a cooling drink called *neera*. It contains many nutrients, such as B complex, potash, vitamin A, vitamin C and other minerals. Frequently referred to in ancient Tamil literature, this drink is called *kallu*.

Prickly Nightshade | Sundakkai

Pericarpium zanthoxyli
Heals ulcers, cancer and stomach ailments

Prickly Nightshade

Prickly nightshade is called *sundakkai* in Tamil. Like black nightshade, it belongs to the eggplant family. As the name suggests, it has tiny prickly thorns and therefore the leaves and stems are not eaten. Only the berries are eaten. It is also known as turkey berry.

During the course of my morning walk, I discovered that this plant grows wild in New Jersey. Although it looked familiar, there were no berries. By the end of August, much to my excitement, the berries appeared.

In south India, the fresh green berries are cooked in *sambar*, *avial* and *kootu*. It is bitter in taste; therefore, salt, jaggery and tamarind or yogurt are included to reduce the bitterness. The dried berries, known as *vathal*, are used in making *vathal kuzhambu* and powders such as *angaya podi* for postpartum diets.

Sun-dried berries have a long shelf life. The berries are first salted and soaked in buttermilk for a day. Then, they are removed from the liquid and dried in the sun. This process is repeated for a few days until there is no more buttermilk left to be absorbed. After the final drying, the *vathal* is ready to be used.

Sundakkai is an important ingredient in Ayurveda and *Siddha* medicine. More importantly, most households keep dried *sundakkai* in their kitchens for using in healthful foods or as medicine. It has minerals such as iron and calcium and an abundance of vitamin A. In Ayurveda, it is used to cure liver and kidney disorders, nerve conditions and night blindness. It is also used to relieve stomach ailments, as a diuretic, for curing stomach ulcers and to rid of intestinal worms.

For stomach problems, my mother used to fry the sun-dried *sundakkai*, add asafoetida and grind it into a coarse powder that was eaten with rice and ghee. For a dry cough, *sundakkai* is roasted in ghee and eaten one at a time until the cough subsides.

Saffron | Kumkumappoo

Crocus sativus
An aphrodisiac

Saffron

Saffron is called *kumkumapoo* in Tamil and *kesar* in Hindi. It belongs to the crocus family.

The stigmas of the flowers are used as the spice. It is the most expensive spice in the world, costlier than gold. Saffron grown in Spain is the most prized, while good saffron can also be found in Kashmir. Saffron possessing the more brilliant shades of red is the best quality.

Saffron has a bitter, pungent taste and a pleasing aroma. It can be used in rice dishes and curries. Saffron is used to flavor almond halvah and other sweets. When used in sweets and drinks, the saffron becomes more fragrant the next day.

Water boiled with a pinch of saffron and two crushed pods of cardamon, with or without honey, makes a refreshing tea, hot or iced. A cup of milk boiled with a pinch of crushed saffron and sweetened with honey makes a good bedtime remedy for insomnia. When my mother used saffron, she always took a pinch and soaked it in half a teaspoon of warm milk or water for a couple of hours. Then, she mashed it with the back of a spoon or with her finger to extract as much pulp and color as possible.

Saffron is considered an ancient herb and is important in Ayurvedic medicine and some consider it even to be a magical herb. It is a cardiovascular tonic, aphrodisiac, stimulant, nerve tonic and sedative. It is stomachic and reduces inflammation. It is a cure for skin problems, diseases of the mouth, eye problems, cough, cold and asthma. It is used as an antidote for poisons. Many Ayurvedic skin creams contain turmeric and saffron.

Saffron is an abortifacient. Therefore, pregnant women must exercise caution while using it. However, after childbirth, women may take saffron as it improves the health of the uterus by healing and supporting contraction.

It also contains crocetin, a natural carotenoid that has been shown to inhibit cell proliferation and tumor formation in pancreatic cancer.

Sesame | Ellu

Sesamum indicum
Cures joint pains

Sesame

Sesame is called *ellu* in Tamil and *til* in Hindi. It is an annual plant that can grow up to three feet tall.

For more than five thousand years, this important herb has been used in ancient medicines. It is perhaps one of the oldest crops to have been cultivated. In most of the Ayurvedic formulas, sesame is the key ingredient. It is used in the form of seeds, oils, paste and powder. This powerful herb contains vitamins B1, B6, E and K and minerals such as calcium, zinc, copper, iron and magnesium. It is rich in fiber, omega-6 fatty acids and anti-oxidants. As an anti-inflammatory, it is prescribed for rheumatoid arthritis. Sesame helps aid digestion, clears stomach ulcer and improves memory.

Sesame seeds are good for the health of the heart. The black sesame is the most nutritious. It is known as *krishna*. It relieves arthritic and joint pains. It is used in many Ayurvedic preparations. The cream-color seed is a *sattvic* food that provides clarity of thinking and wisdom.

I learned much from my father who never missed a chance to educate us about the food we ate or grew in the garden. We were fortunate to have such an enthusiastic parent, as it made us appreciate the abundant gifts and beauty of nature. He would lovingly sit with my mother and they would make sesame laddus for us. Sesame has the highest oil content among other seeds and comes in many colors. In south Indian cuisine, the white and the black are most popular. Sesame oil is considered a stable oil as the smoke point is high and good for frying, and it is the most common oil used in south Indian cooking.

Sesame oil is used in baths and massages to relieve arthritis and skin diseases. For babies, the oil massage strengthens the bones, muscles and joints.

The black seeds are used in death rituals to attract the deified souls of the ancestors. The white seeds are considered to be the most desired offering to Lord Ganesha. Sesame seeds represent prosperity and immortality. Sesame oil and sesame seeds are said to appease the twin planets, Rahu and Ketu.

Stone Apple | Vilaam

Limonia acidissima
Attain longevity and bliss with this storehouse of nutrients

Stone Apple

Stone apple is known by many names, monkey fruit, curd fruit, wood apple and Bengal quince. *Vilaam* is the Tamil name for this sacred tree, which is native to India. In Hindi, it is called *bel* or *bael*.

The fruit has a hard shell. Its pulp is tasty and the aroma is a combination of jasmine, rose and orange. It can also be eaten dried. The shoots and tender leaves can be eaten raw in salads.

A refreshing drink called *bel pana* is made out of the fruit pulp. This popular drink from Bengal is made with *vilaam* fruit, sugar and lime juice. I substitute the sugar with palm sugar or honey. Jams and syrups are also made with the fruits.

The fruits, which have therapeutic value, are rich in riboflavin, carotene, thiamine, phosphorus, iron and vitamin C. The fruit, stem, bark, root and leaves of *vilaam* are used in Ayurvedic medicines and home remedies. The ripe fruit is used as a purgative as it cleans the intestinal tracts and has antibiotic and anti-inflammatory properties. The raw fruit is eaten as medicine to stop purging.

The fruit is paired with *kadukai* (see *Triphala*) to prevent the constipating effect of raw *vilaam*, and can be made into juice with palm sugar. It is considered to be good for the brain.

The juice from the *vilaam* leaves controls diabetes.

Place *vilaam* leaves in a copper vessel, add fresh mineral water and leave it overnight. Drink this in the morning. It will clear all toxins from the stomach and heal ulcers.

The stone apple fruit is used against black magic. Sometimes we have a tendency to eat anything that looks appetizing which could turn out to be toxic for the body and in turn cause indigestion, ulcers, skin problems and allergies. To clean the body of these undesirable (black magic) toxins, the fruit of the stone apple is eaten in the form of a *pachidi*. It is a mouth-watering, fragrant dish but it is made only in the months of August and September. It is made as an offering to Lord Ganesha, the obstacle remover, during the festival of Ganesh Chathurthi.

Tamarind | Puli

Tamarindus indica
Cures liver troubles, corrects bile flow

Tamarind

Tamarind is called *imli* in Hindi and *puli* in Tamil. It is grown as a shade tree along most rural roads. The branches form a canopy over the road and provide shade for wayfarers. It also grows wild in backyards, forests and parks. A tamarind tree can grow up to 80 feet high and live for over 500 years. A 60 foot tree can produce enough pods to supply a whole town.

The sour pulp inside the tamarind pod is removed from the pod, deseeded and used in south Indian cooking. It can be used fresh or aged and stored for years. It contains citric and tartaric acid in combination with potash. My father used to say that vegetables cooked in tamarind juice would retain the vitamin C. It also counteracts the sliminess of vegetables such as ladies' finger.

Tamarind is seldom eaten by itself, though I have eaten it straight from the tree, as many children do. I liked the sour taste and the fresh fragrance. It is like sucking on lemon drops. Of course, it is best when used in combination with other spices. Tamarind is used as the main flavor in *sambar* and *rasam*. A delicious sweet and sour drink is made from tamarind. Fresh tamarind and tamarind candy are available in many ethnic grocery stores. Tamarind concentrate is sold in jars in Indian grocery stores.

Tamarind is considered a disinfectant, antiseptic and cooling agent. It curbs liver problems and corrects the bile flow. My mother used to make a *rasam* with tamarind when we had fever, flu, bronchitis or cough and cold. It also reduces fever. The leaf and bark are made into a paste with mustard oil and used as poultice for rheumatic pain and swellings.

Tamarind is a natural cleaner for brass, copper and bronze pots. Take a little tamarind paste and rub it all over the piece until it glows.

Folk wisdom says that no one should spend time under a tamarind tree during dusk and night as "evil spirits" are said to lurk there. This myth could have started because tamarind trees emit acids from their sour leaves and pods.

Triphala

1. Kadukai - *Chebulic* myrobalan
2. Dandrikai - *Beleric* myrobalan
3. Nellikai - *Emblic* myrobalan

For detoxification and rejuvenation

Triphala

Triphala is a mix of three herbs: *kadukai* (*Chebulic* myrobalan), *danikai* (*Beleric* myrobalan) and *nellikai* (*Emblic* myrobalan). It is an age-old recipe that is antibacterial and anti-inflammatory.

My mother prepared *triphala kashayam*, a decoction, by crushing the dried ingredients to small pieces and simmering them in water. She would then force the unappetizing, bitter-sour purgative on us. She would say, "It's good for you, all your toxins will purge away. You will look slim and beautiful!" We would hold our noses and quickly gulp it down. Within an hour, we would be running to the toilet. The unusual morning ritual then led to a sumptuous *milagu rasam*, specially prepared as a tonic, blood purifier and rejuvenator and eaten with rice and ghee. We looked forward to this heavenly meal after having cleansed our bodies. The benefits of this safe laxative are immeasurable. It is a great colon and liver cleanser. It cures stomach ulcers and boosts immunity. When the intestines are clean, the body is rejuvenated. Therefore, *triphala* is known as a preventer, protector and preserver.

Ayurvedic pharmacies now make tablets and powders with the three ingredients of *triphala* that are sold in markets worldwide.

Kadukai

Kadukai, an ingredient in *triphala*, known as *haritaki* in Hindi, is the seed of the fruit from a deciduous tree. It is used mostly to balance *vata* disorders of the body. It aids in digestion and stimulates and heals liver disorders. It also promotes the health of the central nervous system. *Kadukai* is used to treat asthma and eye diseases. It is an astringent and an anti-inflammatory. It helps the sexual organs and controls white vaginal discharge. A mix of herbs with *kadukai* powder is used as a bath scrub to eliminate body odor.

Danika

Danika, an anti-aging herb, is the nut of *Terminalia* bellirica, a deciduous tree. It rejuvenates the body cells and strengthens the organs. It is used to relieve joint pains and swelling. It is a laxative that cleanses the colon. Danika is antibacterial and antiviral. Research shows that it inhibits viral growth in leukemia patients. It is tonic and astringent and helps stop blood flow from an injury. To control falling hair, the tender seed is ground to a fine paste and applied on the hair. It also promotes new hair growth.

Nellikai / Indian gooseberry

Nellikai is the third ingredient in *triphala*. See section on Indian Gooseberry.

Turmeric | Manjal

Curcuma longa
The mysterious herb, the queen of herbs, what can you not heal?

Turmeric

Turmeric belongs to the ginger family. In Tamil, it is called *manjal* and in Hindi, it is called *haldi*. Indigenous to Southern Asia, this miracle plant grows wild and is also cultivated. Powdered turmeric is deep yellow or orange and easily stains the skin or clothes.

Considered a holy plant, turmeric has been in use for thousands of years by the womenfolk of southern India. It is part of their daily lives, be it for a quick wound healing, cough, cold, beauty treatment, cooking or for auspicious occasions and spirituality. Many times, as I walked along the the villages in southern India, I would see women with yellow face and feet. It is fresh turmeric that adorns them. If you were to walk into their homes, you would see turmeric painted on the door step, turmeric near the altar, turmeric in the kitchen. Turmeric, turmeric everywhere!

Turmeric contains an ingredient called curcumin, a miracle healer. It has antibiotic, antiseptic and antioxidant properties. It heals ulcers in the stomach and intestines. A poultice made with turmeric and hot rice dough helps break and heal mature abscesses on the skin. Turmeric milk relieves cough, cold and sore throat.

Regular use of turmeric keeps the skin free of pimples and eczema. My grandmother, like many people in India, rubbed turmeric on her face and legs before bathing to eliminate unwanted hair.

Before a wedding, a bride participates in a ritual rejuvenating process starting with an oil massage and a cleansing scrub made of turmeric and sandalwood.

My grandmother was very particular that our new clothes, new books and musical instruments should be touched with an auspicious dot of turmeric. Horoscopes and wedding invitations are traditionally stained at the corners with turmeric. Temple priests sprinkle water energized with turmeric and sandalwood on the assembled devotees. Any auspicious occasion or prayer starts with an image of Lord Ganesha (remover of obstacles) made of turmeric paste.

A friend in New Jersey gave me capsules of turmeric to try and said that they were expensive, but worth it. She did not realize that I come from a place where turmeric is ubiquitous, playing an integral part in our daily lives and customs. At home, I grow it in a pot and use this turmeric when cooking.

Some corporations try to patent and claim exclusive ownership of herbs and grains that have been used by the indigenous cultures of the world for ages. These and other entities have even tried patenting the use of turmeric, neem and other Indian herbs. Recently, there has been a controversy over patent issues. Sad what greed can do! Needless to say, turmeric is now being commercialized and exploited.

Vetiver | Khus Khus

Vetiveria zizanioides
Cooling aromatherapy

Vetiver

Vetiver is the Tamil name for this perennial plant. It is also called *khus-khus grass*, sometimes spelled cuscus in English.

The root fibers of *vetiver* have an intoxicating aroma and its uses are mainly therapeutic. In the hot summer months, my father would spray water on window shades woven from *vetiver* roots, then he would run the fan. The room was kept cool and air-conditioned in a natural way. The scent and the accompanying breeze made us feel calm and tranquil. My aunt, who at times suffered from insomnia, always slept well when we had *vetiver* fragrance in the house.

My mother would wash a few roots and immerse them in an earthen water pot. It was refreshing to drink this water in the summer as its cooling properties energized and rejuvenated the body. She also wrapped dried roots in sachets to leave in our wardrobes to keep our clothes smelling fresh. The oil distilled from the root of this plant is used in perfumes and medicines and also as an essence in cooling drinks and ice cream. While I was in Paris, at the airport I found a perfume called "Vetiver" at the duty free shop. I was thrilled to find that the fragrance was indeed the *vetiver* herb from India. I had to buy it at any cost. I brought some back to my friends in New Jersey who loved the scent as much as I do!

Vetiver is used in Ayurveda. A liquid made from the roots mixed with milk is applied externally for headaches and heat stroke and for delirium caused by high fever in cases of typhoid, pneumonia and meningitis. The roots are also used to treat anorexia, flatulence and jaundice. *Vetiver* is used to curb attention deficit disorder, hyperactivity, and schizophrenia. Arthritic and rheumatic conditions can be relieved from its use as well.

Water Hyssop | Neer brahmi

Bacopa monnieri
For brain alertness and preventing Alzheimer's disease

Water Hyssop

Neer brahmi is called *Bacopa* monnieri, thyme-leaved gratiola and water hyssop. The name "neer brahmi" came about because this plant grows in the marshlands of India near ponds and lakes; *Neer* meaning water and *brahmi* from the word Brahma, the supreme God—the creator of the brain, the mind and the soul. *Brahmi* is the preserver of memory. *Brahmi* is known as the Herb of Grace.

Brahmi is an important herb in ancient medicine. It is considered a wonder medicine having been in use for thousands of years. *Brahmi* is used as a brain tonic, one that enhances alertness. The tonic is an elixir for the nerves, regenerating these cells. Also taken to relieve anxiety, *brahmi* is an important all-encompassing rejuvenating herb.

It is a miracle herb for Alzheimer's disease. My neighbor in Chennai, Kalpana, swears that it can also help bring back past memories. It is also excellent for diabetes. Although bitter in taste, it is an amazing natural medicine which can treat a myriad of disorders. You may have noticed that most herbs that are bitter in taste are the most beneficial to health. We pick the *brahmi* herb from the garden and eat it like a salad. Our pet dog Manikandan also eats the herb!

My neighbor's daughter is a student, who, sadly has a degenerative retinal disorder causing her to lose her faculties of vision. She asserts that drinking *neer brahmi* juice has enhanced her ability to concentrate and retain information during class lectures. She felt more alert and was able to remember most facts with ease enabling her to do her case study analysis without any struggle. This indicates that *neer brahmi* may be useful in combating attention deficit disorder as it aids in promoting focus and concentration.

I remember a childhood ritual that I hated, but that my mother was determined to perform, which was to have my scalp massaged with *brahmi* oil after I had the *de rigueur* Sunday oil bath. I did not like oily hair but was told that one must pay a price if one wanted to have a healthy scalp and brain. Reluctantly, I would succumb to my mother's adamancy—the *brahmi* oil massage of the scalp.

Brahmi balances all three *doshas*: *vata*, *pitta* and *kapha*.

Winter Cherry | Ashwagandha

Withania somnifera
One that destroys disease and maintains youth

Winter Cherry

Winter cherry, universally known as *ashwagandha*, is also called *amukara* in Tamil. It is a shrub that grows wild in many parts of India and is now cultivated purely for medicinal purposes. The roots and berries of this wonder plant are truly a blessing from the gods to be used as medicine.

In Ayurveda, *ashwagandha* is used to rejuvenate and strengthen the body, while calming the nervous system. It is said to improve memory and mental health. It is also an aphrodisiac and a natural steroid that gives energy and strength. It alleviates the *vata* and *kapha* imbalances of the body and strengthens the immune system. It is known as a *rasayana* herb in Ayurveda, which means one that mitigates the effects of old age.

Ashwagandha relieves pain and strengthens the nervous system in those who have trigeminal neuralgia. An adaptogen herb, it balances and maintains the health of the thyroid gland.

Dried *ashwagandha* roots were regularly stocked in our pantry. My grandmother would boil the roots in water for 15 to 20 minutes with holy basil or mint and mix the strained tea with honey as an energizing drink. It is anti-bacterial and antifungal and therefore protected us from infections and free radicals. It is also high in antioxidants.

Ashwagandha is available in health food stores and other vitamin stores in the form of pills. But it is best taken in the form of powder. *Ashwagandha* powder can easily be made at home. Mix one cup of water to one cup of milk in a steamer. Steam the *ashwagandha* twigs covered with a cloth for 20 minutes. Dry and then powder the twigs.

For a nightly drink to boost the immune system, mix a quarter teaspoon of *ashwagandha* powder in half a glass of cow's milk or almond milk that is cold or at room temperature. Add honey, stir well and drink. When mixed with warm milk, the powder solidifies. Adding a pinch of crushed cardamom will mitigate the strong aroma and taste of the drink.

Ashwagandha also has cosmetic uses. To use *ashwagandha* as a hair tonic, add a few twigs in coconut oil and let it stand for a few days. Then use the oil to massage the head and hair. It helps relieve stress, strengthens weak falling hair and prevents premature greying. For a cleansing skin scrub, mix *ashwagandha* powder with *mung* flour. This aids in clearing dry skin conditions and rejuvenates the skin.

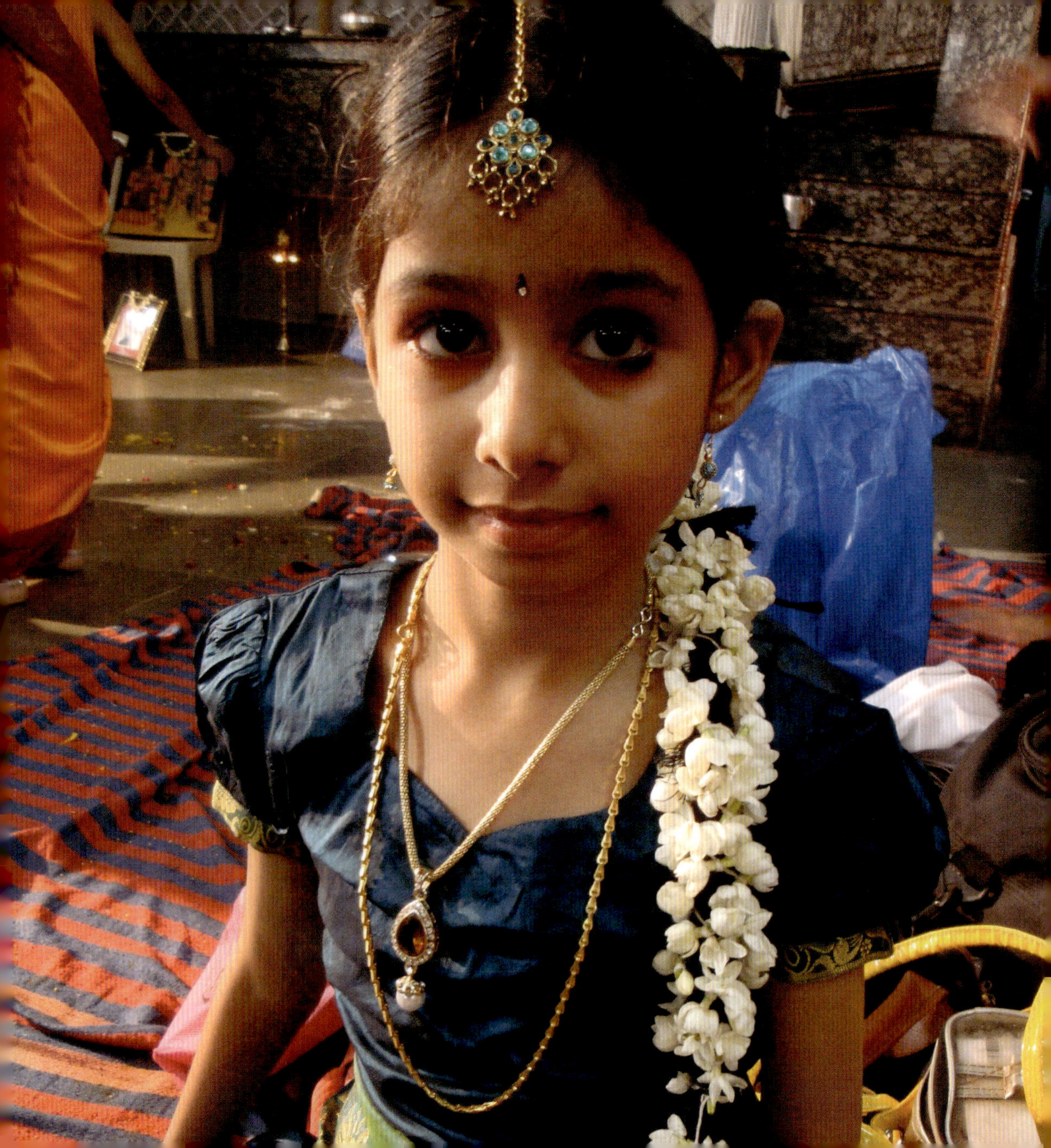

III. The Power of Scent

Although we think of herbal medicine mostly in terms of herbs and spices, many flowers are also healers. Their fragrance may have a stimulating or relaxing effect and some flowers, such as rose and hibiscus, are even edible. In south India, flowers are the natural perfume that women wear and flowers are valued more for their fragrance and aromatherapy. People here cannot live without their flowers. The evening markets near the temples and shops are filled with jasmine, rose, other fragrant flowers and herbs. The beautiful aroma that permeates the streets follows the womenfolk into their homes. Most of all, the ritual associations of these flowers remind one of the spiritual beliefs and mystical connections with higher powers. In addition to those described here, there are many others such as frangipani, known as the plant of immortality, and the unusual *parijatham*, also called night-flowering jasmine, that are frequently planted in gardens and used in worship and aromatherapy.

Jasmine

Many flowers fall under the name of jasmine, some tiny and delicate, some fuller and aromatic, and some simply intoxicating. Jasmine is called *malli* in Tamil and *moghra* in Hindi. It is the trademark of south India. Jasmine vendors are seen everywhere but most visibly near the temples. Jasmine is an offering to the gods and is said to bring wealth and knowledge into the home.

Why do women wear jasmine flowers in their hair? These fragrant flowers produce oxygen and this constant aromatherapy aids in revitalizing the brain. Jasmine flowers tied to the breasts will stop the milk flow of the mother. *Mullai malli*, another variety of jasmine, is used as a depilatory agent along with *korai kazhangu* (coco grass) and turmeric.

Lotus

The Lotus or *padma,* or *thamarai* in Tamil, is the national flower of India. In Hindu iconography it is, among other things, the throne of goddess Lakshmi, who represents prosperity. *Padma* is the confidence and determination on which prosperity rests. It is believed that lotus offered to goddess Shakti will endow powers beyond one's imagination.

According to traditions of meditation and spiritual practice, lotus petals represent the seven chakras of the spinal column. The root chakra that grounds one to the earth has four lotus petals that are the *nadis*, better known as subtle nerves. The kundalini serpent power resides here. When this power is awakened, the serpent uncoils and travels through the spinal column to reach the crown chakra. The crown chakra on top of the head has a lotus of a thousand petals or *nadis*.

Fragrant Screw Pine

The fragrant screw pine is called *thazham poo* in Tamil and *kevra* in Hindi. The essence of this plant is used as flavoring for sweets. The oil is made into perfumes. It is the most intoxicating fragrance I know and has kept me cheerful and full of energy. Growing up in India, my hair was adorned with a mix of flowers called *kadambam* that included *thazham poo*.

Persian Violet

Marukozhundu herb, known as persian violet, is similar to marjoram. It has a beautiful fragrance and the oil is used in perfumes. It is an aphrodisiac and relieves depression. It is used in aromatherapy as a calming and soothing agent. It is one of the plants woven into the breathtaking mixed garlands, *kadambam*, that are offered in temples or worn in the hair. Oh, how I miss this scent!

Rose

Rose, called *roja poo* in Tamil, is adored throughout the world. It is the flower of the heart. In south India, the most popular variety is the damask rose or *paneer roja*, for its heady fragrance.

Dr. Frankie Hutton has beautifully rendered the glory of the rose in her book, *The Rose Lore: Essays in Cultural History and Semiotics*, in which I have contributed a chapter on rose.

Rose is a calming flower but also an aphrodisiac. Rose water is sprinkled to welcome guests during weddings since the essence calms the nerves and the mind producing positive thoughts so the wedding arena has a happy atmosphere. Rose petals are strewn on the bed of the nuptial room.

With sincere devotion, the devotees string the rose garland in reverence to the gods in temples. Rose garlands adorn the deities. Some believe that when rose flowers are offered in worship to the goddess, one could live like a king or queen appreciated by all.

A rejuvenating elixir called *gulkand* is made from honey, rose petals and ghee. Chewed with betel leaves, it is considered an aphrodisiac.

An unusual use of rose is to flavor *rasam* with it to make a divine starter. Make *paruppu rasam*. (See the *Recipes* section.) Instead of garnishing it with coriander leaves at the end, dip the fragrant *paneer roja* in it for a few minutes. Before serving, remove the flower.

A refreshing drink is also made from roses. Take one cup of yogurt, add 1 teaspoon honey and the petals of a whole *paneer roja*. Puree everything together in the blender. Serve cold.

Bullet wood

The tiny flowers of the evergreen bullet wood tree are called *magizham poo* in Tamil or *maulsari* in Hindi. The flowers can be strung like beads. The fragrance is intoxicating. A few strewn on the bed can drive one to ecstasy.

The flowers also have medicinal use. Chew a few flowers for 4 to 5 minutes, spit them out, and gargle with warm water to cure loose teeth and toothache. The flower is used to relieve the discomfort that arises from teeth grinding.

Manoranchitham

Manoranchitham is known as *Artabotrys hexapetalus* or *hari champa* in Hindi. It is a climbing woody shrub with fragrant yellow flowers. The name literally means "tranquility of the mind." Breathing in the fragrance of *manoranchitham* calms the mind, relieves stress, brings down blood pressure and finds one more tranquil. *Manoranchitham* is often included in garlands of *kadambam*.

The importance of the fragrant herbs and flowers are so beautifully depicted in ancient stories such as the great epic *Ramayana* and a classic called *Shakuntala*. In *Ramayana*, exchanging the rose garlands solemnized the wedding of Rama and Sita. Shakuntala, in the eponymous classic, was adorned solely with flowers. South Indian weddings exemplify the grandeur of the ceremony with fragrant rose and jasmine garlands that provide tranquility to the bride and the groom during the elaborate rituals of the wedding.

Fragrant jasmine flowers are given to all the female attendees and rose water sprinkled on all the guests as a gesture of welcome, friendship and for wishing prosperity. During the wedding ceremony, the guests shower the bride and the groom with rose petals to bless them.

The bride is pampered with rose and sandalwood fragrances and the length of her long braided locks are adorned with jasmine and rose flowers.

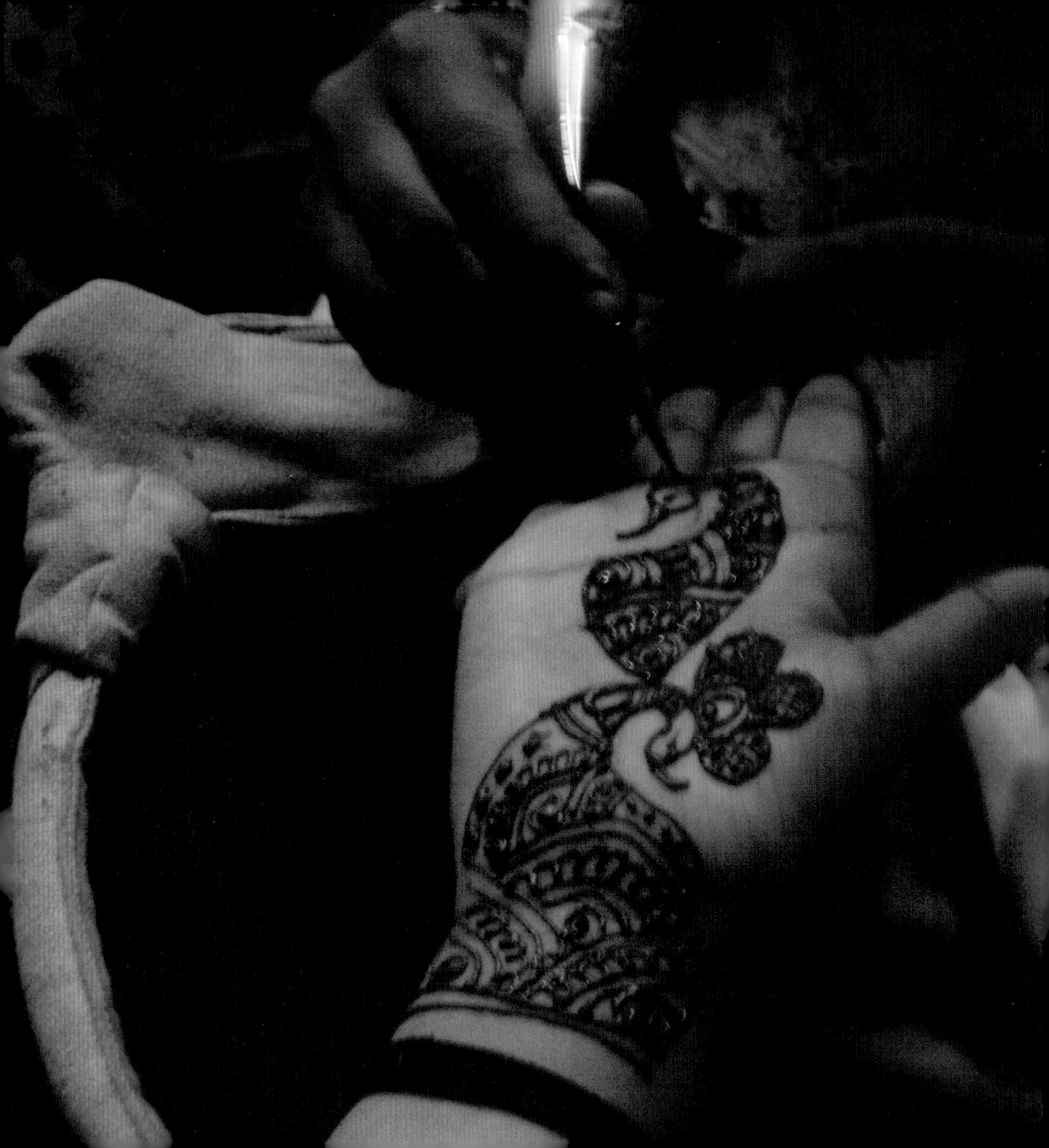

IV. Recipes that Rejuvenate and Make You Radiant

Everyone wants to look young. We are constantly searching for new products that will miraculously reverse the aging process. So, pharmacologists developed botox, doctors suggest plastic surgery, and the markets are full of chemical products that promise to keep one's appearance youthful.

What did people do in ancient times? When Ayurveda and *Siddha* were being developed, the kings and queens sent rishis and *siddhars* out in search of wonder herbs that could keep them youthful. The herbs discovered for this purpose were intended not only to enhance outer beauty but to cultivate the beauty that radiates from within. It is this combination that gave the royal families the aura and charisma with which they ruled.

Herbal oils, herbs, spices, fragrant flowers, muds and minerals are the secrets of ancient people to rejuvenate and nurture the mind, body and soul. Internal cleansing and energizing along with external cleansing and rejuvenation go hand-in-hand with maintaining eternal youth and beauty. I have attempted here to identify and give recipes for time-tested beauty enhancing agents.

The scrubs and masks described should be mixed with water for normal skin, with milk or aloe vera juice for dry skin and with yogurt for oily skin.

Water Hyssop

Water hyssop or *neer brahmi* heals psoriasis. Make a paste and apply it on the affected area. To control hair loss, put the leaves in coconut oil and massage the scalp with this oil.

Henna

Henna, known as *mehndi* in Hindi and *mardani* in Tamil, grows wild in tropical and subtropical climates. The leaves are used to boost hair growth and as a hair dye.

A special wedding ritual consists of ornamenting the hands and feet with henna dye. Fresh henna leaves are ground to a paste and intricate designs are drawn on the hands using a cone, as one would put icing on a cake. After a few hours, the henna leaves a beautiful orange-red dye that lasts a week or two. The women of the bridal party spend much of the day together waiting for their henna to dry, socializing, singing and dancing.

Hibiscus

When we were children, my cousins and I gathered henna leaves for this purpose and made designs on our own hands. My mother used to yell at us to be careful not to stain our clothes but she herself mixed henna in hair oils for its cooling effect.

Henna also dyes the hair a reddish to deep brown color while making it silky smooth.

Henna is now packaged and sold in many health food stores and Indian grocery stores as hair dye and for tattoo, but, of course, with added chemicals.

Keeping a henna plant in the house is believed to help balance the five elements and energy fields of the universe.

Hibiscus, called *sembarathai* in Tamil, has been in use in Ayurveda and *Siddha* medicine for ages. It contains antioxidants and is found to reduce cholesterol and triglycerides in the blood. Hibiscus is offered to goddess Durga, an avatar of Shakti or strength.

Hibiscus is a good hair tonic when taken as tea and also used externally in hair oils. The flowers promote hair growth and darken the hair. Just add a few flowers in coconut oil, let it stand for a few days and massage the scalp with the oil.

Leaves of hibiscus should be boiled in water and taken as tea to get rid of the white discharge in women. The flowers, when boiled and taken as tea, help heal kidney infection.

Flowers, dried and powdered, will improve the libido. Take one ½ teaspoon daily as tea or in milk.

False daisy

False daisy or *Eclipta* alba is called *bhringraj* in Hindi and *karsilanganni* in Tamil. The plant with the yellow flower is called *Widelia* chinensis in English, which is a different variety of *karsilanganni*. It grows as a weed in temperate and tropical climates.

In Ayurveda, false daisy is considered a *rasayana* herb, rejuvenating the system and promoting longevity. False daisy stimulates hair growth. It has antifungal and antidandruff actions. It prevents premature graying. A few leaves are added to coconut oil and left to steep. Then, the scalp is massaged with the oil before a shower.

The leaves secrete a black dye and therefore, darken the hair.

It is a cooling herb which removes stress and helps one sleep better. The herb is used in Ayurveda to calm the mind and relieve mental disorders. It is also used as a liver and spleen tonic. The juice of the leaves is taken with buttermilk or milk to treat hepatitis. A few drops of this herb with 8 drops of honey will cure edema. It is also good to treat earache.

In Ayurveda, false daisy is used to treat a variety of eye problems.

Butterfly Pea

Shangupushpam, known as butterfly pea in English, is good for the eyes. These blue flowers also enhance brain power.

Cosmetics Recipes

Eye Makeup

My mother used the leaves of false daisy or the flowers of the butterfly pea (*shangupushpam* in Tamil) to make the traditional eye makeup called *mai* in Tamil and *kajal* in Hindi. We never bought *mai* from the store. Making *mai* is an art, but it is easy. Here's how we did it:

We sterilized a small piece of muslin, an oil lamp, a steel plate and a small silver container. We made fresh juice from the herb. We soaked the muslin in it and let it dry. We soaked it again two or three times and let it dry. Then, we filled the lamp with castor oil, twisted the muslin into a wick and lit it. We held the plate above the lamp to let the soot gather on the plate. Then we scraped off the soot into the silver container. We then added a tiny bit of almond or castor oil to form the *mai*.

Eye Mask

It was so common to see my sisters, friends and relatives using a slice of cucumber on the eye lids to relieve stress and dark circles. Simply lie down with cucumber slices on your closed eyes, stay in a meditative state for 20 minutes and observe how calm and relaxed you feel. Look at your eyes and marvel at the glow of your face without dark circles! If you combine cucumber in a paste with Indian madder, *manditti* in Tamil, you can apply it around the eyes to remove wrinkles. *Manditti* powder, mixed with a little honey, is another way to heal wrinkles. In Ayurvedic practices, *manditti* is known to remove skin infections and discoloration of the skin.

Cleansing Scrubs

I often use a facial, body cleanser and scrub containing sandalwood and turmeric developed from an old family recipe that comes from the Tanjore district of southern India. Centuries ago, the Tanjore princesses used this bathing powder for blemish-free, glowing skin. Turmeric is an antiseptic and aromatic that controls signs of age. The cooling, aromatic sandalwood with its aphrodisiac and beautifying qualities makes a sensuous cleanser, providing a setting for a fairy-tale romance.

Since Vedic times, turmeric has been hailed as a rejuvenating and healing plant, whether used internally or externally. New brides are encouraged to use the combination of turmeric and sandalwood for its alluring qualities.

The *Kamasutra*, an ancient treatise on love and sex, explains in depth how a man and a woman should bathe in aromatic oils and soothing herbal powders before coming together if they wish to experience ecstasy and bliss.

An ancient skin care formula, which contains sandalwood, turmeric, *manditti* and legumes such as *mung* (to provide nutrition), *vetiver*, neem, *paneer roja*, bullet wood flower and several other rare herbs is a perfect concept in skin care with the ideal balance of nutrition, cleansing agents, antiseptics and aromatics.

The ancients and my ancestors used this to clean their face and body. A small amount of the mix is combined with water to form a paste and then used as a scrub for face and body. I apply this mask for 10 minutes and rest while the nutrients go to work on my skin. Because this mixture is also a cleanser, there is no need for using soap. Once a week, when we took the oil bath, we used this scrub to clean the oil from the body. A *shikakai* and fenugreek mix was used to clean the hair.

Directions for Use:

For your face, take half of a teaspoon of the scrub and mix with water to make a paste and wash your face with warm water. You may leave it on for 10 minutes as a mask before rinsing. Do not use soap. Use daily for lasting results.

For your body, take 2 tablespoons of the scrub and mix with water to make a paste. In the shower, first wet your body and then scrub with the paste. Do not use soap. Let the herbs work on your skin and delight yourself with the lingering aroma. One could also take an oil bath once a week and clean the body with the scrub.

Shikakai

Shikakai, a powder made from the pods of *Acacia concinna*, is a healthy substitute for soap or shampoo. It removes oils without stripping the skin and it also controls dandruff. When I grew up, we washed our hair with a paste made from *shikakai* and water and we scrubbed our bodies with a mix of *shikakai*, fenugreek and green gram or with the sandalwood-turmeric scrub.

Almond and walnut shell powder is sometimes used in facial scrubs as a natural rejuvenator, increasing the blood circulation. It is most effective when ground coarse. Legumes such as *mung* and Bengal gram are also powdered or ground into a coarse paste to be used as scrub and soap. They are natural oil removers, rejuvenating the skin and giving it a healthy glow. Newborn babies in India are often given an oil massage and bathed with *mung* flour instead of ready-made soaps.

Face Masks

The compounds in many fruits and spices naturally cleanse and rejuvenate the skin.

Papaya, rich in vitamins A and E, is said to delay aging. Simply purée a fresh papaya, apply it to your face and let it rest for 15 minutes. Wash off with warm water.

A purée of fresh tomatoes and carrots can be combined to make an effective anti-wrinkle mask. Tomato has a natural tightening effect on the skin. The carotenoids in tomatoes and carrots not only slow the aging of skin, but also protect it from ultraviolet rays.

Cloves and carom mask with fenugreek is an excellent home remedy for pimples. Take one teaspoon each of cloves and carom seeds with a pinch of fenugreek, then soak and blend into a fine paste. Apply to the face once a week until the pimples disappear. Cloves and carom by themselves may give the skin a burning sensation, so, fenugreek is added to keep the skin cool.

A mask made of honey and holy basil with almond or sesame oil helps control wrinkles. Another way to heal the skin and rejuvenate the internal organs is to eat a spoon of tulasi leaves that have been soaked in honey. Do this every morning.

A mask made of holy basil and neem helps remove acne and blackheads. Take equal amounts of holy basil and neem powder, add a pinch of turmeric and make it into a paste by adding water. Apply this on your face for 15 minutes every alternate day.

A paste made of black caraway and sesame oil is often applied as a face mask to clear skin disorders.

There are no words to describe the benefits of aloe vera gel for skin care. It was Cleopatra's secret for blemish-free skin. Aloe clears dead cells, refreshes and tightens the skin. It acts as a sun screen, a good moisturizer and a healer. Use fresh aloe gel on your skin every day as moisturizer and watch the wrinkles fade away. It is also a natural deodorizer. Rub aloe under your arms to get rid of body odor. A good moisturizer and anti-wrinkle formula can be made by pairing honey and ghee.

Sometimes, we cleansed our skin by culling the butterfat (*yedu* in Tamil) from heated milk and applied this to our face. Rub *yedu* on your face to clean pores and eliminate blackheads.

Depilatory

Sugar or jaggery with lemon and turmeric can be used to make a natural wax to remove unwanted hair. Heat a ½ of a cup of sugar in 4 tablespoons of water until it forms a thick syrup. Remove from the heat and add half a teaspoon of lemon juice. Apply a thin layer on areas that need to be depilated, place a cloth on top, press down until it sticks firmly and then pull the hair off.

Oils for Massage

In Ayurveda, coconut and sesame oils top the list in skin care formulas. Massaging the body and head with sesame oil before bathing rejuvenates the skin cells. Coconut oil is used in herbal compounds for both body and hair. Almond oil is rich in vitamin E and antioxidants. It rids skin of free radicals and helps retain moisture. With regular use, it reduces wrinkles.

A word of caution: Test for allergies first and choose the herbs or oils that best suit you. Generally, most natural products do not cause allergies and it is the chemical additives and unknown ingredients that have those effects. Still, before using any cosmetic, always test for allergies using a small amount. It is your body—listen to it—and when and if you need guidance, consult a certified doctor who practices natural healing.

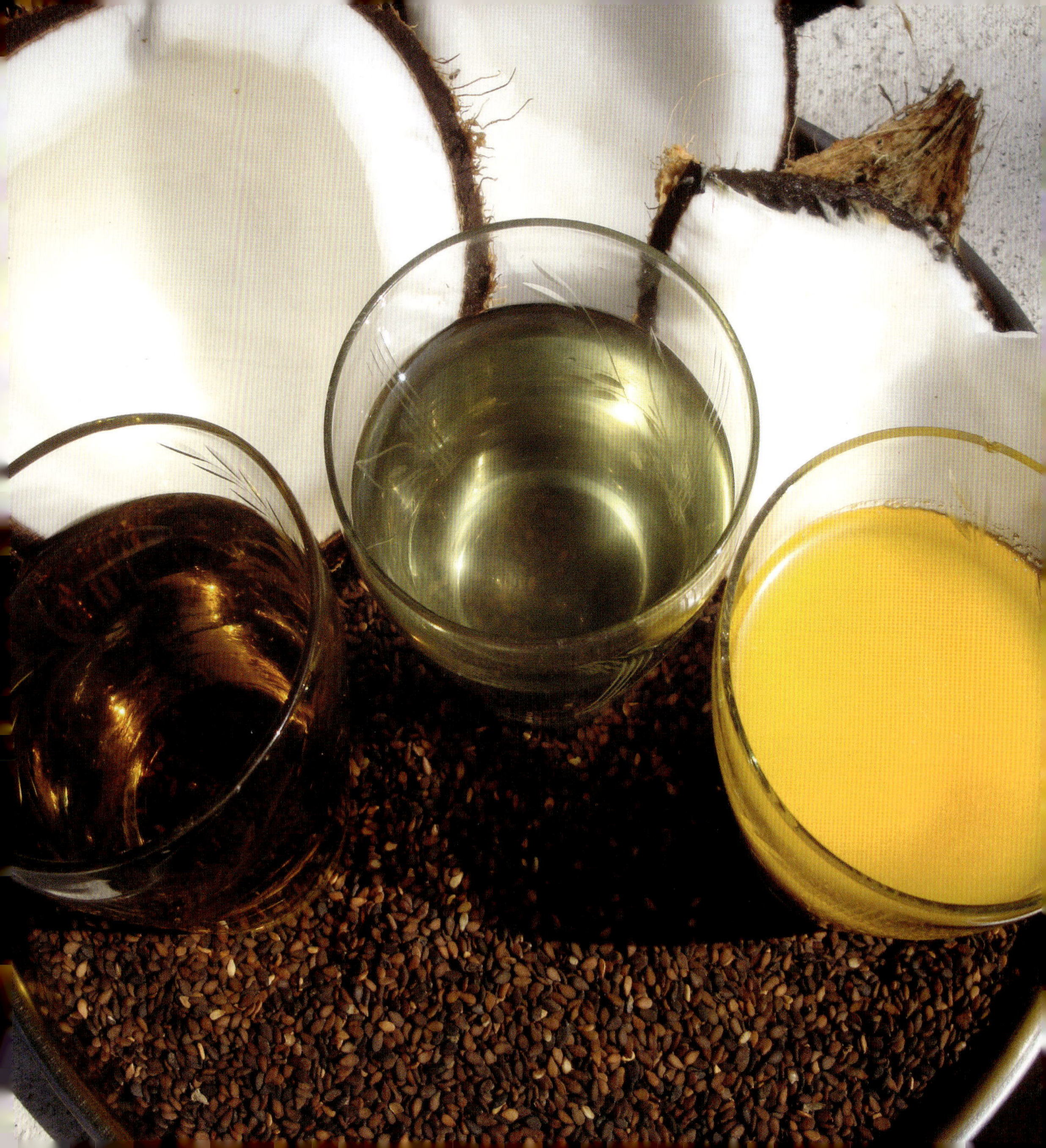

V. Energizing Food Enhancers

Cooking Oils

Ancient medicine gives a lot of importance to the fats we use in cooking. Not all oils and fats are meant for heating and cooking. Some oils, when heated over and over again, become carcinogenic and cause cancer, carotid artery and other artery blockages, leading to heart attack and stroke.

One can find all kinds of oils in the store, extracted from corn, sunflower, canola, olive, coconut, sesame, flax, almond and many other plants. Then we have fats from animals and milk. Some oils are processed to remove their natural fragrances, and in some, fragrances are added. We also have artificial fats, added colors, margarine and things that taste like butter but are far from it.

Apart from their use in cooking, oils can be ingested raw or rubbed on the body for therapeutic and cosmetic purposes. In Ayurveda and other natural systems of medicine, the naturally extracted base oil is as important as oils in which particular herbs have been added. The oils traditionally used in India for centuries are extracted from sesame, peanut and coconut. Olive oil is now being used in Indian cooking. A special cooking medium that has been used for millennia in India is ghee, or clarified butter.

My family in India always used first cold pressed sesame oil for cooking. In Tamil, we call it *nalla ennai* which means the good oil. It has a slightly yellowish color. In the far east, sesame oil is pressed from roasted seeds. It is dark brown and has a stronger fragrance. Food cooked or fried in sesame oil is delicious. However, it is seldom used in sweets or desserts because of its strong fragrance. The antioxidants in sesame oil help control the cholesterol level keeping one healthy.

Sesame oil is also used externally. It contains vitamin E which keeps the skin moist, rejuvenated and youthful. It acts as a sunscreen and is antibacterial and anti-inflammatory. In our family, once a week, we bathed with sesame oil. I looked forward to my Sundays when the lady who we knew as *dai* would come to massage my body and hair in the early morning when the sun was still cool and the courtyard serene. I would make up stories to tell the *dai* while she massaged me. I would tell her about my athletic skills and how hard I had to work and why my limbs were always aching. She would then feel sorry for me and do an even better job. The oil was usually washed off with *shikakai* and herbs powder. The oil and *shikakai* kept my skin smooth and blemish-free.

After we migrated to America, it took me years to figure out how to take oil baths without slipping or leaving a greasy mess in the tub.

Sesame oil used on the hair is considered cooling. It has a good effect on one's eyes as well. For healthy sinuses, two drops of sesame oil can be put into each nostril every night.

Families who cannot afford sesame oil often use peanut oil. Peanut oil controls the cholesterol level and contains vitamin E. Its qualities are similar to those of olive oil and sesame oil, but unlike olive oil, peanut oil can be heated to a high temperature. Peanut oil contains a polyphenol antioxidant which is a preventive against cancers and degenerative nerve disease.

Coconut oil, a staple in the southwestern Indian state of Kerala, is derived from mature coconuts that are dried and turned into *copra*. The oil is then extracted from *copra*. The oil solidifies in cold weather and quickly melts in temperatures above 70°F.

It is used in cooking, cosmetics and medicine. Many ayurvedic massage oil formulas for the hair and body have a coconut oil base, with different herbs added for specific purposes. The people of Kerala are known for thick and lustrous hair that stays dark well into old age.

My mother used to fry *appalams* (lentil fritters) in coconut oil to give them a special taste and aroma. She also made the famous Kerala stew of mixed vegetables known as *avial* and at the end she sautéed a few curry leaves in coconut oil to garnish. The aroma was awesome.

Coconut oil is now known to be a healthy oil for cooking since it is stable enough to withstand high temperatures. It is antibacterial and the lauric acid in it supports the immune system. The body converts lauric acid into monolaurin which has antiviral, antibacterial and anti-protozoan properties. Finally, scientists have tested the use of coconut oil on animals and have declared it highly beneficial—what indigenous people have known all along.

Olive oil has a similar texture to sesame oil. However, it is not healthy when heated. You cannot use olive oil for frying. I always get first cold pressed organic olive oil and use it raw in my salads, bread and sometimes steamed vegetables.

I have saved the best of all the fats for last—Ghee! The favorite of the gods and especially Lord Krishna, who would ignore ghee? According to Ayurveda, food cooked in ghee has pure energy and the body can assimilate all its nutrients from it. Ghee, which in essence is clarified butter, helps us digest our food properly.

Ghee is best made from butter of pure cow's milk.

I learned the art of making ghee from my mother and grandmother, and here's how we did it:

First, we make yogurt with cow's milk. The milk is boiled and cooled to room temperature. For a quart of milk, a teaspoonful of yogurt culture is added and the milk is left at room temperature for 6 to 8 hours until it sets into yogurt. Yogurt culture is simply yogurt that has already been made. You do not need to buy artificial cultures.

Once the yogurt is set, the butter fat is skimmed from the top. We save this fat every day until we have enough to nearly fill a bottle. Then we add some water in the bottle and shake it until the butter solids separate and float to the top.

The butter solids are removed and heated in a wok at medium heat until all the water evaporates and it stops hissing and bubbling. A dark brown crust will remain at the bottom and the ghee needs to be filtered so that only the clear part remains. This is pure, unadulterated ghee and it does not have to be refrigerated.

An easier way to make ghee is from store-bought unsalted organic butter. Heat the butter to remove the water content until the bubbling stops and when it cools, filter and store.

Food cooked in ghee tastes amazing. Ghee can be used to sautée vegetables and to sputter mustard, cumin or curry leaf as garnish. It can be used instead of butter in making sweets, cookies and cakes. Ghee is also eaten with rice and millet.

Ghee is an important aspect of spirituality. It is a key ingredient during the sacred ceremony of invoking the gods through the ritual known as *homam* or *havan*. This invocation is performed to invite the forces of nature and universal energy to purify the space of negative elements, thoughts and energy. The sun's energy is invoked through fire. This fire, in turn, is further energized by the ritual pouring of ghee, the symbolic pure matter. This pure energy permeates the space, invigorating and energizing the chakras of the people who are present, thus dispelling dark energies.

Ghee is also used in a ritual called *abhishekam* in temples. This is the "pampering of the gods" through bathing them in ghee, milk, buttermilk, sesame oil, honey, sandalwood water, and fruit juices. Hindus believe that God resides within oneself. Clearly, we can deduce that we too can pamper ourselves with these ingredients to enhance our personal radiance and vitality.

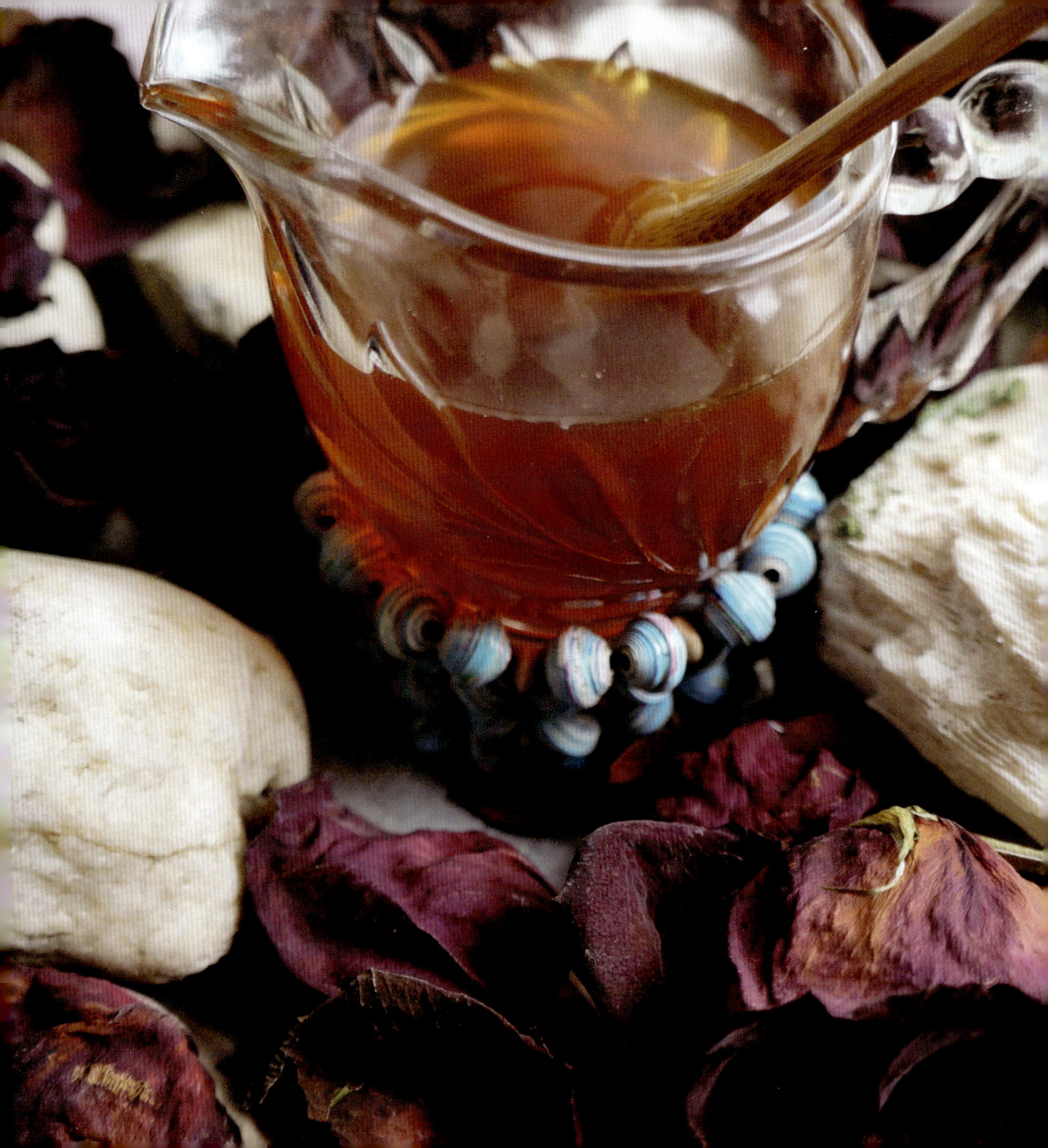

Honey

Honey, called *madhu* in Hindi and *thain* in Tamil, has been in use in Ayurvedic medicine for thousands of years. Its nutritional values and medicinal properties are well documented.

At lower temperatures, honey forms dextrose crystals that settle. This is a sign of pure honey. Pure honey pours like a serpent, unlike adulterated honey which will fall straight. Manuka honey from New Zealand is considered to be the best quality. However, excellent honey, prized for its medicinal value, is cultivated in Kashmir—near the lakes where the lotus blooms, in the valleys where saffron is grown, and also in the Nilgiri forests of the south.

Honey contains powerful antioxidants. It has antibacterial and antiseptic properties. It heals wounds on the skin by producing hydrogen peroxide when mixed in with the body fluids. Honey contains minerals such as iron, sulphur, phosphate, magnesium, potassium and calcium and many different types of vitamins depending upon where it was produced.

Honey is nutritive, demulcent and a preservative.

Honey, in combination with cinnamon, is used in the treatment of many diseases (see *Cinnamon*). Honey mixed into carrot juice is a drink that can improve eyesight. Honey and ginger together make an effective expectorant.

A traditional bedtime drink for children is warm milk with honey. I drank it when I was young and continue to do so quite often. It ensures sound sleep, mental health and overall rejuvenation of the body. Do not mix honey with hot milk or hot water. When honey is heated, it loses its nutritional value and becomes toxic.

Honey plays an important role in rituals. It represents the oneness of everything in the universe. Honey is known as the nectar of the sun and its powers are absorbed not only internally but externally. It is one of the five nectars offered to the gods, the other four being ghee, milk, palm sugar and buttermilk. In temples and homes, the gods are bathed in honey, along with other elixirs. In certain rituals, a food called *panchamritham*, which means the five elixirs of life containing honey, is offered to the gods and then served back to worshippers as *prasadam*, or blessed food.

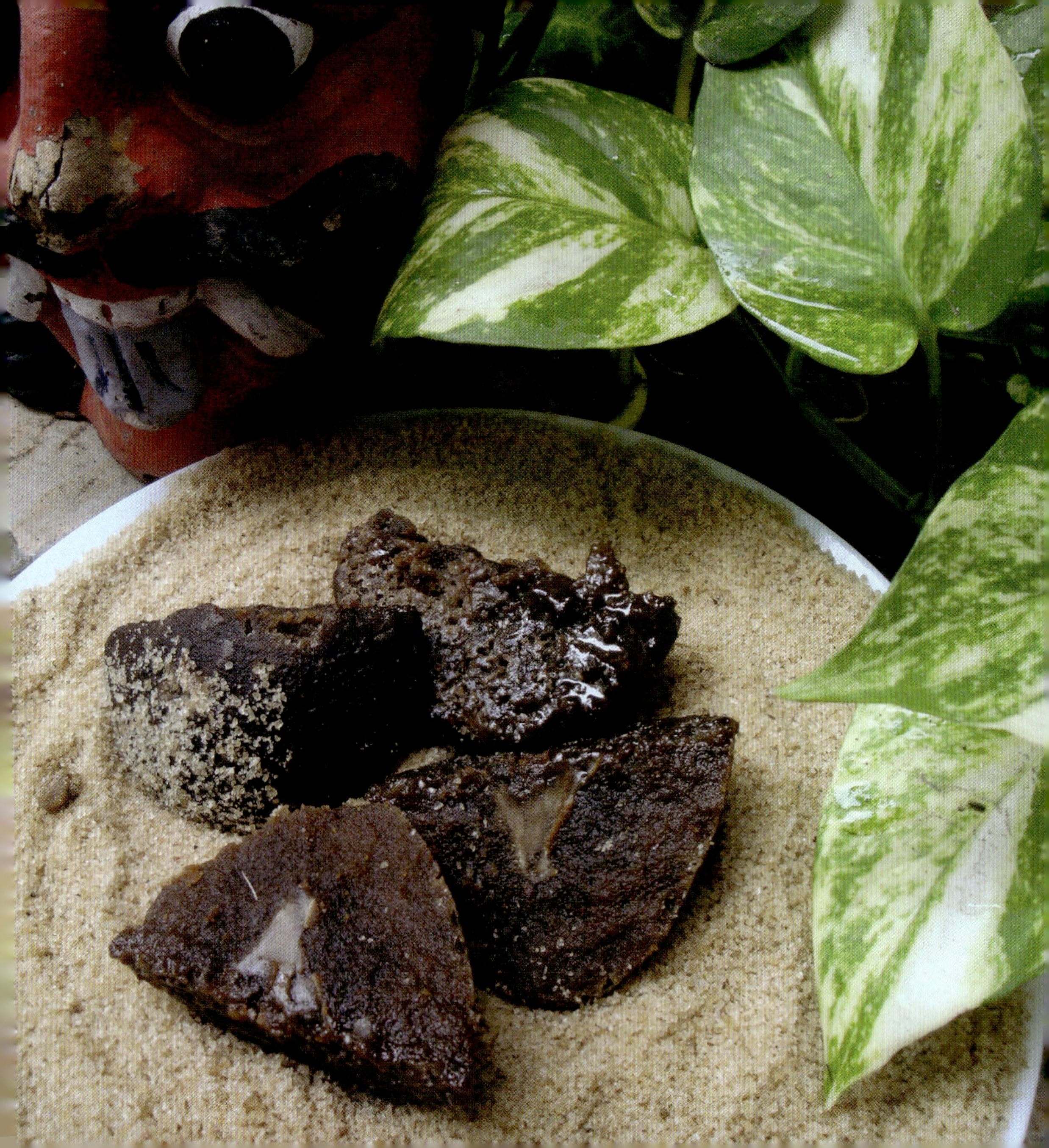

Sugar

What is the difference between jaggery, palm sugar, molasses, brown sugar, raw sugar and white sugar?

Jaggery, known as *vellam* in Tamil and *gud* in Hindi, comes from unrefined cane or palm sap. It is the sugar that is extracted without the removal of molasses and sugar crystals.

Palm sugar is made by evaporating the sap of palm trees.

Molasses is made from sugar cane stalk and sugar beets. The molasses is extracted from the sugar cane in three stages. The third stage of extraction is the most valuable. From the sugar beet, the by-product of the first extraction stage is molasses.

Brown sugar is refined white sugar with added molasses, coloring and flavoring. Dark brown sugar has more molasses added to it.

Raw sugar is a natural unrefined sugar made from sugar cane.

White sugar, which I consider a poison, is refined cane sugar that has gone through a chemical process to make it flow freely and it is bleached to look snow white. It is sad to see the organic sweeteners that promise healthfulness give way to this evil masquerading as pure "snow white". Processed white sugar is heat producing, has high glycemic index and is harmful to diabetics and cancer patients. Also, high fructose corn syrup is not a better choice; as a matter of fact, it is even more harmful than white sugar.

Palm sugar is called *pana vellam*, *pana kalkandu* and *vellam*. It is the only sugar that is unrefined and natural, and it is packed with nutrients. It is light brown and is sold in the form of sugar crystals. It dissolves and acts like refined sugar and tastes amazing with a slight caramel flavor.

Four kinds of palm are used for extracting sugar: date palm, coconut palm, sago palm and palmyrah, which is also known as the *nongu palm*. Slits are made in the palm inflorescence and the sap is collected in an earthen pot tied to this. In coconut palms, slits are made in the base of the flower buds. The sap extracted is heated until most of the water content evaporates to make *pana karupatti* which is the raw sugar. The fresh sap is also used as a nutritional drink called *neera*.

Palm jaggery

Palm sugar is full of nutrients, minerals and vitamins. It has thiamine, riboflavin and vitamin C. It has concentrated amounts of vitamin B12, B1, B2, B3 and B6, which are rare in plant products. It is an energy builder, having low glycemic index. It contains iron, potassium and magnesium. It is good for the health of the heart as it keeps the blood pressure under control. Coconut palm sugar has similar nutritional properties to the palmyrah variety, although it lacks vitamin B12. The sap of coconut contains an abundance of calcium, amino acids, vitamin C and minerals like potassium, phosphorus, magnesium, zinc, iron, and vitamins C, B1, B2, B3 and B6.

Palm sugar is used in Ayurveda to decrease *pitta*. Palmyrah sugar and date palm sugar are preferred to coconut sugar.

South Indians use palm sugar and jaggery in sweetened rice dishes and in homemade medicinal recipes. An ancient dish is *thinai maavu* or foxtail millet flour mixed along with palm sugar. In the temple offering (*prasadam*) at the Murugan shrine in Pazhani, palm sugar is included as one of the five nectars, the other four being honey, milk, banana and ghee.

One can make delicious syrups with coconut palm jaggery and palmyrah palm jaggery. This syrup can be used for making sweets and for garnishing the pancakes, cakes and any sweet.

To make the syrup, take a cup of jaggery and add a ½ cup water. Heat it in a pan until it forms a syrup without any lumps. Store this in an airtight container for up to a week. The syrup can be flavored with cardamom, vanilla, cinnamon and any other flavoring of your choice. One can also add fruits such as pineapple, apple, blueberries and strawberries while making the syrup. The consistency should be like that of molasses that is sold in stores.

The jaggery syrup goes well with coconut. Coconut milk and jaggery syrup makes a delicious drink. This is a combination that was a favorite of the ancients. Grated coconut in jaggery syrup with ghee makes a great filling.

A favorite dish of Lord Ganesha, *kozhukattai*, is made once a year during the Ganesh festival as an offering. *Kozhukattai* is a steamed sweet dumpling. The outer covering is made of rice flour and the inside filling is made from grated coconut and palm sugar jaggery.

Palm sugar

Can artificial sugars be a substitute for diabetes and weight loss? Aspartame is a chemical found in artificial sweeteners. It has been shown to cause brain tumors and convulsions. The research conducted indicates that those who drank sodas and drinks containing artificial sweeteners for weight loss actually gained weight. For diabetics, it did nothing for them as they had to be on insulin or Metformin® anyway. So what is the solution to the sugar dilemma?

Possibly, the answer is stevia, a plant-based natural sweetener. In addition to sweetness, it is packed with nutrients and it actually aids in the fight against diabetes. Fortunately, it seems Mother Nature does provide us with all that we need.

Stevia, known as honey plant, is a small feeble perennial shrub. In Paraguay, the native Guarani Indians use it as medicine for stomach problems. They boil stevia leaves in water and drink it as tea. Stevia has antibacterial, antifungal and antiviral properties. It is considered a diuretic and is taken for cardiac health and high blood pressure.

It not only acts as a sugar substitute but actually controls diabetes. And of course, as a sugar substitute, it also helps in weight loss, as this is the only natural sweetener with zero calories.

Himalayan Rock Salt

Salt

Salt is an important nutrient for the body. This electrolytic is a combination of a metal and non-metal substance. Our bodies do not produce salts; we get salt from fruits, vegetables and legumes. We also harness salt from rocks and seas and then chemically process it, adding other nutrients such as iodine.

Salt is as important as water in the body. If the body dehydrates due to illness, saline water is quickly administered. In tropical countries, people have to replenish the salt they tend to lose from perspiration. Too much salt causes water retention which affect the kidneys.

A dash of iodine is essential for production of thyroid hormones. Iodine deficiency in pregnant women affects the newborn child. On the other hand, too much iodine is risky. What foods naturally contain iodine? Seafood, seaweed such as kelp and dairy products such as yogurt, milk and cheese contain iodine. Just one helping of any of these foods supplies more iodine than the daily requirement of 150 micrograms. Besides these, potatoes, strawberries, cranberries and some legumes contain iodine. Do we need iodized salt then? Absolutely not.

Salt is a preservative. Fish, meat and vegetables are salted and dried for a longer shelf life. Pickles also contain large amounts of salt.

In the recipes I have provided in this book, I always recommend rock salt. The rock salt I am referring to is Himalayan crystal salt also known as mountain salt or gray salt. According to ancient medicine, it is said to be good for blood pressure, heart ailments and ulcers. It is recommended for detoxification. Best of all, rock salt has natural iodine. As a child, I only remember seeing rock salt at home. We called it *kallu uppu* or *induppu* in Tamil.

My father used to say that sea salt was as good as rock salt. It has a mild ocean fragrance. *Kala namak* or black salt is commonly used in cooking in the northern part of India. It is called *sanchal* in Hindi. It is a volcanic rock salt with a strong taste and sulfur flavor that is used in exotic dishes.

White processed table salt raises the blood pressure and makes the body retain water, causing puffiness of the eyes and ankles. However, rock salt has medicinal uses. A half teaspoon of salt in 6 ounces of warm water is an effective gargling solution for a sore throat.

To relieve stress and exhaustion, soak your feet for 30 minutes in warm water with rock salt in it. To treat puffiness around the eyes, dip cotton in warm salted water and apply as poultice.

Salt absorbs moisture and is an excellent remedy for stings and poisonous bites. Salt applied as a poultice to the area will extract the poison. You can also use inexpensive refined salt to put on spills that cause stains. Toss some salt on the spill, wait until it absorbs all the moisture, then vacuum the salt.

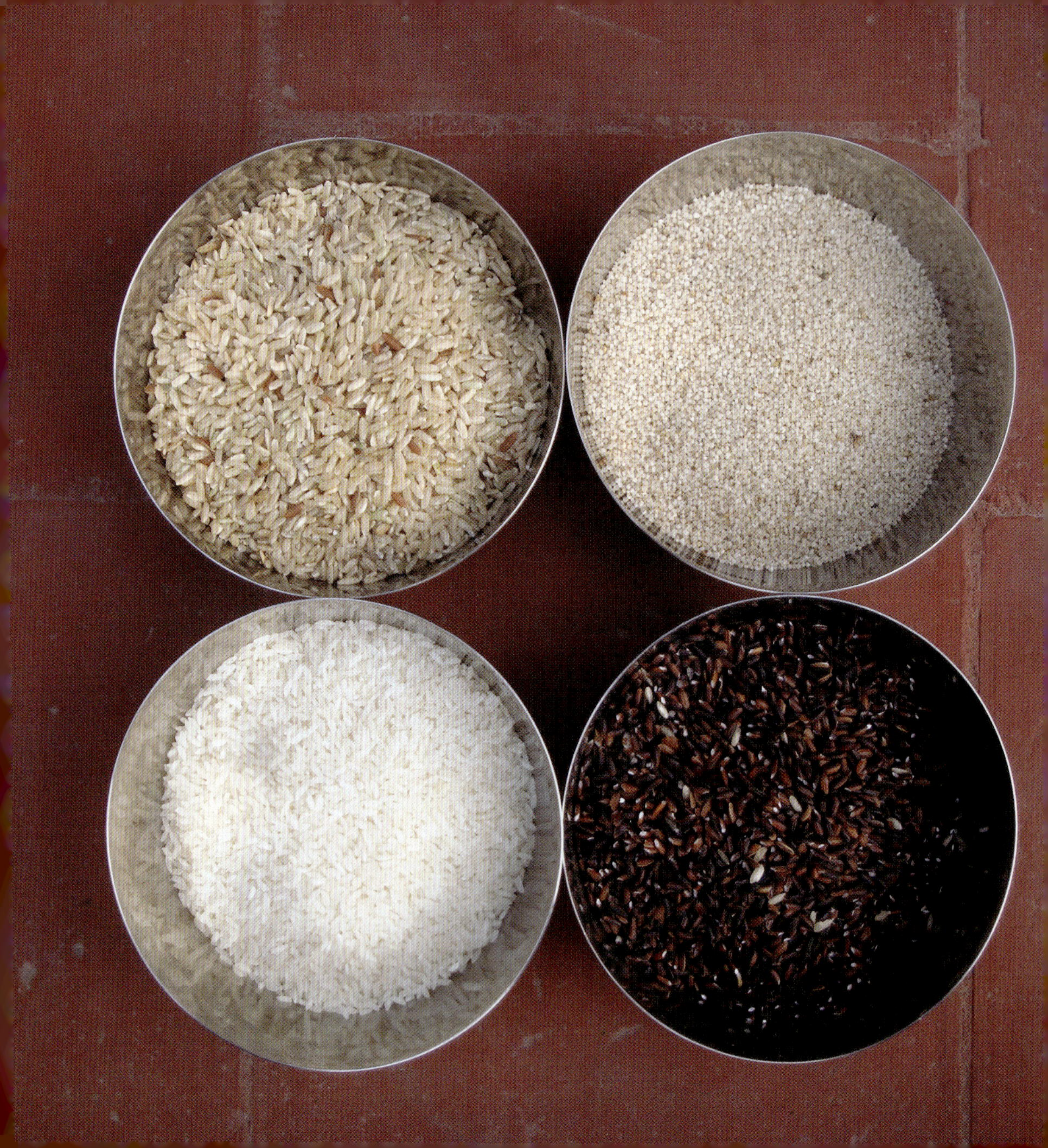

Grains

What are the secrets of longevity pertaining to grains? Let me share what I know about the varieties of grains that contribute to overall healthful living with youthful body, sharp mind, stamina and vigor. Grains belong to the grass family.

Rice

Rice is called *annam* in Tamil. It is a sacred grain in south India, a symbol of prosperity and fertility. Rice is worshipped as *Annalakshmi*. Rice is a symbol of Lakshmi, the goddess of wealth. Rice, stained with turmeric, is an offering to the gods and is used to bless newlyweds, children, books, musical instruments and just about everything during festivals and rituals. *Shankranthi* is a festival that celebrates the harvest of grains. At the same time, the elements Earth, Water and Sun are also worshipped because it is these that make the harvest of life-sustaining foods possible.

Rice is a staple food in many parts of the world. There are many varieties such as the long grain, medium grain, short grain and aromatic rice. We also have brown rice, red rice and wild rice of different sizes and flavors. In all, there are more than 40,000 varieties of rice in the world.

Rice is a complex carbohydrate and is known as *the* energy food. It is rich in vitamin B and iron. The ancients used unpolished grains with the husk removed, while still keeping bran and germ layers intact. Eating unpolished rice aids digestion and helps one avoid constipation. In this modern age, we have polished white rice that has been shorn of most of its nutrients.

Parboiled rice is rice in its natural form that is steamed and dried. It is full of amino acids and vitamin B complex. A fermented batter of parboiled rice and black bean legume is used in making *idli* and *dosai*. *Idli* is given to sick and convalescing patients because it is easy to digest and has lots of nutrients. *Idli* can also be made with rice alone. My father-in-law was diabetic and ate *mung idli* prepared without rice.

Hand-pounded rice is full of vitamins. It has more fiber and is an energy food. It is digested slowly, thereby controlling hunger and it is recommended for people with diabetes. Beaten rice is called *aval* in Tamil and *poha* in Hindi. During this process, the rice is dehusked and soaked in water. The soaking enhances the B vitamins. It is then flattened and dried.

A gruel called *kanjee* is an ancient food that can be made with any grain or millet, but is commonly made with rice. In Tamil, the word *kanjee* means starch. In Sanskrit, it means "formed in water", referring to rice fields, which are always growing in standing water.

Villagers commonly cook rice with a lot of water and drain the water into a container. The starchy water is then stored overnight and consumed the next day with buttermilk for quick energy to sustain them while they worked in the fields. The fermented *kanjee* is full of vitamin B complex. *Kanjee* relieves inflammation of the mucous membranes of the mouth and intestines.

My mother used to add water to leftover rice or millet and let it ferment overnight. We called it *pazhayadu*, meaning old rice. The next day, she would mix it with yogurt and garnish with curry leaves, asafoetida, green chili and salt. It tasted heavenly and we were energized due to its abundance of B vitamins.

Kanjee is made in different ways these days. Some people cook rice in a large quantity of water and mash it and eat with their favorite accompaniment.

Kanjee, made with finger millet, pearl millet, foxtail millet or oats, is even more nutritious. Packaged ready-mix *kanjee* powders are available in stores. However, they contain sugar and additives. At home, people prefer to flavor *kanjee* with jaggery and milk. Honey can be substituted for jaggery as long as it is not heated. *Kanjee* can also be eaten with a little salt added and some pickle on the side.

During my childhood, we also used the rice *kanjee* to starch our cotton clothes. It was a natural starch that did not irritate the skin.

Wheat

Wheat has benefits similar to those of pearl millet (*kambu*) but contains gluten. Wheat is healthy only when you consume the whole seed containing the bran and the fiber. When you buy ground whole wheat, you have to make sure that it is whole grain.

Wheat is often processed to remove the wheat germ and outer bran layers. Pearled wheat is used to make flour and farina. It is further refined to make white flour. White flour contains gluten and is the most unhealthy form of wheat.

Oats

Oat, or *Avena* sativa, is an important grain in Ayurveda. It is known as *jowar* in Hindi and *kanni* or *pularisi* in Tamil.

Oat is hailed as containing the secrets of longevity and believed to be an aphrodisiac. It is a complete grain that is full of minerals such as zinc, copper, magnesium and iron, and essential vitamins such as vitamin E. Oat has many health benefits, especially a high content of soluble and non-soluble fiber. Non-soluble fiber helps reduce carcinogens in the gastrointestinal tract and soluble fiber reduces high blood pressure. Regular intake of oats helps regulate bowel movements and reduces risk of heart problems. It lowers the estrogen levels, preventing hormone-related diseases such as breast cancer, prostate cancer, and ovarian cancer.

We grew up on oats *kanjee*, eating it at least once a week. Unlike rice *kanjee*, oats *kanjee* is not fermented. Sweet oats *kanjee* is the same as the oatmeal. However, it can be further fortified by adding walnuts, almonds, raisins, fruits and a bit of spice such as cardamom and cinnamon. Instead of sugar, add honey or palm sugar. The oats can be cooked in milk instead of water for a richer taste.

My sister Shashi makes the best savory oats *kanjee*. Whenever I visit her in South Carolina, I insist that we have *kanjee* made by her.

Oats is also used as fodder for cows.

Barley

My mother was big on barley. Even though her formal education stopped at the fifth grade level, perhaps because of my father and her ancestral influences, she seemed highly knowledgeable about the health benefits of foods and knew recipes for everything. Once in a while, she would make a pot of barley water. She would add 1 tablespoon of organic barley to about 4 quarts of water and simmer for half an hour. She would drink barley water as a diuretic and also because it is rich in nutrients.

This barley drink helps to lower blood cholesterol levels. Barley can also be cooked in soups.

Barley tea with mint, basil or hibiscus is highly rejuvenating and helps control weight.

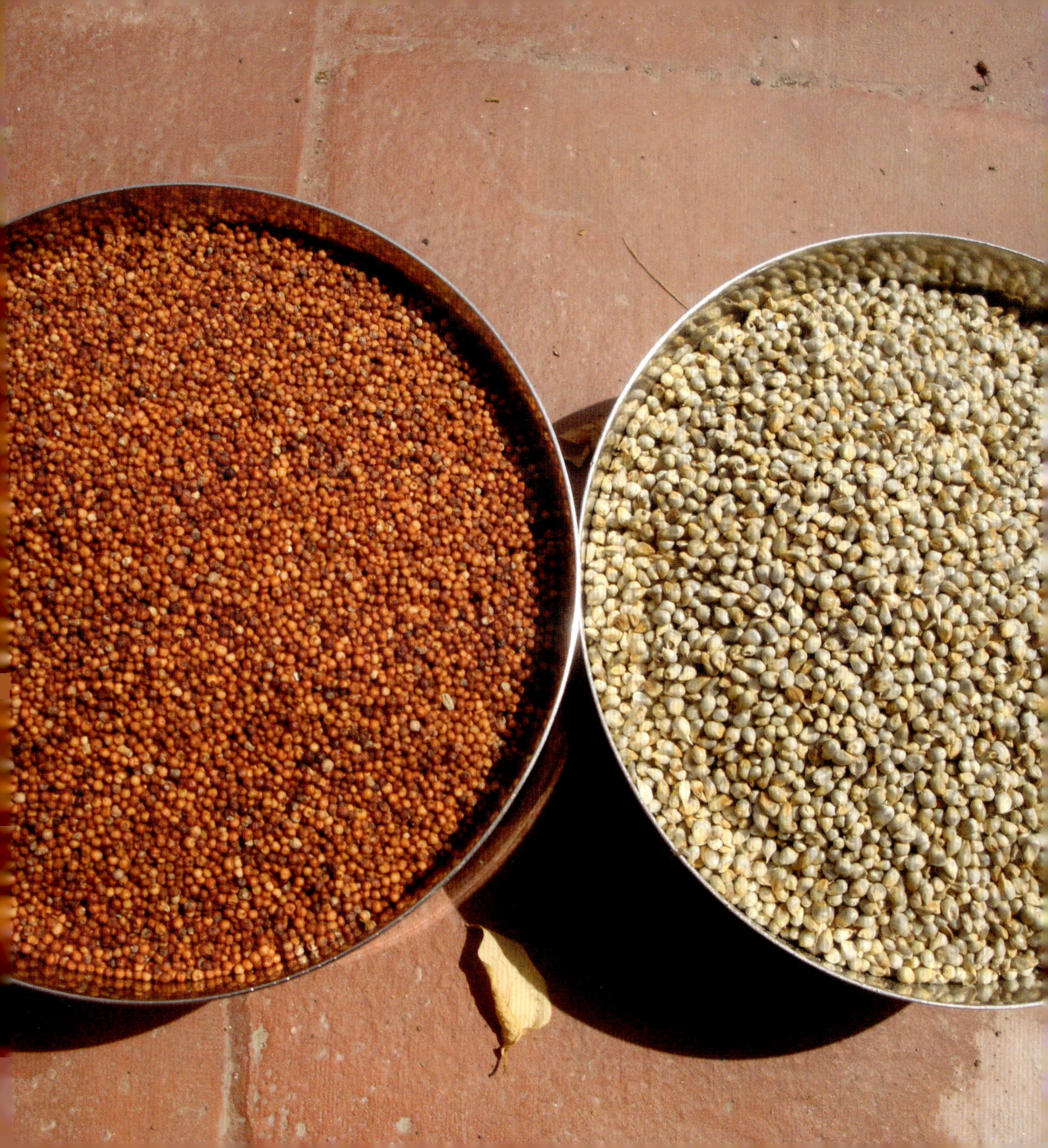

Millets

The word "millet" refers to a wide variety of grains, some of which have been used since Vedic times. Millet is gluten-free and nutritious, being high in magnesium, phosphorus, calcium, iron and potassium. Millet is stomachic and makes a good substitute for rice and wheat.

Finger Millet

Ragi or finger millet (*mandua* in Hindi) is full of iron and calcium and is a good source of gluten-free protein and fiber. One of the staples of south India, it is called *kelviragu* in Tamil. It has high amounts of calcium—ten times that of rice or wheat. It takes longer to digest and therefore is good for weight loss. It helps control degenerative diseases and slows the aging process. *Ragi*, made into a *kanjee*, is one of the foods recommended after fasting. It is also one of the foods fed to cows. Sadly, *ragi* is considered a low-status food. It is not cooked during weddings and festivities the way rice is. Cultivation of *ragi* is therefore declining since farmers are pressured to grow rice, wheat and other cash crops. Still, the merits of *ragi* are not forgotten. In one folktale regarding rice and *ragi*, the two grains visit Lord Rama and ask him to declare which is greater. He locks both of them up to see which can best survive the ordeal. As the months pass, rice rots away while *ragi* endures. Recent interest in *ragi* as a health food may revive its popularity and make it more widely available.

Foxtail Millet

Thinai or foxtail millet (*kangni* in Hindi) has long been used for food and fodder. *Thinai* can be substituted for rice and eaten as a grain to accompany meats, vegetables and legumes. It is made into cereal and found in baked items such as breads and cakes. Traditional *thinai* dishes include *upma*, *dosai*, *puttu* and *kozhukattai*. It is rich in protein, is gluten-free, and often recommended for women as it is considered to keep the uterus healthy. It is also high in fiber and makes a good diet food for weight reduction.

Pearl Millet

Kambu or pearl millet, known as *bajra* in Hindi, contains protein, calcium, iron, zinc, phosphorus, folic acid, fiber and vitamins. It is similar to wheat but without the gluten. Therefore, anyone allergic to gluten can safely consume *kambu*.

Kambu, an ancient grain, is popular among farmers as it energizes and cools the body. A favorite meal of the farmers in the south is *kambu* grain cooked in the same way as rice and mixed with spiced buttermilk. It helps the farmers to bear the heat while working in open fields. *Kambu* is also fed to the cows as a nutritious meal for healthy milk production. Once a month, we would drink *kanjee* or *koozhu*, a kind of boiled flour, made of *kambu*. My grandmother would make *dosai* with *kambu* flour. As a veterinarian, my father was particular that the cows were fed *ragi* and *kambu* regularly.

Barnyard Millet

Barnyard millet is *kudiravali* in Tamil and *jhangora* in Hindi. A nutrient-rich, gluten-free grain containing antioxidants, fiber and minerals. This millet has a low glycemic index making it a super food for diabetics. Barnyard millet is a great alternative for rice and couscous. One can cook the millet and add vegetables and spices to make a great dish. It can be made into porridge, pancakes and breads.

Kodo Millet

Kodo millet (*kodra* in hindi) is a popular grain in southern India where it is called *varagu* in Tamil. It has high amounts of phosphorous and many other minerals. It is also rich in fiber and antioxidants. It is cooked the same manner as rice. Delicious dishes such as lemon kodo, tamarind kodo, coconut kodo, and kodo *pongal* are all favorites of mine. One can also make *kanjee* with it.

Little Millet

Little millet, *samai* in Tamil and *kutki* or *samo* in Hindi, looks and tastes like rice, but is tiny. Rich in iron, protein and vitamins, soaking it overnight increases the vitamin B content. It reduces cholesterol levels and strengthens bones and muscles. According to folk medicine, it regulates menstrual problems.

Little millet is cooked like rice but one must watch to make sure the bottom does not burn as this grain cooks quickly—allow just a few minutes to cook. Cooked rice is soaked overnight to ferment. Soaked millet can be made into *kanjee*, sweet porridge or to make a thick gruel; add buttermilk, salt and pepper to taste.

Sorgum

Sorgum is known as *cholam* in Tamil (*jowar* in Hindi). It resembles a corn plant but it is formed from the beautiful flowers blossoming at the top of the plant. It is rich in fiber, vitamin B and protein. Said to improve the functionality of the liver, it is also beneficial for weight loss.

Sorgum cooks fast and can be made into a morning breakfast cereal. It can be soaked, blended and made into pancakes. Use your creativity and try different combinations with any of the millets. You can also mix different varieties of millets for making breads and pancakes.

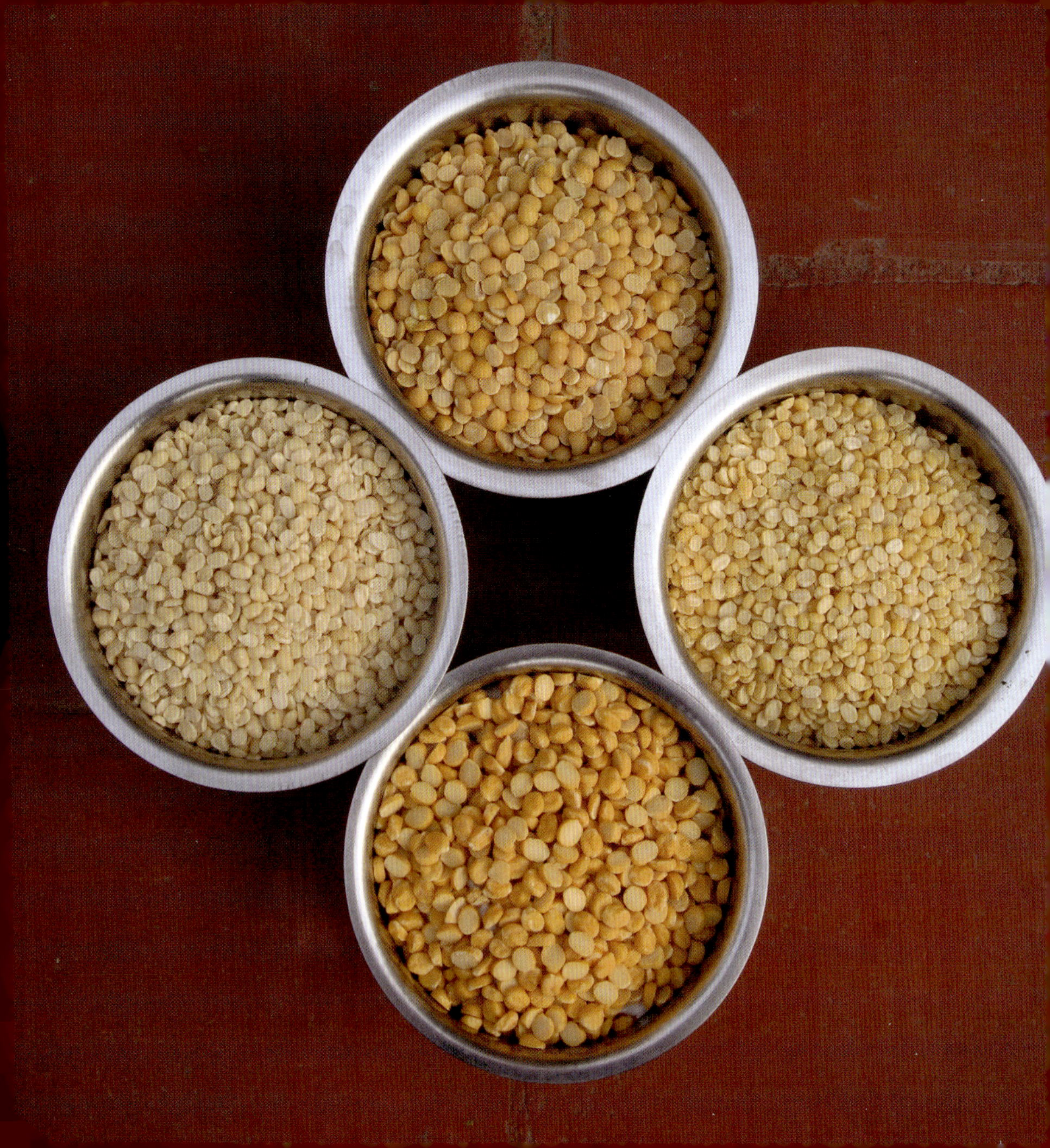

Legumes

Legumes are also known as pulses. Beans and lentils come under the legume family. They are an important source of protein especially for vegetarians. I grew up as a vegetarian, except that as children we ate eggs. My father made certain that we had enough protein in our diet. He also made sure that my mother included different varieties of lentils and legumes in the meals.

Legumes are a better source of protein than red meat, which is heat producing. Legumes have been part of the diet for thousands of years throughout the world. Every south Indian kitchen stocks the four main pulses: split red gram (also called pigeon peas), split black gram, *mung* beans and split Bengal gram.

Yellow pigeon peas, mung beans, Bengal gram, chickpeas (garbanzo beans), split or whole black gram, black beans, black-eyed beans, lima beans and kidney beans are rich in manganese, phosphorus, potassium, magnesium, copper and iron. They are a good source of vitamins A, B1, B2, B6 and K as well as folate, the naturally occurring form of vitamin B9.

Americans and Europeans hesitate to eat legumes mainly because they fear it will cause intestinal gas, but legumes cooked in south India always include asafoetida or cumin seeds to combat this problem.

Legumes are recommended for those who have diabetes. They prevent food cravings by providing energy and nutrients without causing the pancreas to flood the body with insulin. Foods and substances such as high fructose corn syrup, sugar, refined flour, white rice and other refined carbohydrates cause the pancreas to secrete large amounts of insulin and within hours the blood sugar level drops, causing food cravings.

Yellow pigeon pea (red gram) is called *thuvaram paruppu* in Tamil. What we buy in the market is husked and split. *Thuvaram paruppu* is used in making *sambar* and it is also an important legume in Ayurveda.

Yellow pigeon pea (Red gram lentil)

Black gram is called *ulundu* or *ulutham paruppu* in Tamil. It is used in making *idli*, *dosai*, and *vadai*. It is available husked, split or whole. The south Indians use the husked, split white lentil for their food preparations. It is of the same family as the small black beans and large whole black beans used in Mexican cooking.

Mung bean is called *paitham paruppu* in Tamil. The *paruppu* form is husked and split and looks yellow. Whole mung with the skin still intact is green. Mung is *sattvic* food and is a blessing from the gods. Ayurvedic diet for convalescents incorporates mung. It is healthy, high in protein, and good for diabetics and does not cause any gas.

Split Bengal gram, which is husked and looks yellow, is called *kadalai paruppu*. Whole Bengal gram is used in making *sundal*.

Peanut is a poor man's food throughout India. It often adds protein to vegetable dishes and grains. Other legumes include red kidney beans, chick peas and black-eye peas. During the festival of *Navaratri*, known as the Nine Nights Celebration, a different legume *sundal* is prepared on each day as an offering to the goddess Durga.

Black gram

Mung bean

Bengal Gram

Uma Swaminathan

Tropical Fruits

Mango

The incredible, edible mango, considered to be the king of fruits, has hundreds of mouthwatering varieties, each with a distinct taste and flavor. Some popular ones are *bangarapalli, neelam, alphonso, benishan, mulgo*a and *rumani* from southern India, *langda* and *dusseri* from the north, and *kesar* from Gujarat. There are mango festivals during the harvest season.

Even though mangoes are heat producing, one cannot resist eating them all summer long. I can say without guilt that as a child I used to steal mangoes from the storeroom of my own house and eat at least three or four a day. My brother, who would catch me in the act, would taunt me saying that I would get pimples on my face from eating all of those mangoes!

Mango trees grow wild and are also cultivated in groves throughout India. Many household gardens have mango trees along with jackfruit trees, coconut trees, papaya and banana plants.

The fruit is eaten both raw and ripe. Mangoes are also made into *pachadis* and soups that accompany the main meal. They are made into desserts and drinks. A wide variety of salty, spicy and sweet pickles are made from mangoes. A particularly popular pickle in the south is made from the whole tender mango or *vadu* and is best eaten with yogurt rice. Another favorite pickle is called *avakai urugai*. Mangoes are also used all year long in the form of jams, dried fruit strips and dried powder.

Mango has many nutritional and medicinal properties. The fruits are full of calcium and magnesium. They contain vitamins such as A and C as well as antioxidants such as beta carotene, and foods that are rich in antioxidants are known to diminish the risk of cancer and heart disease. According to Ayurveda, mango helps curb miscarriages in pregnant women.

Ritually, mangoes represent fortune, love, abundance and fertility. Mango leaves are strung and hung at the door to symbolize festivity and happiness and to welcome guests during auspicious occasions. The leaves are also used during offerings. According to legend, when little Ganesha, son of Lord Shiva, displayed a great act of wisdom, he was rewarded with a mango.

Uma Swaminathan

Banana / Plantain

Banana belongs to the grass family. Banana is called *vazhai* in Tamil and *kela* in Hindi. Once a banana plant has matured, there is only one stalk that bears the fruits and flower. After a few rows of fruits are formed, the rest of the flower is removed to help those newly formed fruits to grow faster. A plant bears fruit only once. So, once the plant has fruited, it is removed to allow the new corms at its base to grow. Most types of cultivated banana have no seeds. Wild varieties do have seeds.

Most varieties of banana are eaten ripe as fruit. Some varieties of banana, often called plantains, are cooked while still green and served as a vegetable. Parts of the banana flower can also be prepared like a vegetable. After the fruit bunch is harvested and the plant is cut down, the center of the stem is chopped and cooked as a vegetable. Plantain slices are fried into chips to make a popular snack.

Red banana (*sevvazhai* in Tamil) has beta carotene and vitamin C. It also provides fiber and 20 percent of the daily requirement of vitamin B6. Red banana fruits are wrapped in hay and stored in barrels underground to make Ayurvedic medicines.

The cooking bananas as well as *rasthali*, *yelachi* and *malai* (hill) varieties are good for overall health and are packed with vitamins. The nutrients in them rejuvenate the body and boost immunity.

The roots and stems are anthelmintic and astringent. Ripe bananas act as laxatives for children, though banana can also be binding. It is given to babies as one of their earliest solid foods.

Blend the raw stalk together with pepper and cumin and a pinch of salt to make a drink to improve the health of kidneys and liver. The stalk can be made into soups, salads and *kootu*. It is a diuretic and helps in weight control.

Banana flower is said to be good for the uterus and ovaries.

Although bananas are mostly beneficial, *Siddha* specialist, Kalpana Premkumar, notes that there are caveats. The varieties *karpuravalli* and *puvam* can cause chills and fever if eaten during the rainy season. Beware of overripe yellow or green bananas as they may have worms inside that are not visible to the naked eye.

An unusual use of banana leaves is as packaging. Food and flowers are often packed in banana leaves and also some Ayurvedic herbs and mud packs. How much healthier is this than the plastics and chemically treated paper that package so many foods! The compounds in the leaf are said to energize the body and eliminate toxins. Some foods are steamed in banana leaves. Banana leaves are ritually used as plates and are considered particularly hygienic. When eating from a banana leaf, the food must be served hot so that it absorbs the nutrients from the leaf. The food also absorbs the fragrance of the leaf, giving the meal a special taste.

The juice from the stem is used for ear infections. The fiber that comes out of the stalk is used as medicine for skin problems.

The dried scales of the banana stump are used to string flowers into garlands and to tie packages. Now, cloth is also being made from this fiber including the fabric for beautiful saris that almost look like silk.

For important occasions in south India, especially weddings, whole banana plants with the fruit and flower are tied on either side of the main entrance to the venue. Symbolically, the bride is wedded under a banana tree. The plant represents Lakshmi, meaning wealth, and Shakti, meaning strength or power. The presence of the plant also bestows a blessing on the married couple that they will prosper and grow as abundantly as the banana plant grows. "*Vazhadi vazha valaranam*," is the Tamil phrase for this wish.

Guava

Guava is called *goyya pazham* in Tamil. It is considered a poor man's food because it grows wild. One can see guava trees in cities, villages and roadsides in India. As a child, I used to climb trees and roofs to get guavas. Sometimes, the squirrels and parrots would get to them first. I even broke my nose chasing them down!

There are many varieties of guavas. They are mostly round with white or red flesh inside. The sweet, oval, seedless variety that I used to delight in seems to have gone extinct. Guavas have a jasmine-like fragrance and taste delicious. They have twice as much vitamin C as oranges and also contain antioxidants. They contain high amounts of potassium, magnesium, and vitamins A and B3. Ripe guava helps clear worms from the intestines and toxins from the body. Guavas can be eaten as a fruit or slightly raw in salads. Some eat guava sprinkled with black salt and red chillies.

This "super fruit" is credited with many healing properties and in folk medicine, it is recommended for health of the prostate.

Papaya

Papaya is called *papali* in Tamil. The papaya plant is a straight stalk that grows to a height of 8 to 10 feet. In south India, practically every household garden has a papaya plant. The sweetness of the fruit is unsurpassable. When Christopher Columbus first tasted it, he reportedly called it "fruit of the angels".

Like many of nature's bountiful fruits, papaya has loads of nutrition and medicinal properties.

It contains vitamins A and C, and B vitamins, fiber, carotene and minerals such as phosphorus, calcium and iron.

Papaya can be cooked or eaten raw to lose weight. It improves the digestion and removes toxins from the body. It helps heal inflammation of the liver and spleen and is also anthelmintic. Raw papaya juice is taken to cleanse the intestines. The enzyme papain which is found in papaya, along with the concentration of lycopene it contains, help prevent prostate cancer. The milky substance from raw papaya has tremendous medicinal properties. It is used in curing ulcers of the mouth. Incidentally, the white milky substance is also used in making chewing gum.

Pregnant women should not eat papaya in the early months, as it is a natural abortifacient.

Sapodilla

Sapodilla is known as *sapota* in Tamil and *chikku* in Hindi. The tree is widely grown in India and has a delicious, sweet fruit rich in fiber, vitamins A and C, and minerals such as iron, potassium and calcium. Eating sapota is said to help improve the vision and promote healthy skin.

Sapota contains antioxidants. The tannin content in the fruit makes it antiviral and anti-inflammatory as well as antibacterial and antiparasitic. Therefore, it is thought to reduce some of the risk factors for cancer. It has simple sugars such as fructose and sucrose and provides quick energy. Its high sugar content makes it unsuitable for diabetics.

Jackfruit

Jackfruit is called *palapazham* in Tamil. It can grow to be a whopping 15 to 30 pounds, 20 inches long and a foot in diameter. The ancient Tamil texts hail jackfruit, banana and mango as the "trinity fruits".

Inside the jackfruit, there are lots of small fruits with a seed inside each one. The fruit is soft and succulent and the aroma is breathtaking. It can be found in Indian and Oriental grocery stores when in season.

The young, raw fruit is cooked as a vegetable. The coarse, rough skin gives out a sticky white resin that is difficult to clean. Many people rub oil on their hands first so that the resin is easier to remove afterwards. I wear gloves when cutting the vegetable. The seeds of mature jackfruit are cooked and eaten and are rich in protein and other nutrients. Simply boil the seeds and add to any dish of your choice.

Jackfruit has vitamins A, B6 and C and minerals such as potassium, manganese, and iron. It has antioxidants that help the immune system.

The nutrients in jackfruit are credited with slowing down the degeneration of cells.

Pomegranate

Pomegranate is a small tree belonging to the family of plants called *punicaceae*. In Hindi, it is called *anar* and in Tamil it is *madulam*.

Each seed is encased in a ruby red, edible pulp. The seeds are often added to yogurt dips and salads. Dried seeds give a tart taste to Indian dishes. All parts of the plant are used in medicine. The leaves and the fruit are full of antioxidants, vitamins and minerals. Pomegranate fruit contains vitamins A, C and E.

Pomegranate promotes digestion and healthy bowel movement. It is good for diabetics and enhances blood sugar support.

The tree, including the root, is cooling, diuretic, aphrodisiac, stomachic and an astringent. Pomegranate juice is a natural medicine to control diarrhea. My mother gave us pomegranate when we had stomach problems. I helped a friend with our family remedy when she had an upset stomach with diarrhea. I gave her fresh pomegranate and well-cooked rice and ghee mixed with fried and powdered prickly nightshade (*sundakkai*). I supplemented this with 1 teaspoon of fenugreek seeds in ½ cup yogurt. The seeds are swallowed with yogurt. To hydrate the body, she had coconut water. Within a few days she was well.

Pomegranate is often thought to have magical powers. A pomegranate tree in one's garden is said to bring wealth, luck and fertility.

Pineapple

Pineapple is called *ananas* in Hindi and *anasipazham* in Tamil. The fruit is made up of a whole bunch of flowers surrounding a central core. The outer shell is rough, with eye-like protrusions all around it. It is a delicious, juicy fruit that is nutritious and medicinal.

The juice and stems of pineapple contain bromelain, which helps digest proteins. Bromelain also acts as a blood thinner. Pineapple has high amounts of vitamin C and manganese. It is high in antioxidants and is an immune booster.

In Ayurveda, it is used to treat digestive disorders, kidney stones and bronchial conditions, including pneumonia. It is also used to relieve inflammations and swellings of the joints and gastrointestinal tract. It is used after surgeries to contain infections and relieves the swelling and stuffiness from sinusitis.

Eating pineapple keeps the intestines healthy and free of worms. Drink a glass of pure fresh pineapple juice or eat fresh pineapple whenever possible.

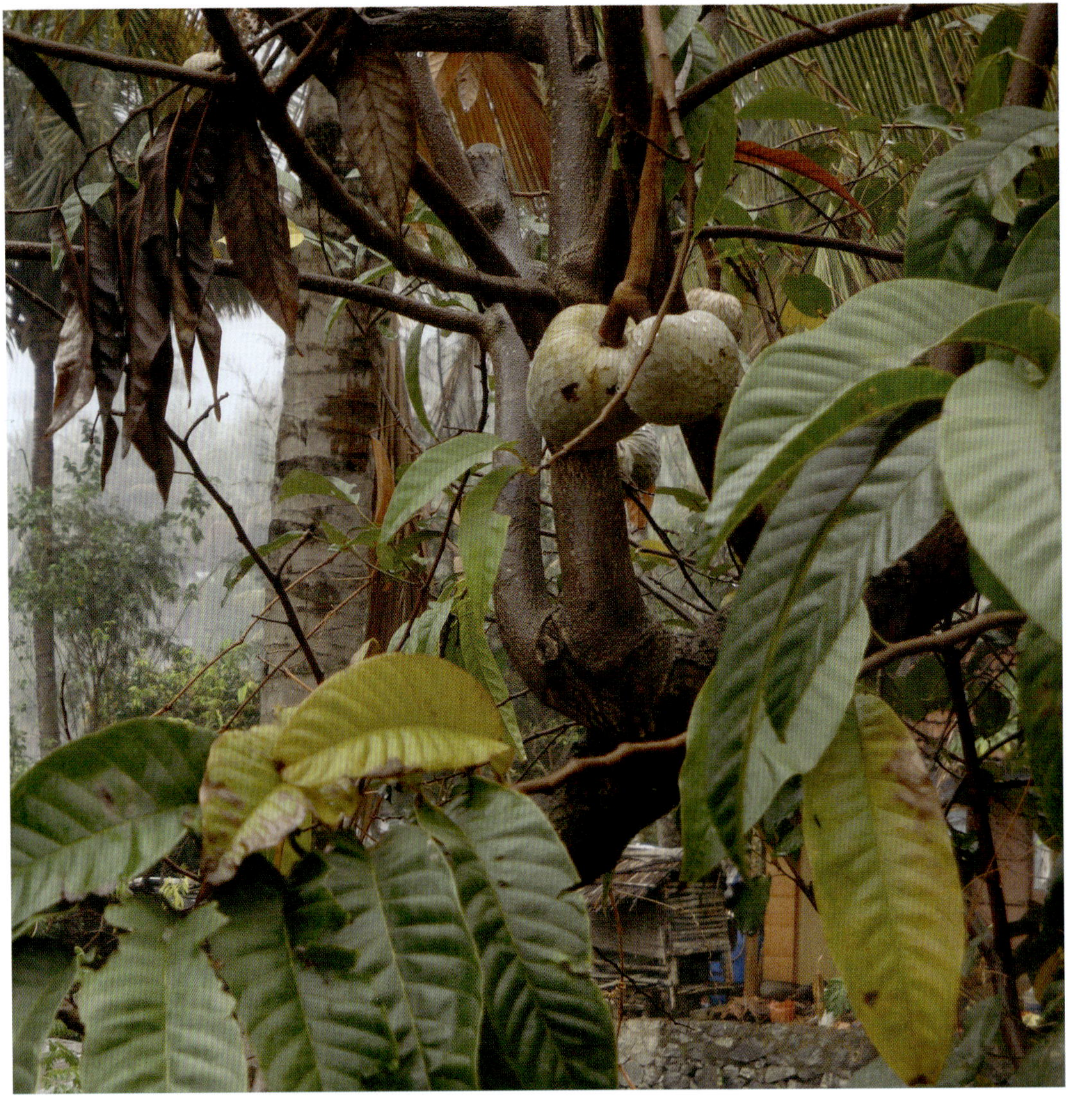

Soursop

Soursop, also known as guanabana, cherimoya and graviola, belongs to the family *Anona* muricata.

There are many varieties of soursop and the one that grows in abundance in India is called *sitapazham* in Tamil and *sitaphal* in Hindi. Its botanical name is *Anona* squamosa. Found in tropical regions, it is known as custard apple or sugar apple in English.

The fruit is a rich source of vitamins A, C, vitamins B1 and B2. The antioxidants that it has are beneficial in promoting longevity. It has minerals such as calcium, phosphorous and iron. All parts of the fruit are credited with healing and rejuvenating properties. A paste made with the fruit is used to get rid of boils and ulcers of the skin. The tree bark is ground and used to strengthen the gums and alleviate toothache.

The seeds are powdered and used as insecticide and to remove head lice. The roots are used as purgatives and the root extract has been used by the folk people as abortifacient. The fruit and the leaves are miracle healers and preservers of the immune system. Eating the fruit helps strengthen the bones and keeps one from getting arthritis. While being able to calm the nerves, it improves the blood count and controls blood pressure.

That is why it is called the miracle fruit. Now, the secrets of the fruit are being unveiled! The ancients understood the healing powers of the plant and ancient medicine used this to preserve and sustain life. The leaves and fruit are blessed with phytochemicals called annonaceous acetogenins. It is a cure for cancer and is believed to be as potent as chemotherapy. The bark has tannins and astringent properties and the fruit alkaloids that are beneficial in controlling cancer. The research still goes on, so always check with your doctor.

Sitapazham has dark brown seeds the size of pumpkin seeds with sweet white flesh around it. It is a delicious fruit and, in season, we ate a lot of them even though the seeds were a menace and had to be spat out. My brother again would tease me that I was going to get fat. The fruit which has high amounts of fructose is supposed to help gain weight!

Tropical Vegetables

Ash Gourd

Ash gourd is also known as white pumpkin or winter melon. In Tamil it is called *pushnikai*. It has a light green skin and is white inside.

Ash gourd contains an abundance of vitamins B1, B2 and C and is cooling to the body. It is a laxative, a natural diuretic, weight reducer, aphrodisiac, and anti-periodic. It is used to treat hemorrhages of internal organs. It is used in Ayurveda to treat epilepsy and nervous diseases. It is beneficial in getting rid of white vaginal discharge. It strengthens the heart and improves the health of the blood. Ash gourd juice is used in treating diabetes and digestive ailments.

Ash gourd is ritually used to ward off evil. On the day of the new moon, the ash gourd is taken to the front entrance of a house, moved in a clockwise circle three times and smashed on the ground. It is believed that all of the evil will enter the broken pieces and leave the house free of negativity. At south Indian weddings and other auspicious occasions, ash gourd is always part of the menu.

Snake Gourd

Snake gourd, known as *podlangai* in Tamil, comes in two varieties: one that can grow up to 6 feet long and truly looks like a snake and the other type which is a short variety that only measures up to one foot long. It is another favorite of the south Indians.

Snake gourd is mentioned in the ancient Ayurvedic textbooks as a medicinal plant. It is a cooling vegetable used in the summer months. It has high water content and fiber. It is good for diabetics. It also contains minerals and vitamins, but is best known for its anti-inflammatory effect.

Kootu and *kari* are made out of snake gourd.

Pumpkin

Pumpkin is known as *parangikai* in Tamil and *kaddu* in Hindi.

It contains loads of antioxidants, minerals and vitamins. The red variety has many benefits. The seeds are ground up and given to those who have stomach infections. It helps clean the bladder of all toxins and rejuvenates all organs, especially the prostate, and increases sperm count. It can control diabetes.

October is the pumpkin harvest season in America. There are pumpkins everywhere and the celebration of Halloween is not complete without a pumpkin. People make pumpkin pie, yet the many health benefits of pumpkin are not widely known.

In India, pumpkin flowers have ritual uses. During the *Pongal* season in January they are used to decorate the *kolam* that is drawn in front of the house, a custom that welcomes wealth into the home. *Sambar* made with pumpkin is popular. During *Thiruvadarai*, a south Indian festival, a special dish that celebrates the pumpkin called *yezhukarikootu*, or the *kootu* with seven vegetables, is prepared. The other vegetables included are ash gourd, raw banana, sweet potato, broad beans, lima beans and colacasia. Sometimes, *chayote* (Bangalore eggplant) is used.

Bitter Gourd

Known as *pavakai* or *parkai* in Tamil and *karela* in Hindi, bitter gourd is eaten throughout India and in the Far East. The Indian variety looks different from the Chinese variety.

Bitter gourd has vitamins B1, B2, B3 and C. It is a good source of thiamine and riboflavin and contains many minerals, including magnesium, zinc, phosphorus, beta carotene, calcium, iron and manganese. It also has folic acid and high amounts of dietary fiber.

In Ayurvedic medicine, bitter gourd plays an important role. It is a blood purifier, builds the immune system and helps improve vision. My father-in-law controlled his diabetes through home remedies and one item that he ate quite often was bitter gourd. It contains lectin and a polypeptide similar to insulin that is known as plant insulin.

Ridge Gourd

Ridge gourd, called *peerkangai* in Tamil, is also known as sponge gourd because of the spongy flesh inside. Mature gourds get quite fibrous and are familiar to us as loofah, the exfoliating sponge sold around the world. Tender gourds are eaten as vegetable. The green outer skin is peeled before the flesh is cooked in a *kari*, chutney or *kootu*. It cooks very quickly and has a high moisture content *(photo, above right)*.

Ridge gourd is a good source of fiber and has vitamin C and B vitamins. It is also rich in minerals such as iron, zinc and magnesium.

In Ayurveda, it is considered a cooling food as it is alkaline. All parts of the plant are used in medicine. The seeds are used as a laxative and the seed oil to treat skin diseases. It is also used in treatment of diabetes. The gourd releases natural insulin that regulates blood sugar levels. The juice of ridge gourd is used to treat jaundice. The beta carotene in the vegetable improves vision and the juice taken daily strengthens the immune system.

Lady's Finger

Lady's finger is also known as okra. It is called *vendakai* in Tamil and *bhindi* in Hindi. It is known as brain food in many traditional families. My grandmother always urged us, "Eat, eat! It's good for the brain."

Lady's finger contains tremendous amounts of valuable nutrients. It is rich in antioxidants. It has a lot of soluble dietary fiber in the form of gums and pectins that lower cholesterol, and it reduces the risk of heart diseases. It has vitamins A, K and C. It also has minerals such as iron, calcium, magnesium and manganese.

When cooked, lady's finger turns slimy. The fiber and sliminess of lady's finger relieve constipation and regularize the bowel movement. My father used to say that if your digestion is good and your intestines and colon are clean, you will never get sick. A healthy digestive system also reduces the risk of any digestive tract cancer.

Lady's finger also lowers blood sugar levels. Diabetics can soak the vegetable in water overnight and drink the water in the morning.

Lady's finger should never be overcooked or fried in a lot of oil, as many restaurants do. I wash and dry tender lady's finger and sauté it in a little ghee with cumin seeds until it is half cooked and crispy. This should be eaten fresh and hot. The taste is divine. *Sambar* is also a delicious way to eat the vegetable since the tamarind in the *sambar* takes away the sliminess of lady's finger.

Brinjal

Brinjal or eggplant is called *kathirikai* in Tamil and *baingan* in Hindi. It belongs to the nightshade family.

There are many varieties of brinjal, including the long purple brinjal, the green large round brinjal, the small round purple brinjal, the green small brinjal, the white large brinjal, the Italian brinjal, and the Chinese brinjal.

The purple variety, which is good for the blood, is packed with iron, potassium and vitamin D. Brinjal contains a rare enzyme that helps control inflammation of the liver and lungs. It is *not* recommended for people with kidney or gallstone problems.

The purple brinjal skin is a potent antioxidant that rejuvenates the cell membranes. It has anticancer, antimicrobial and antiviral properties. It has manganese and vitamin K, which are good for the bones. It also contains vitamins A, B6 and C. Brinjal has high water and fiber content, as well as potassium and iron.

Brinjal is popular throughout the world and is prepared in many different ways. Delicious, familiar dishes are Italian brinjal Parmesan, Chinese sautéed garlic brinjal, and Greek and Jewish baked brinjal with olive oil and garlic.

Beans

Four varieties of beans are eaten throughout the world: broad beans (fava or Indian broad beans), flat beans, string beans, and long beans. Flat beans and string beans have similar health benefits, whereas broad beans and long beans have more healing powers.

Broad beans, also known as Italian green beans, contain high amounts of potassium. They help the heart function properly, relieving stress and lowering blood pressure. They also have amino acids and fiber, which helps dissolve carcinogenic build up in the body and, therefore, diminish the risk of cancer. Broad beans are cholesterol-free and high in protein. Because broad beans, known as *avaraikai* in Tamil, has a low glycemic index, they are good for diabetics. They can be steamed and made into a drink for that purpose. String, long, and flat beans can also be prepared this way.

String beans are full of vitamins, antioxidants and phytonutrients. They can be cooked the same way as broad beans. Boil the beans and blend to add to soups or make a simple crispy bean dish as follows: Boil a pound of beans in water for 2 minutes. Drain and set aside. Heat ghee in a wok and add ½ teaspoon cumin. When the cumin has browned, add the beans and sauté briskly for a minute. Add rock salt to taste.

Flat beans have a strong fragrance and are absolutely divine when cooked. They have health benefits similar to those of broad beans.

Long beans are also known as snake beans or long podded cowpea. They contain vitamins C and A, and antioxidants. They are recommended for patients who want to lower their blood pressure.

Root Vegetables

Among the root vegetables catagory, elephant yam, sweet potato and colacasia are favorites in south India. They are often served during weddings and festivals.

Elephant Yam

Elephant yam, known as *karna kazhangu* in Tamil, is cooked like other yams but also used as medicine in Ayurveda and *Siddha*. Elephant yam has a low glycemic index and so is good for diabetics. It relieves piles and constipation. Besides being a rich source of fiber, it also contains vitamins and minerals such as nitrogen. This yam has very little fat in it and is considered a diet food. The outer fibrous skin of elephant yam is removed before it is cooked.

Elephant yam contains oxalic acid that may cause itchiness of the throat and mouth. Adding a little tamarind in the cooked yam will help combat this characteristic. Before cutting the yam, you can also rub oil over your hands to prevent itchiness.

Colacasia

Colacasia known as *sepakazhangu* in Tamil is also called taro. It is a corm which is an edible root vegetable. The leaves called *patra* are also edible. Colacasia roots are steamed and the outer fibrous skin is removed before making dishes with it. The inner potato-like flesh is cut and sautéed. Sometimes, it is mashed like mashed potatoes. It is a bit slimy, but when sautéed with spices, it turns out to be a delectable dish; high in fiber, antioxidants and minerals, including potassium.

Greens

All varieties of greens are an excellent source of minerals and vitamins. At least one helping should be eaten every day for good health.

Drum Stick

Murangai in Tamil or drum stick, is widespread in south India and grows in other warm regions. The cooked leaves are considered good for the eyes and act as a blood purifier. The tiny, fragrant flowers are said to be an aphrodisiac. The long seeds or beans are cooked and eaten as vegetable.

Spinach

Spinach is called *palak* in Hindi and *pasalai keerai* in Tamil. It is an important green that we must include in our meals. As anyone who has watched the famous cartoon *Popeye* knows, a person who regularly eats spinach gains strength and valor. It is a storehouse for iron, vitamins and antioxidants. It contains anti-cancer properties such as phytonutrients that protects one from cancer.

Black Nightshade Leaves

Black nightshade leaves (*photo next page top left*) are good for mouth and stomach ulcers. Sauté the tender leaves and berries for a delectable dish.

Fenugreek

Fenugreek greens fight diabetes.

Agathi Keerai

Another popular green is *agathi keerai*, (*photo, above right*) also known as *aathi keerai*, it is harvested from the tree *Sesbania* grandiflora. The bark, gum, leaves, and flowers of the tree are all medicinal. The greens are diuretic, emetic, tonic and is an emmenagogue. They are used in folk remedies for bruises, skin sores, cataracts, sore throat, fevers, headaches and dysentery. It is part of the diet recommended after breaking a lunar cycle fast.

Amaranth

Amaranth (*mulai keerai* in Tamil) is also known as Chinese spinach, garden amaranth or fountain plant. The leaves contain minerals and vitamins. They are antibacterial, stomachic and a febrifuge. Other popular greens used in south Indian cuisine are spleen amaranth (*arai keerai* in Tamil) and tropical amaranth (*siru keerai*).

– Trove of heirloom recipes in Tamil script

VI. Classic Recipes for Vitality and Health

When I was growing up, I remember having a three-course meal served in the morning, always before 10 AM, as our main meal of the day. The classic south Indian meal starts with rice and a teaspoon of ghee, *sambar*, and a vegetable side dish as a first course. *Rasam* is mixed along with rice as a second course rather than served in the beginning as a soup. Salads are served like any other vegetable. The sweet pudding known as *payasam* made for festive occasions is served after *rasam*. The meal is finished with rice and yogurt accompanied by a spicy or salty pickle as a third course. But, we were strange people in my house. My parents cooked millets, oats and ancient recipes that we ate with *sambar*, *rasam* and yogurt. The recipes in this book do not strictly follow the traditional sequence that has become the norm in the last century or two, but instead reflect the focus on healthy eating. We start, therefore, with drinks that are healing and cooling or otherwise therapeutic and end with the special postnatal diet. Most orthodox families, like the ancients, do not use onions or garlic in their food. However, one may include them for taste. Garlic is included for medicinal purposes in the diet of lactating mothers, while onions are avoided.

Note: Most recipes will serve approximately four to six people.

Drinks & Tonics

Asafoetida Buttermilk Drink
Neer Moru

Yogurt: 1 cup
Asafoetida: ⅛ tsp, powdered
Curry leaves: 1 sprig
Mustard seeds: ¼ tsp
Sesame oil: ½ tsp
Rock salt: to taste

Neer moru is a refreshing and nutritious drink taken any time of the day, especially in summer. It is calming, healing and prevents flatulence.

Blend yogurt, salt and water to form a thin buttermilk drink. Heat the oil in a sputtering ladle. Add mustard and pop the seeds. Add asafoetida and curry leaves and mix it in the buttermilk. If you like it spicy, garnish the buttermilk with chopped green chillies.

Ginger Buttermilk Drink
Inji Neer Moru

Yogurt: 1 cup
Water: 3 cups
Ginger: a small fresh piece
Curry leaf: a few
Asafoetida: a few pinches
Rock salt: to taste

The following recipe is a slightly different neer moru featuring ginger.

Wash, peel and finely chop the ginger. Blend all the ingredients. Transfer to a jug. Cool and serve.

Bermuda Grass Drink
Arugampul Saru

Bermuda grass: 4 ounces
Black pepper: ⅛ tsp
Buttermilk: 8 ounces

A morning drink of bermuda grass or arugampul acts as a blood purifier and promotes weight loss.

Blend the ingredients in a blender, strain and drink first thing in the morning. Do not eat for a couple of hours. Drink at least 3 to 6 glasses of fluids or plain water during the day. Do this for at least two weeks and surprise yourself with a healthy, rejuvenated, slim and youthful body!

Cardamom Drink
Elakai Kashayam

Water: 2 cups
Cardamom: 4 pods, crushed
Ginger: 1-inch cube, grated
Lemon: 1
Palm sugar: 1 tsp

My mother used to make this delicious drink with cardamom for coughs and colds.

Boil all the ingredients except lemon in 2 cups of water, strain, add lemon juice and drink. It should be sipped hot.

Cardamom Holy Basil Tea
Tulasi Kashayam

Holy basil leaves: 2 tsp
Cardamom: 4 pods ground
Ginger: 1-inch cube, grated
Black pepper: ¼ tsp
Milk/almond milk: 1 cup
Water: 2 cups

The famous masala chai of India (tea) contains cardamom, but the ancients did not drink tea which is a modern substitute for holy basil. This drink removes toxins and helps rejuvenate the body.

Heat all the ingredients and bring to a boil. Reduce heat and simmer for 2 minutes. Remove from heat, strain and drink. One may add palm sugar if desired.

Clove Cinnamon Tomato Drink
Girambu Kashayam

Tomatoes: 8 medium size, washed and chopped
Onions: 1 medium size, chopped fine
Cloves: 8
Black pepper: ½ tsp
Cinnamon powder: ½ tsp
Rock salt: to taste

This drink is recommended for diabetics.

Sauté the cloves and black pepper lightly in a dry pan. Grind to a fine consistency in a coffee grinder and set aside. Sauté the onions in a little butter or ghee, add the chopped tomatoes and sauté further. Cool and puree the mix. Add the cinnamon, ground cloves, palm sugar and salt. Blend to mix. Pour this in a pot. Add 4 cups of water and bring to a boil. Remove and serve.

Edible Stemmed Vine Drink
Perendai Saru

Perendai roots
Milk: ½ cup

For healthy bones and osteoporosis.

Dry *perendai* roots in shade. Powder and store in a dry, cool place. Add ½ teaspoon of the powder in ½ cup of milk, stir and drink twice a day for 4 to 6 weeks..

Galangal Drink
Sukku Chitharathai Kashayam

Galangal: 2 pieces, 1 inch long
Jamaica licorice: 2 pieces, 1 inch long
Dry ginger: 2 pieces, 1 inch long
Black pepper: 1 tsp
Cardamom: 10 pods
Coriander seeds: 1 tbsp

This decoction is recommended for sore throat and chest congestion.

Sun dry all the ingredients for a few hours. Cool and grind them to a coarse powder and store in an airtight jar. When needed, take a spoonful of the powder and add 8 ounces of water, then boil. Reduce heat and simmer for 3 minutes. Strain and drink with honey.

Alternate Galangal Drink

Galangal: ½ cup
Jamaica licorice: ½ cup
Turmeric: 1 tbsp
Carom seeds: 2 tsp
Black pepper: ½ tsp

Sun dry the ingredients for a couple of hours. Cool and grind to a fine powder and store in a jar. Mix a ½ teaspoon in hot milk to relieve cough and chest congestion. You can add honey for taste. One can also suck on a piece of dry galangal to relieve cough and cold.

Sweet Ginger Drink
Panagam

Galangal: ½ cup
Palm sugar/jaggery: 2 tsp
Ginger: 1-inch cube
Cardamom: 4 pods, crushed
Water: 2 cups

A cooling summer drink; it helps digestion.

Peel and chop ginger. Blend all of the ingredients, strain and serve cold.

Ginger Clove Drink
Inji Grambu Kashayam

Jaggery: 1 tbsp
Ginger: 1-inch cube
Raisins: 1 oz.
Cloves: 4

This drink has a cooling effect on the body, it aids digestion and improves metabolism.

Peel and chop the ginger. Blend all of the ingredients in 2 cups of water. Let stand for 10 minutes, strain and drink the clear liquid.

Lemongrass Ginger Tea
Karpurapul Jalam

Lemongrass: 2 stalks
Ginger: one 2-inch piece

This tea helps to relieve painful menstruation.

Chop lemongrass and crush it in mortar. Chop ginger into small pieces and crush it in mortar. Add the ginger and lemongrass to a quart of water and bring it to a boil. Reduce heat and simmer for 5 minutes. Drink this tea plain or with honey.

Coconut Lemongrass Drink
Karpurapul Thengai Kashayam

Coconut: 1
Turmeric: ½ tsp
Lemongrass: fresh chopped, ½ cup or 1 tsp powdered
Rock salt: to taste
Lemon: juice of ½ lemon
Coriander leaves: a few
Green chilli: 1 (optional)

This delicious drink makes a soothing tonic, reducing stress and calms the nerves.

Take a whole coconut and grate the white meat from it. Blend and strain to extract the milk of the coconut. Add turmeric and crushed lemongrass to the coconut milk. Add 4 cups of water and bring to a boil. Reduce and simmer for 5 minutes. Add rock salt to taste and the lemon juice. If you like spicy you can add a teaspoon of crushed ginger and green chilli. Garnish with coriander leaves. Crushed fresh lemongrass can also be added to other soups and vegetable dishes as flavoring.

Lemongrass Drink
Karpurapul Kashayam

Lemongrass: 2 stalks
Ginger: 1-inch cube, peeled and chopped
Tomatoes: 3 medium, crushed
Turmeric: 1 tsp
Red chillies: 3
Cumin seeds: ½ tsp
Ghee: 1 tbsp
Juice of one lemon
Coriander leaves: handful
Rock salt: to taste

This drink improves functioning of the nervous system.

Cut the red chillies in half and set aside. Cut stalks of lemongrass into small pieces and pound it in mortar. In 2 quarts of water add lemongrass, tomatoes, ginger and turmeric. Bring to a boil. Lower the heat and simmer for 7 minutes. Add one more glass of water and simmer for 2 more minutes. In a sauté pan, heat ghee, add the cumin and let it pop and get brown. Now, quickly add the red chillies and pour it in the soup. Add freshly chopped coriander leaves and lemon juice.

Cumin Tamarind Drink
Jeera Panagam

Tamarind juice: ½ tsp
Dates: 4, pitted
Black salt/rock salt: to taste
Asafoetida: 1 pinch
Ginger: 1 piece, ½-inch long, peeled
Cumin: ½ tsp

Cooling and stomachic.

Roast cumin until it turns brown. Add 1 cup of water to dates and grind. Add one more cup of water and all the other ingredients and blend to liquefy. Add ice and one more cup of water, blend to stir and enjoy a smooth, cooling drink.

Tamarind Sweet Drink
Panagam

Jaggery or palm sugar: ¼ cup crumbled
Ginger: ½ tsp, peeled, grated or dry powder
Tamarind juice: ½ tsp
Cardamom: 4 pods peeled and crushed
Water: 4 cups

For liver health and bile flow.

Liquefy all of the ingredients in a blender. Add ice and drink cold or at room temperature.

Carom Drink with Betel Leaves
Omathi Neer

Carom seeds: ½ tsp
Betel leaves: 2
Water: 1 cup

To relieve colic pain and stomach disorders.

Blend the ingredients in a blender and strain. You can add honey to make a soothing drink. Give ¼ cup to children and ½ cup to adults as an appetizer and digestive aid and to clear phlegm in the lungs. Betel leaves work as antiseptic of the respiratory tract, carminative, expectorant and stimulant.

Carom Neem Drink
Omam Kashayam

Black pepper: ½ tsp
Cumin: ½ tsp
Carom: ½ tsp
Long pepper stem: ½ tsp
Dried ginger: ½ tsp
Dried neem flower: ½ tsp
Coriander seeds: ½ tsp

For stomach ailments, blood circulation, rejuvenation.

Roast all the ingredients except neem flowers in a pan. Roast the neem flowers separately until they are dark brown. Grind all of the ingredients together to a semi-coarse powder. Mix the ground powder to 4 cups water. Bring to a boil, reduce heat and simmer until the water reduces to 3 cups and then drink it.

Carom Drink
Omam Rasam

Carom: 1 tsp
Cumin: 1 tsp
Tamarind: 1 tsp
Tomato: 4 chopped
Palm sugar: 1 tsp
Rock salt: to taste
Ghee: 1 tsp
Turmeric: ⅛ tsp
Rasam powder: ½ tsp
Asafoetida: a small piece or a few pinches

It aids digestion and controls flatulence.

Roast carom and cumin and grind to a powder. In a 2 quart pot, add 1 quart water and all the above ingredients. Bring to a boil. Reduce heat and simmer for 5 minutes. Drink warm as needed.

Almond Milk
Badam Kheer

Almonds: ½ cup
Milk: 3 cups
Water: 3 cups
Saffron: 2 pinches
Raw sugar: ½ cup
Edible camphor: 1 pinch, smaller than the size of black pepper

An aphrodisiac, rejuvenator, and brain food.

Soak almonds in hot water for a couple of hours. Peel the skin and blend into a fine paste with 3 cups of water. Pour into a 2 quart pot and simmer. Add 3 cups of milk and raw sugar. Heat to a boil then simmer for 5 minutes. Add the saffron. It is a good idea to crush the saffron before adding it to the almond milk. Remove from stove and add crushed camphor. My mother used to add sliced pistachio as garnish. Can be taken hot or cold. For those who are lactose intolerant, just add a few more cups of water instead of milk.

Turmeric Milk with Black Pepper

Milk: 2 cups
Turmeric: ½ tsp
Black pepper: ¼ tsp, crushed
Dates: 2 dried, pitted and crushed
Honey: 1 tsp

A half cup of warm turmeric milk taken three times a day relieves cough and sore throat. One can substitute almond milk in place of cow's milk. Taking it everyday improves the overall health.

Bring all of the ingredients to a boil, except honey. Reduce the heat and simmer for 5 minutes. Strain, cool, add raw honey and drink. It can be made without honey.

Turmeric Cardamom Drink

Milk: 2 cups
Cardamom seeds: ¼ tsp, crushed
Hot milk: 1 glass
Turmeric: ¼ tsp
Black pepper: ⅛ tsp
Honey: 1 tsp

This soothing, warm drink is good for a sore throat and also tastes divine.

Mix all the ingredients in hot milk and drink.

Payasam and Sweets

The following recipes are a very small sampling of the many sweet dishes that are popular in south India. I have selected a few that are made as offerings to deities and ancestors, these are considered worthy of the divine. *Payasam* is not just another sweet dish, but is considered to be a symbolic *"elixir of life"* that is made as an offering to the gods. It can be served hot or cold. *Payasam* is always made with the purest ingredients without any additives and oils. It is low in calories.

Organic raw rice: 1 cup
Milk: 1 quart
Raw sugar or jaggery: ½ cup
Cardamom: 6 pods, peeled and powdered
Cashews: ¼ cup roasted in ghee

Milk Payasam

The devout believe that if you offer milk payasam to the cosmic energy, you will be granted any wish. This payasam is said to be Lord Shiva's favorite food.

Cook rice and mash it. Boil milk and add the mashed rice and sugar. Simmer at low heat for 5 minutes. Add cardamom and cashews. Eat hot.

Camphor Payasam

Camphor is very potent and has a strong flavor; use sparingly. Follow the recipe for milk payasam, add a pinch of edible camphor at the end.

Mango: 1 large
Milk: 2 cups
Raw sugar: ¼ cup
Cashew nut: ¼ cup roasted in ghee
Saffron: a pinch

Mango Payasam

First, peel and puree a ripe mango. Mix together all of the ingredients except the cashews and heat in a pot until it comes to a boil. Reduce the heat and cook for a couple of minutes more. Remove from heat and add roasted cashews.

Oats Payasam

Oats: 1 cup
Milk: 3 cups
Raw sugar: to taste
Cardamom: 8 pods, powdered
Saffron: a pinch

A complete grain full of minerals, it lowers the estrogen levels, preventing hormone-related diseases. It is also good for blood pressure.

Dry roast oats for 2 minutes. Add 3 cups of water and cook for 2 minutes. Add milk and sugar, bring to boil and simmer for a couple of minutes. Add saffron and cardamom. Drink hot or cold.

Almond Halwah

Almond: 1 cup
Ghee: 3 tbps
Raw sugar: 1 cup
Saffron: 2 pinches

A brain food.

Soak and peel the skin of the almonds. Blend to a thick paste. In a wok, put ½ cup water and sugar and heat until the sugar dissolves into the water. Add the almond paste and keep stirring for 10 minutes and add 1 tablespoon ghee. Stir again until it comes together. Add 1 tablespoon of ghee and saffron and stir again until the almond paste pulls away from the sides of the wok without sticking to the sides. Pour on a plate greased with ghee, let it cool and cut into to 1 inch squares. For those who like less sweetness, reduce the raw sugar to half a cup. Diabetics may substitute stevia for sugar.

Sesame Laddus
Ellu Urundai

Sesame seeds, black or white: 1 cup
Palm sugar: ½ cup
Ghee: enough to moisten your hand

Sesame seeds are full of antioxidants, minerals, and vitamins E and B. It relieves arthritic pain.

Roast the sesame seeds until they turn golden. Cool and grind the seeds until they are coarse. Add palm sugar and blend to mix them together. Remove and shape into balls, moistening your hands with ghee.

Add roasted cashews and crushed cardamom for variety.

Ginger Honey Candy
Inji Morabba

Honey: ¼ cup
Ginger: 1 cup, peeled, washed and cut

This candy relieves indigestion, heartburn and cold.

Steam ginger until it is cooked. Cool and transfer to an airtight jar. Add honey and let it soak for 10 days before eating.

Foxtail Millet Sweet Pongal
Thinai Sakarai Pongal

Foxtail millet: 1 cup
Bengal gram: 1 tbps
Mung split: ¼ cup
Palm jaggery: ¾ cup
Ginger: a small piece, peeled and chopped fine
Cardamom: 6 to 8 pods, crushed
Cashew nuts: ¼ cup, roasted
Edible camphor: 1 tiny pinch
Ghee: ¼ cup

Gluten-free, high in fiber, rich in protein.

Dry roast the millet, Bengal gram and mung in medium heat for a few minutes. Wash and add 4 cups of water and cook it. Mash the cooked millet and set aside. In a wok, add palm sugar and ½ cup water. When this turns into syrup, add the cooked millet and let the mixture come together. Add a tablespoon ghee and the ginger. Mix and add ghee again until the mix does not stick to the pan. Add cashews, cardamom and camphor and stir. Remove from heat and serve hot and top with a spoonful of ghee.

Finger Millet Halwah
Ragi Halwah

Finger millet: 1 cup, cracked
Almond flour: ½ cup
Almond milk: 1 cup
Ghee: ¼ cup
Raw sugar: ¾ cup
Cashew nut: ¼ cup, chopped

Gluten-free, high in calcium.

In a wok, add 1 tablespoon ghee and roast the finger millet slightly. Add 2 cups of water and almond milk, and cook until the millet is soft. Add almond flour, raw sugar and 2 cups of water and stir further. Add the ghee and stir. The halwah is ready when it pulls away from the wok. It should be similar in consistency to pudding. Add more ghee if needed. Add cashews and serve.

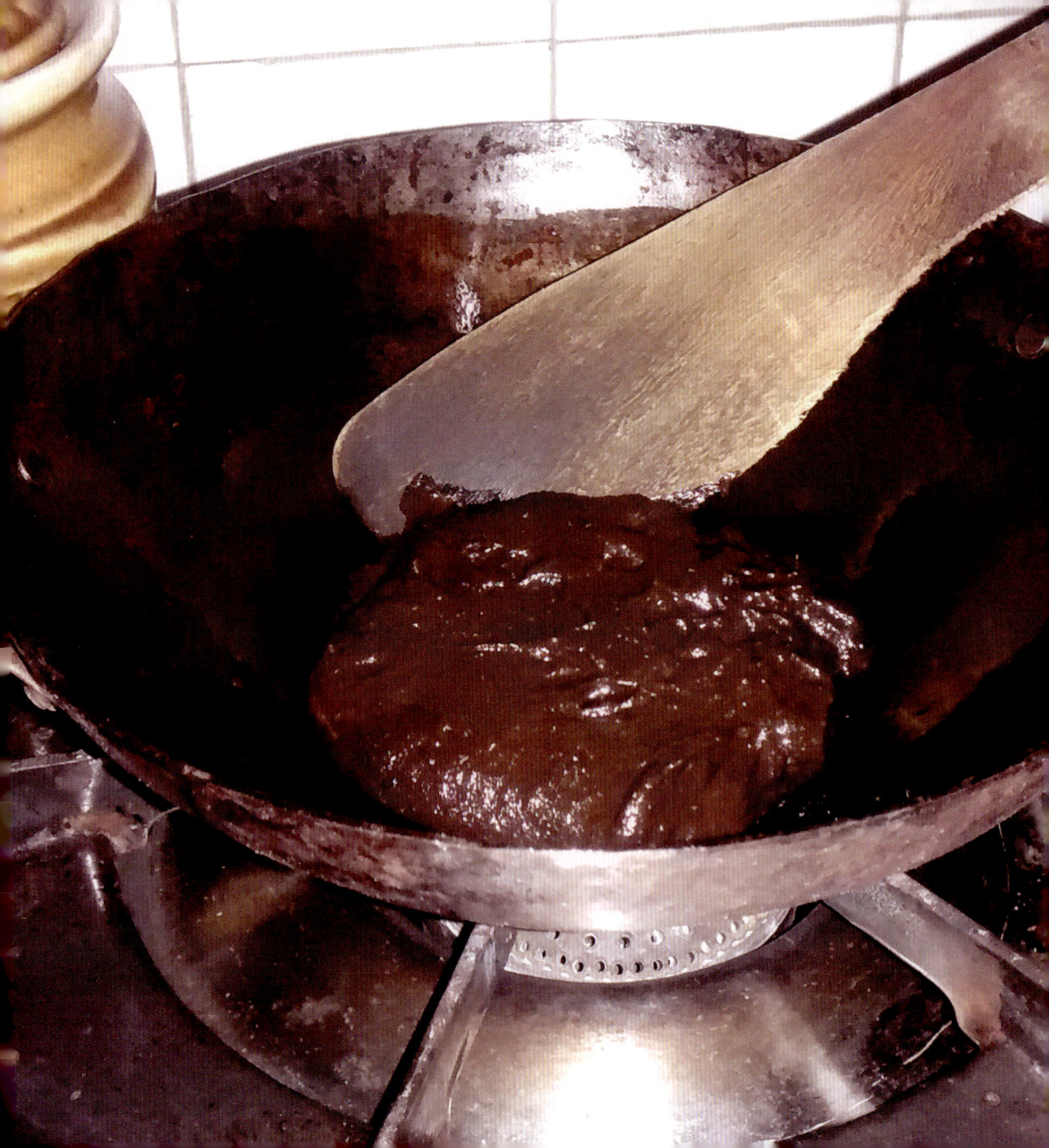

Legiyam

Legiyam is a soft, medicinal paste that has the consistency of halwah. See the postpartum foods for more.

Black Pepper Legiyam
Milagu Legiyam

Black pepper: 1 cup
Milk: 4 cups
Jaggery: ½ cup
Ghee: 1 tbps

Good for anemia.

Cook milk and pepper together at medium heat until the milk evaporates to form a halwah consistency. Remove from heat, cool, and grind to a paste. Add ½ cup of jaggery and blend to mix. Heat 1 tablespoon of ghee in a wok and add the paste. Reduce to medium-low heat and keep mixing until the paste pulls away from the sides. Cool and store in a glass jar. Eat one ½ teaspoon every morning.

Cumin Legiyam
Jeera Legiyam

Cumin: ½ cup
Dry pomegranate seeds: 1 tsp
Palm sugar: ¼ cup
Ghee: 1 tbps

Good for digestion.

Roast cumin seeds, add pomegranate seeds and roast a little longer. Grind them.

In a pan, add ¼ cup water and palm sugar and heat at medium heat for 3 minutes. Then, add the ground cumin and pomegranate; reduce the flame to low. Stir and add the ghee. Mix thoroughly and evenly. Cool and store in a jar.

Take a ¼ teaspoon every morning or before going to bed.

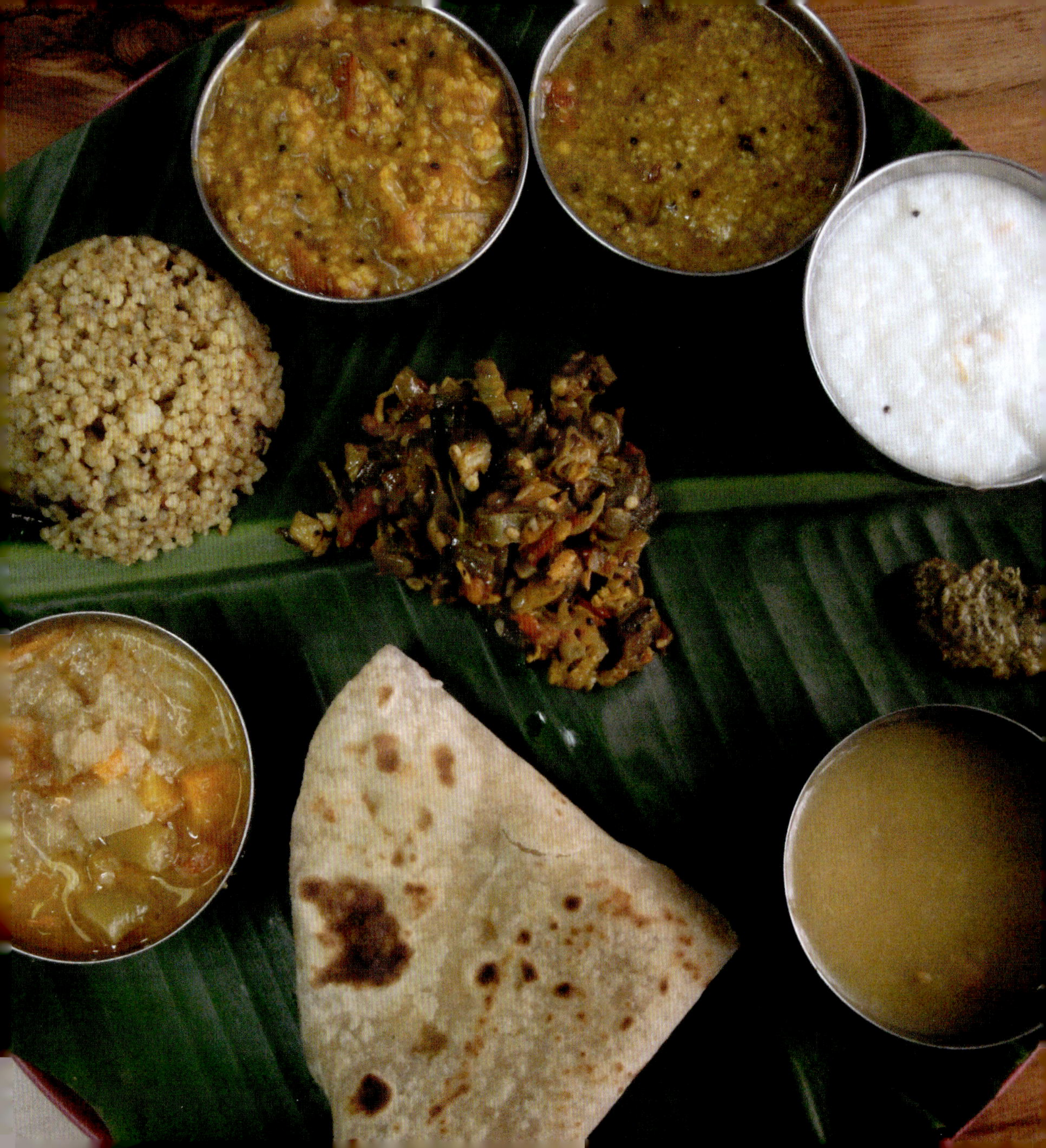

Main Dishes

Grains and legumes are an important part of a wholesome diet. Most main dishes of southern India are made with grains and legumes. In ancient times, the raw rice and millets took center stage. These days, most main dishes such as *idli*, *dosai* and *adai* are made with plain white rice and legumes. We can always break the rules to make healthy foods in order to eat like the ancients. My ingredients do not include polished white rice. I do use parboiled rice, as this is full of nutrients including the B vitamins.

Rice: 2 cups, parboiled, brown or red rice
Split or whole black gram: 1 cup
Salt: to taste
Sesame oil or ghee for greasing the steamer

Idli

Idli is considered a satvic food as it is easy to digest. It is a food prescribed for sick people. It is a popular breakfast food in south India and also eaten as tiffin in the afternoon or a light meal at supper.

Wash and soak the rice and black gram separately for 3 hours or more. Grind them fine with the water that was used for soaking until you get the consistency of thick pancake batter. Add rock salt to taste and mix. Leave it overnight to ferment. Fermenting allows the batter to rise and also produces B vitamins. Grease the *idli* steamer with ghee or sesame oil, ladle the batter neatly into the round depressions and steam for 20 minutes at medium heat.

In cold seasons, adding a pinch of yeast helps the batter to ferment. The batter must also be kept in a warm place overnight. Leaving this inside an oven with the light on is a good option.

Idli is eaten with *sambar*, coconut chutney or a blend of spices and lentils known as *milagai podi*.

Dosai

Rice: 2 cups parboiled rice
Split or whole black gram: 1 cup
Fenugreek: 1 teaspoon
Sesame oil: for griddle frying

Soak rice and black gram separately for 4 to 6 hours. Fenugreek can be soaked along with black gram. Grind them separately to form a thick batter. Add salt to the batter and leave it overnight to ferment and rise. The next day, add water and stir to form a medium thin consistency. Heat a griddle. Baste the griddle with a bit of oil. The *dosais* will not spread evenly with too much oil on the griddle. Take a ladle full of batter and pour at the center of the griddle and spread clockwise from the center to the periphery. Once it is golden brown and a little crisp, turn it over carefully. Cook a few seconds longer, remove and serve hot with *sambar* or coconut chutney.

Rice Adai

Brown or red rice powder mix: 2 cups
Split black gram: 2 tsp
Bengal gram: 1 tbsp
Onion: 1, chopped
Green chilli: 1 or 2, chopped
Cumin: 1 tsp
Curry leaves: 2 sprigs
Sesame oil for frying

Rice adai, a gluten free ancient food, is not very popular anymore.

Add water to rice powder and make a batter with it, adding a little rock salt. Heat 1 teaspoon sesame oil and add black gram and Bengal gram. Sauté until golden. Add cumin, onion, curry leaves and green chilli. Remove from heat and mix this with the rice batter. Let it stand for a couple of hours and then ladle into thin pancakes on a hot griddle basted with oil. Flip and cook the other side, basting it until lightly browned. Eat with your favorite accompaniment such as coconut chutney or *sambar*.

Legume Adai

Split red gram: ¼ cup
Mung: ¼ cup
Split black gram: ¼ cup
Bengal gram: ½ cup
Brown rice: ¼ cup
Red or green chili: 4
Asafoetida: ¼ tsp
Rock salt: to taste
Sesame oil for the griddle

Soak the legumes and rice for 2 hours. Grind this with all the other ingredients, adding water to get a coarse pancake batter. Ladle onto a hot basted griddle as you would a pancake, only thinner. With a spoon, oil the edges around the *adai* and cook until it turns brown. Flip the *adai*, baste, and cook the other side.

Yogurt Rice
Thayir Sadam

Rice: 1 cup
Yogurt: 1 cup
Milk: 1 cup
Green chili: 1 or 2 chopped fine
Ginger: a small piece, chopped fine
Mustard seeds: 1 tsp
Curry leaves: 1 sprig
Asafoetida: a few pinches
Sesame oil: 1 tsp
Rock salt: to taste

Yogurt is a digestive aid because of the bacterial cultures it contains. It also increases the B vitamins in the rice and is soothing to the stomach. Indigenous people ate this and benefited from the probiotics. Some rice takes longer to cook; using a pressure cooker is helpful.

Cook the rice with 3 cups of water and set aside to cool.

In a bowl, mix the rice with yogurt and mash it well. Add milk and salt and mix again. Heat sesame oil in a pan. Add mustard seeds. As soon as it starts to sputter, add ginger, green chili, asafoetida and curry leaves. Sauté for a few seconds and stir it into the yogurt-rice mix. For a variation, you can add finely chopped cucumber and fresh pomegranate seeds.

My mother would add small pieces of raw mango and finely chopped coriander leaves, sometimes grated carrots and even cashew nuts.

Lemon Rice
Elimichampazham Sadam

Rice: 1 cup
Lemon: 1 large
Turmeric: ¼ tsp
Rock salt: to taste
Asafoetida: a few pinches
Mustard seeds: 1 tsp
Bengal gram: 1 tbsp
Red chilli: 2
Ginger: 1 inch cube, peeled and cut into small pieces
Curry leaves: 1 sprig
Sesame oil: 2 tbsp

Cook the rice in 2½ cups of water. Set it aside to cool.

To the cooked rice add lemon juice, 1 tablespoon sesame oil, salt and stir to mix. In a pan, heat rest of the oil. Add mustard seeds. As soon as it starts to sputter, add Bengal gram and sauté until golden brown. Add chilli, asafoetida, ginger, curry leaves and turmeric and stir for a few seconds, then add this to the rice and mix well. Roasted peanuts can be added for a variety. Millet can be substituted for rice.

Pearl Millet Kanjee

Pearl millet: 1 cup
Water: 3 cups

Grind millet until it is the consistency of cracked wheat. Cook millet in water as you would make rice. Eat it with ghee or make a porridge.

Oats Kanjee

Oats: 1 cup
Yogurt: 2 cups
Asafoetida: ⅛ tsp
Curry leaves: 1 sprig
Green chilli: 1, minced
Mustard seeds: ½ tsp

A superfood that controls blood pressure and lowers estrogen levels.

Cook oats in water. Cool and add yogurt to it. Heat sesame oil and pop the mustard seeds. Immediately, add asafoetida, green chilli and curry leaves. Sauté for a few seconds and add to the oats with yogurt. Add salt and mix.

Pearl Millet Adai
Kambu Adai

Pearl millet: 1 cup
Split black gram: ¼ cup
Bengal gram: ¼ cup
Mung: ¼ cup
Red chillies: 3 whole
Asafoetida: a small piece
Fennel: 1 tsp
Cumin: ½ tsp
Curry leaves: 2 sprigs

Soak the millet and legumes in water for 3 to 4 hours. Blend all the ingredients to a medium soft batter. Make *adais* on a griddle with sesame oil. Cook both sides until golden brown. Pair them with your favorite accompaniment. This can also be prepared with vegetables. Chop onions, ginger, carrots and cabbage; stir them into the batter and cook.

Little Millet Pongal
Samai Pongal

Little millet: 1 cup
Mung, split: ½ cup
Ginger: 1 inch piece, chopped
Cumin: 1 tsp
Black pepper: 1 tsp
Ghee: 2 tbsp

Reduces cholesterol, strengthens bones and muscles. It is gluten free.

Wash and cook mung in 2 cups of water. When almost soft, add little millet and 3 cups of water. Cook it with salt until soft. In a wok, heat ghee. Add cumin, black pepper and ginger. Quickly saute and add this to the millet. Turn it over to mix. One can add more ghee or rock salt to taste.

Millet idlis in a steamer

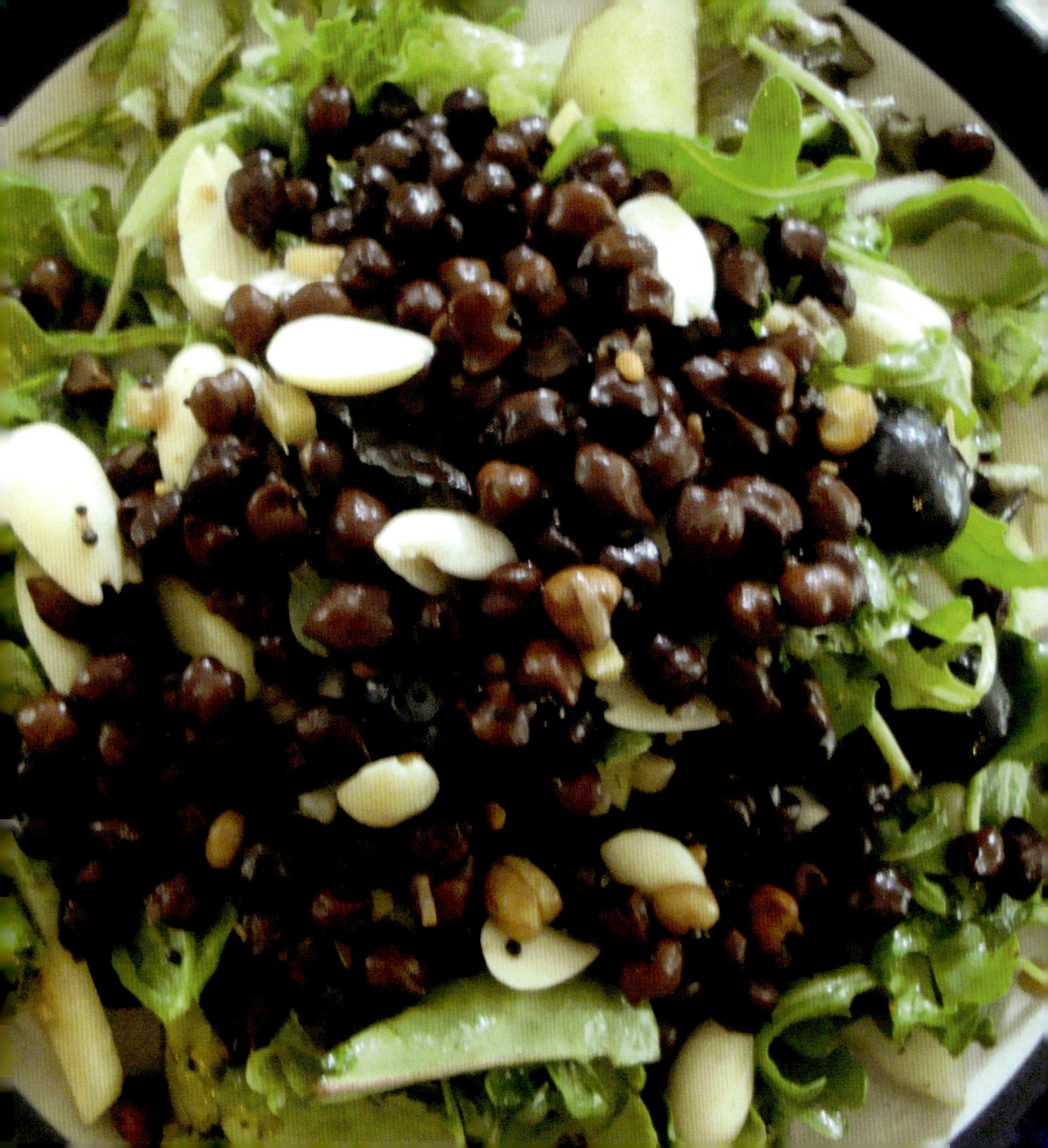

Sundal

Sundal, a simple dish of cooked legumes tempered with mustard and garnished with curry leaves and coconut is an all-time favorite of south Indians. During the Navaratri festival, a different *sundal* is made on each of the nine nights of the festival as an offering to the deities. *Navratri* is a festival where goddess Durga kills the evil demon Mahishasura on the ninth day of fasting and meditation. The tenth day is Vijayadasami. *Vijayam* means victory and *dasami* means the tenth day. It is the day when one has attained pure knowledge.

The house is cleaned for the festival of *Kolu*. This is essentially a women's festival, when elders and young girls of the family build 3, 5, 7, or 9 steps and decorate them with dolls, gods, goddesses, villages scenes, harvest and good food. I remember dressing up every evening in new clothes or special silk clothing and visiting neighbors to invite them to visit our *kolu*. They, in turn, would do the same. Every evening, there was music. This was the time to show off your musical talents. One would sing or play an instrument. *Veena* was very popular among girls when I was growing up.

The significance is that each day, a different *sundal* is made for goddess Durga, who, in Hinduism, is considered to be the supreme power, or *Adi Shakti* and has nine forms: Parvati, Bhairavi, Vaishnavi, Kali, Jagatmata, Mahishasuramardhini, Gauri, Chandi and Uma. The intention is to inspire young girls to empower themselves with strength, power, confidence, determination, knowledge, fearlessness, intelligence, calmness and the ability to destroy evil, as represented by the goddesses. Every day, *sundal* is offered to the *kolu* along with other items such as bananas, coconut, beetle leaves, turmeric and *kumkumam* (the red color put on the forehead by women and girls). The festival inculcates discipline, self confidence, healthy eating, love for nature, neighbors and friends.

In general, legumes are easy to prepare. Chickpeas, kidney beans, black beans, black-eyed beans, whole mung and whole black gram should be washed and soaked overnight. The next morning, add fresh water, salt to taste and add any combination of spices and vegetables and slow cook in a cooker. If you are in a hurry, cook on the stove on medium heat (or in a pressure cooker) until done. Before serving, you can add a little ghee on top. Legumes can be sprouted and used in salads. To sprout legumes, soak overnight, drain the water and leave it in a covered container until you see the sprouts.

Black-eyed Bean Sundal

Black-eyed beans: 2 cups, soaked for a few hours, cooked and drained
Rock salt: to taste
Red chillies/ green chillies: 3 chopped into ½ inch pieces
Mustard seeds: 1 tsp
Ginger: 2-inch cube, peeled and chopped
Asafoetida: a small piece, roasted and crushed
Coconut: ¼ cup, grated
Curry leaves: 2 strands
Sesame oil: 1 tsp

The recipe for black-eyed bean or karamani sundal can be followed using any kind of bean for a simple, healthful and savory snack.

Note: Sundal is always made dry. The water drained from cooking the beans can be saved for *rasams* or soups.

In a wok, heat oil and sputter the mustard seeds. Add the chillies, ginger, asafoetida and curry leaves and sauté lightly. Add the beans, salt and stir for a few seconds. Garnish it with coconut.

The same recipe can be followed to make *sundal* from whole mung, chickpeas, black *chana* or lima beans. These legumes need to be soaked overnight.

Pattani or dried sweet peas *sundal* is a delicacy made in the same way, but with the addition of raw mangoes chopped into small bits.

To make peanut *sundal*, roast a cup of peanuts on low heat for a few minutes to remove the skin. Then soak the peanuts in water for 4 to 6 hours or overnight. Steam it with a little salt. It is now ready to be made into *sundal* in the same way as *pattani sundal*.

Sweet Sundal

Black-eyed beans or mung: 1 cup
Palm sugar or jaggery: ½ cup
Cardamon: 8 pods, peeled and crushed
Ghee: 1 tablespoon

My mother-in-law used to make a sweet sundal using either mung or black-eyed beans.

Soak the lentils for 3 hours. Cook and drain the water. This water can be used for melting the jaggery.

Heat jaggery in ¼ cup water. Once it is dissolved, add the beans and stir until the jaggery gets absorbed. Add cardamom and ghee and stir. Remove from heat and serve warm.

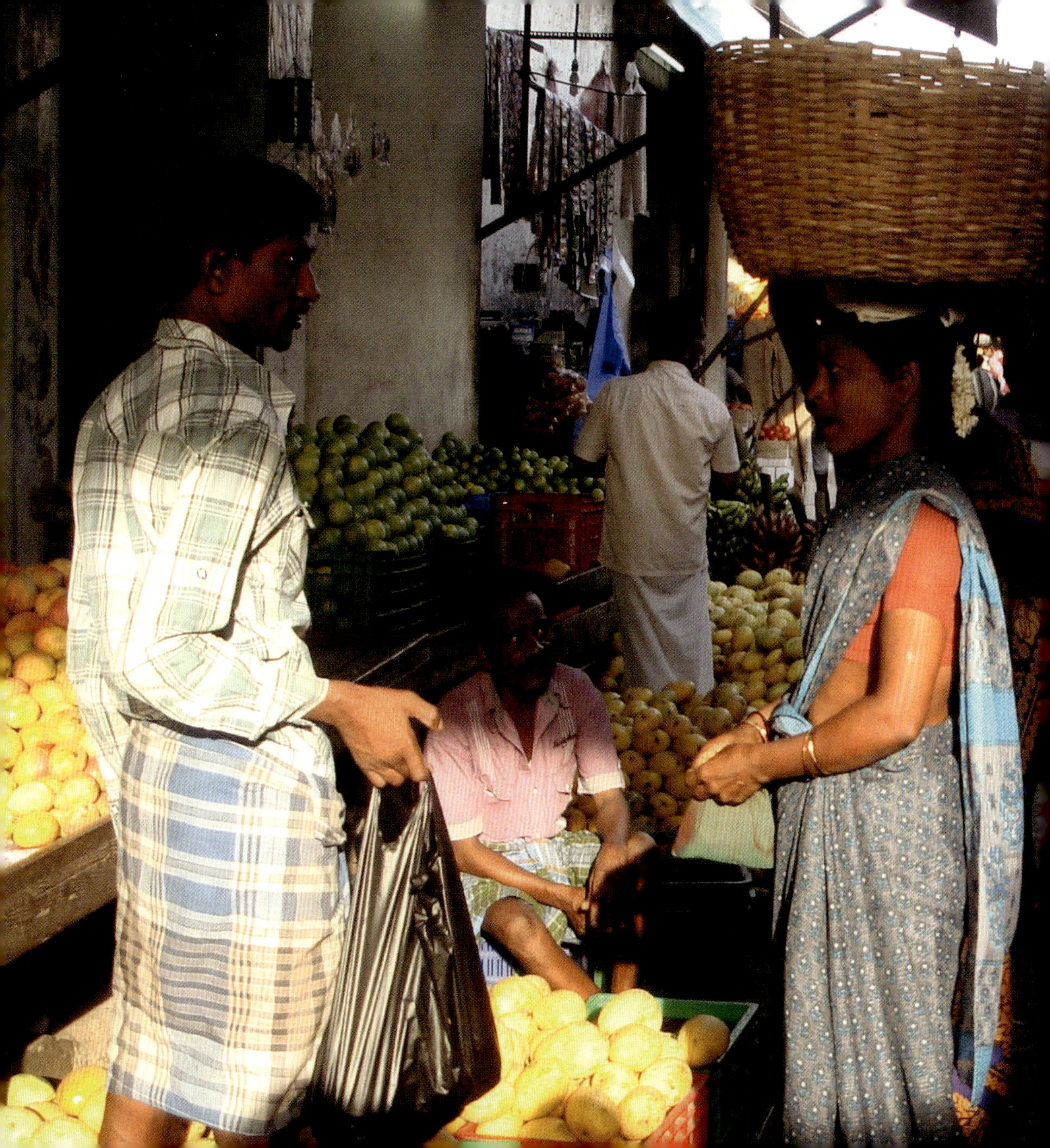

Sambar

Sambar

Kuzhambu is a stew made with vegetables and flavored with a powdered spice mix. The most common type of *kuzhambu* is *sambar* and many people use the two terms interchangeably. Every south Indian kitchen stocks *sambar* and *rasam* powders. One can mix their own powders or buy packaged powders from Indian grocery stores. Each time you make *sambar*, you can create distinct flavors by varying the vegetables, spices or coconut.

The basic ingredients that go in a *sambar*, apart from the vegetables, are tamarind, salt, asafoetida, *sambar* powder and split red gram. You can use any vegetable in a sambar. Most commonly used vegetables are brinjal, ladie's finger, pumpkin, bell pepper, onion, white radish and bitter gourd; each giving a distinct flavor. Sometimes, the *sambar* is made with mixed vegetables. It is eaten with rice as the first course of a traditional south Indian meal. It is very nutritious because it contains protein, vitamins and spices that are stimulants, stomachic and carminative. Along with rice, which is a carbohydrate, it makes for a complete meal. Another type of *kuzhambu* is *morkuzhambu*, in which the source of tanginess is yogurt or buttermilk rather than tamarind.

Sambar Powder, Recipe 1

Coriander seeds: 2 cups
Red chilli powder: 1 cup
Split red gram: ⅛ cup
Bengal gram: ¼ cup
Split black gram: 1 tsp
Black pepper: 1 tsp
Cumin seeds: ½ tsp
Fenugreek: ⅛ cup
Turmeric: 1 tbsp
Asafoetida: 1 tsp

Lightly roast these ingredients separately until the raw smell is gone. Roast fenugreek until it turns brown. Grind all the ingredients to a fine powder and store in an airtight glass jar.

Sambar Powder, Recipe 2

Red chilli powder: 2 cups
Coriander seeds: 2 cups
Bengal gram: ½ cup
Split red gram: ½ cup
Fenugreek seeds: 1 tsp
Turmeric powder: 1 tsp

Roast all the ingredients, grind to a fine powder and store in an airtight glass jar.

Daily Sambar
Kuzhambu

Split red gram: ½ cup
Fresh tamarind pod the size of a lime, or 1 tsp tamarind paste
Sambar powder: 2 tsp
Asafoetida: a small piece
Rock salt: to taste
Mustard seeds: ½ tsp
Fenugreek: ⅛ tsp
Curry leaves: a sprig
Vegetables: 2 cups, diced

In a 2 quart pot, heat a teaspoon of sesame oil. Add fenugreek and sputter mustard seeds. When the mustard sputters and the fenugreek seeds are browned, add asafoetida and curry leaves and sauté. Add 16 ounces of water. Next, add the vegetables along with tamarind, salt and sambar powder. If using tamarind pods, soak in water and remove pulp. Cook the red gram in 1½ cups of water until soft and then puree. When the vegetables are cooked, add the pureed red gram. The *sambar* should be similar in consistency to gravy. Eat with rice and a ½ teaspoon ghee.

Ground Masala Sambar
Araithu Vitta Sambar

Split red gram: ½ cup
Turmeric: ½ tsp
Tamarind: 1 tsp
Asafoetida: a small piece or ⅛ tsp of powder
Coriander seeds: 2 tbsp
Coconut: ¼ cup, grated
Bengal gram: 1 tbsp
Fenugreek: ⅛ tsp
Rock salt: to taste
Mustard seeds: ½ tsp
Sesame oil: 1 tsp
A pound of any of the following: brinjal, ladie's finger, pumpkin, white radish, bitter melon, winter melon

An elaborate version known as arachi vitta sambar, *for a richer flavor.*

Wash and dice vegetables. Cook red gram in 3 cups of water with turmeric until soft enough to mash. I use a pressure cooker to cook them. In a 3 quart pot, add 16 ounces of water, vegetables, *sambar* powder, asafoetida, tamarind and salt. Cook until the vegetables are done. Mix in the mashed red gram.

Roast fenugreek until dark brown, roast Bengal gram until golden brown and coriander until slightly brown. Grind these well with coconut and add to the mix. Bring to a boil. Turn off the heat and garnish with coriander leaves. Sputter ½ teaspoon of mustard seeds and curry leaves in ghee or sesame oil and garnish the dish. Another tasty variation is to add a ½ cup grated coconut, roasted dry, and ground with fenugreek, coriander seeds and Bengal gram.

Prickly Nightshade and Fenugreek Sambar
Sundakkai Mendiya Kuzhambu

Carom: ½ tsp
Fenugreek: ¼ tsp
Split red gram: 1 tbsp
Tamarind: 1 tsp
Sambar powder: 2 tsp
Ghee: 1 tsp
Sundakkai: 1 tbsp (dried)
Palm sugar: 1 tsp
Asafoetida: a small piece
Rice powder: ½ tsp
Rock salt: to taste

A medicinal dish to relieve stomach ailments, pain and diarrhea.

Roast fenugreek until golden brown. Add red gram and fry further until slightly browned. Now, add carom and fry until the fenugreek has turned dark brown. Remove from heat. Cool, then grind coarsely and set aside.

In a 2 quart pot, add 1 quart water. Add tamarind, *sambar* powder, asafoetida and bring to a boil. Reduce heat and simmer for 5 minutes. Add the ground fenugreek powder and palm sugar and bring to a boil. Reduce the flame and heat for another 5 minutes. Heat ghee in a pan, add dried *sundakkai* and fry until dark and crisp. Add to the *kuzhambu* after removing from heat.

Black Pepper Sambar
Milagu Kuzhambu

Tamarind: 2 tsp paste
Coriander seeds: 2 tsp
Sesame oil: 2 tsp
Asafoetida: ¼ tsp
Black pepper: 2 tsp
Mustard seeds: 1 tsp
Split red gram: 3 tsp
Bengal gram: 2 tsp
Cumin seeds: 1 tsp
Jaggery: 1 tbsp
Rock salt: 1 tsp
Turmeric: ½ tsp
Fenugreek: ¼ tsp
Curry leaves: 4 sprigs

Rejuvenator and blood purifier.

Roast fenugreek until dark brown and set aside. Roast Bengal gram and red gram until golden brown and set aside. Roast coriander seeds, black pepper, asafoetida and cumin seeds for a minute in medium heat until golden brown. Blend these ingredients together to a semi-fine powder.

In a 2 quart pot, heat sesame oil. Sputter mustard seeds and add curry leaves. Add 1 quart water. Stir in the tamarind paste, jaggery, rock salt and turmeric. Stir in the blended powder and bring the mix to a boil. Reduce heat and simmer for 20 minutes. You can also add quarter teaspoon of fried fenugreek.

Pitlai Sambar
Pitlai

Bitter gourds: 4
Split red gram: ½ cup
Bengal gram: 1 tbsp
Coriander seeds: 2 tbsp
Split black gram: 1 tsp
Tamarind paste: 1 tsp
Asafoetida: a small piece
Coconut: ½ cup, grated
Cumin seeds: ¼ tsp
Green chillies: 2, medium
Rice: 1 tsp
Sesame oil: 1 tsp
Mustard seeds: 1 tsp
Coriander leaves for garnish

Roast Bengal gram, coriander seeds, split black gram and asafoetida. Grind and set aside. Grind coconut, cumin seeds, green chillies and rice into a fine paste, adding water. Mix in the ground powder and blend again, adding water to form a loose consistency. Set aside.

Bitter gourds should be chopped into thin round pieces. Meanwhile, cook red gram in 1½ cups of water in a pressure cooker.

Heat sesame oil and sputter mustard seeds. Add curry leaves. Stir in the bitter gourd pieces. Add 16 ounces of water, salt to taste and tamarind paste. Cook until the pieces gets tender. Add the cooked red gram and the blended mix. Stir and add water to make a stew-like consistency. Bring to a boil and then remove from heat. Add coriander leaves to garnish.

Concentrated Sambar with Dried Vegetables
Vettha Kuzhambu

Sesame oil: 1 tbsp
Tamarind: 2 lumps the size of a lemon ball, soaked in ½ cup of water, squeezed and strained or 2 tsp concentrate
Bengal gram: 2 tbsp
Mustard seeds: 1 tsp
Asafoetida: a large ½ inch piece
Sambar powder: 2 tsp
Red chili: 3 pieces
Curry leaves: 3 or 4 sprigs
Palm sugar: 1 tbsp

In a 2 quart pot or a wok, heat sesame oil. Sputter mustard seeds, then add Bengal gram and fry until golden. Remove from heat, add the chilies, asafoetida and curry leaves. Put the vessel back on stove at medium heat and add the sambar powder. Turn it over once and quickly add 24 ounces of water, or 3 cups. Add tamarind and palm sugar. Simmer on low heat for 20 minutes.

For variety, you can add dried brinjal, dried lady's finger, or onions. Prickly nightshade or black nightshade is used, but only as a garnish at the end. The nightshade has to be fried dark and crisp before being used as garnish. Vetha kozhambu is best eaten with hot rice and ghee. Sometimes, raw sesame oil is substituted for ghee. My mother's secret recipe included two other ingredients: coriander seeds and sesame seeds. She would roast and grind them and then add the mixture while the kuzhambu was simmering.

Mango Buttermilk Sambar
Mampazha Morkuzhambu

Mango: 1 large, medium ripe
Buttermilk or yogurt: 2 cups
Coconut: ½ cup, freshly grated
Green chillies: 2
Cumin seeds: ¼ tsp
Coconut oil: 1 tbsp
Rice: 1 tsp for binding, soak in water
Curry leaves: 1 sprig
Rock salt: to taste

Cut mango into large pieces. Grind coconut, green chillies, rice, cumin seeds to a fine paste. Add yogurt or buttermilk and salt and blend together. Heat coconut oil in a pot. Add curry leaves and mangoe pieces. Stir and then add the yogurt mix to it. Heat on low flame until it comes to a boil. Remove from heat and serve as a soup or with along with rice.

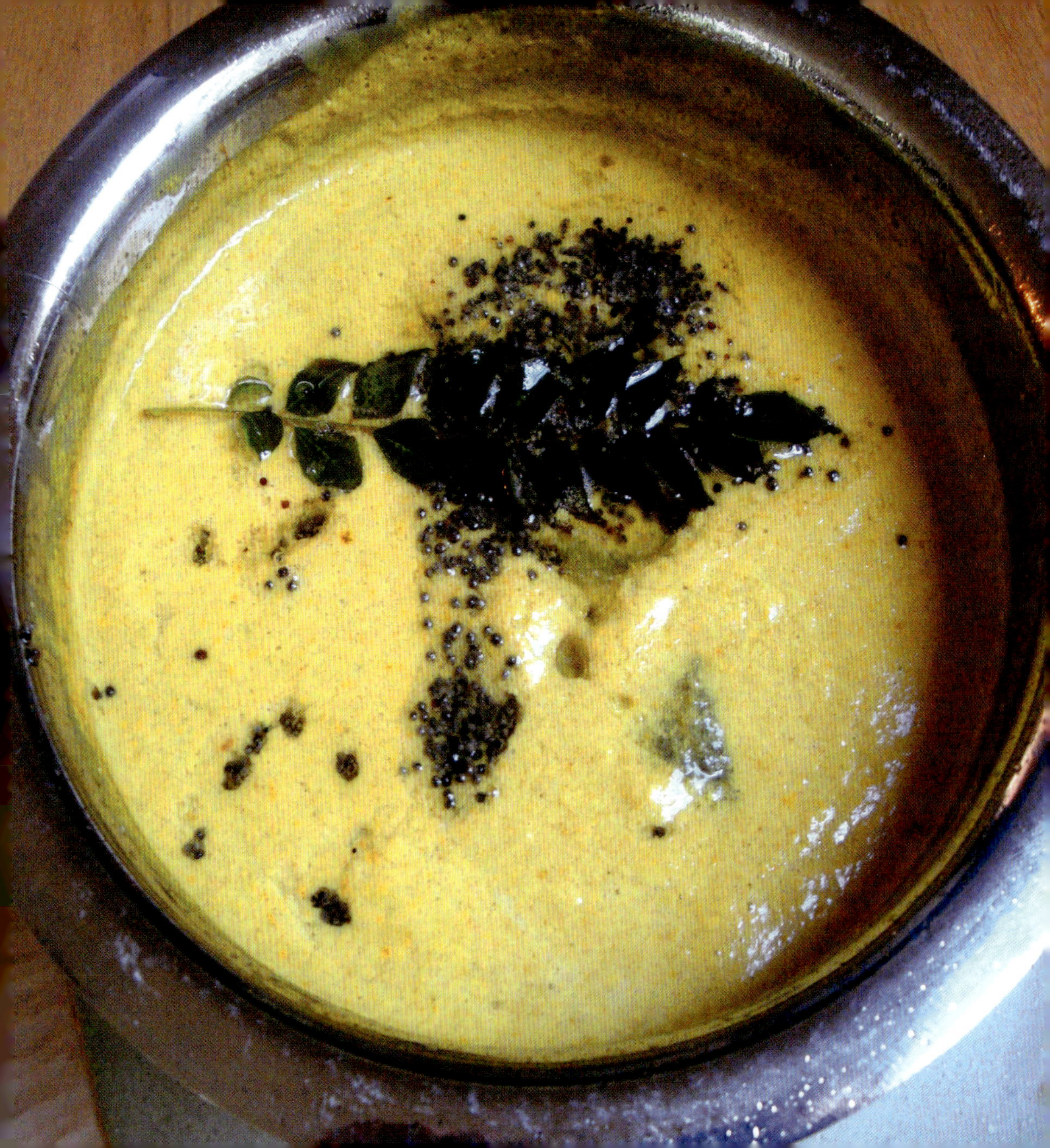

Buttermilk Sambar with Ash Gourd
Morkhuzhambu

Ash gourd: 2 cups, peeled, deseeded and diced
Turmeric: ¼ tsp
Buttermilk: 1 quart, made from yogurt
Coconut: ¼ cup fresh, grated
Green chillies: 2, small (use one if you prefer mild heat)
Bengal gram: 1 tsp soaked for 2 hours
Cumin: ½ tsp
White rice: 1 tsp soaked, for binding
Turmeric: ¼ tsp
Curry leaves: 1 sprig
Rock salt: to taste

Grind coconut, green chillies, Bengal gram, cumin and white rice to a fine paste adding water. Mix in the buttermilk and blend again until all the ingredients mix well together. Set it aside.

In a 2 quart vessel, cook the ash gourd with just enough water and turmeric until it becomes tender. Add the buttermilk mix to it. Bring to a boil and switch off the stove. Overcooking will curdle the buttermilk.

For a variation, you can add coriander seeds and ginger. Fry the coriander seeds and blend the seeds and ginger with the rest of the ingredients and follow the recipe above.

My mother used to add fenugreek seeds. Fry a quarter teaspoon of fenugreek until dark brown and blend with the rest of the ingredients.

This dish is served with various rice recipes such as lemon rice, coconut rice, tamarind rice and plain rice. I also serve it as a soup or with rotis (Indian flat bread).

Rasam

Rasam

Rasam comes from the Sanskrit word *rasa*, meaning juice. In Tamil, the word means "a thin liquid with legumes and herbs". It is like a thin, clear soup. It has never a thick or of creamy consistency. *Rasam* is traditionally eaten with rice as a light second course. For a tablespoon of rice, a cup of *rasam* is added. Some people like more rice with less *rasam*, but it is still taken thin. For most *rasams*, the *rasam* powder is the spice base. South Indian kitchens stock *rasam* powder and *sambar* powder in their pantry, just as north Indians keep curry powder and *garam masala* in their pantry. These are all my family recipes. Most *rasam* recipes are made with lentils or legumes. Wash and soak lentils for several hours first, then replace with fresh water and add turmeric before cooking. Add 3 cups of water to 1 cup of lentils for cooking.

Rasam Powder

Black pepper: ¼ cup
Cumin seeds: ¼ cup
Coriander seeds: 1 cup
Split red gram: ½ cup
Red chilli pepper: 5
Asafoetida: ½ tsp
Turmeric: 1 tbsp
Curry leaves: a handful

Roast split red gram in medium heat until slightly brown and set aside. Roast all the other ingredients slightly, except turmeric. Grind all of the ingredients together to a fine powder and store in an airtight jar.

Black Pepper Rasam
Milagu Rasam

Tamarind: ½ tsp
Tomatoes: 2 medium, chopped fine
Split red gram: 1 tbsp
Black pepper: 1 tsp
Cumin: ½ tsp
Rock salt: to taste
Ghee: 1 tsp
Palm sugar: 1 tsp
Asafoetida: a small piece
Coriander leaves: a small bunch, washed and chopped

Black pepper rasam found its way into Indian restaurants in the West in the form of Mulligatawny soup. This is a rasam made with milagu *(black pepper) and* tanni *(water in Tamil). The British, during their occupation in India, had embraced this dish, giving it the name Mulligatawny soup. Today, restaurants have adopted this wording, having created their own version of the gourmet dish, which is far from authentic.*

Milagu rasam is good for coughs and colds and makes a great soup for winter months. It improves blood circulation and can be taken as an appetizer. It is also given to patients who have fever. Mixed together with a little mashed rice and ghee, it energizes the body and brings down fevers.

Roast lentil, black pepper and asafoetida. Add cumin and fry a little more. Cool and grind the ingredients to a coarse powder, similar to cream of wheat. Set aside. In a 2 quart pot, add ghee and pop the mustard seeds, add 1 quart of water. Stir in the tamarind paste, salt and tomatoes. Bring to a boil. After a couple of minutes, reduce heat and add palm sugar and the ground-up mix. Simmer for 3 minutes. Remove from heat, garnish with coriander leaves. Drink it as a soup or eat it with rice and ghee.

Split Red Gram Rasam
Paruppu Rasam / Thakkali Rasam

Split red gram: ½ cup, cooked in 1½ cups water
Tamarind: ¾ tsp
Rasam powder: 1 tsp
Asafoetida: a small piece
Tomato: 2 medium
Rock salt: to taste
Palm sugar: ½ tsp
Ghee: 1 tsp
Mustard seeds: ¼ tsp
Coriander leaves: a handful, washed and chopped

Sometimes this rasam is called thakkali rasam because tomatoes are added as well. This is a favorite rasam of the south and is served almost daily.

In a 2 quart pot, heat ghee, pop the mustard seeds and add asafoetida. Add 1 quart of water, tamarind, rasam powder, tomato, palm sugar and salt. Bring to a boil, reduce heat and simmer for 5 minutes. Add the cooked red gram. Add a little more water to get a thin consistency. Simmer for 2 minutes. Remove from heat and garnish with coriander leaves.

Long Pepper Rasam
Kandathipli Rasam

Tamarind: 1 tsp
Split red gram: 2 tbsp
Black pepper: 1 tsp
Long pepper: 5 pieces
Long pepper stems: 1 tbsp
Cumin: ½ tsp
Asafoetida: 1 small piece
Palm sugar: 1 tbsp
Rock salt: to taste
Mustard: ¼ tsp
Curry leaves: 2 sprigs
Ghee: 1 tsp

Kandathipli rasam was eaten regularly in my home. It is a nutritious, medicinal rasam. It relieves fever, flatulence, indigestion, constipation and stomach problems. Usually, it is eaten after a fast or after detoxifying the body with triphala decoction.

Roast red gram, black pepper, long pepper and long pepper stems until the red grams are golden brown. Add asafoetida and cumin, stir once and remove from heat. Grind the ingredients and set aside.

In a 2 quart pot, heat ghee. Pop mustard seeds and add curry leaves. Add 1 quart of water. Stir in salt and tamarind. Bring to a boil. Add palm sugar and the ground mixture. Stir well and simmer for 3 minutes.

Cumin Rasam
Jeera Rasam

Tamarind: 1 tsp
Split red gram: 2 tbsp
Red chillies: 2 medium
Cumin seeds: 2 tsp
Rock salt: to taste
Asafoetida: a small piece
Ghee: 1 tsp
Mustard: ½ tsp
Palm sugar: 1 tsp
Curry leaves: 2 sprigs
Coriander leaves: a handful, chopped

The divine jeera rasam is another traditional favorite. It goes down easily and prevents dyspepsia. It also relieves cough and cold and is beneficial for liver disorders.

Soak red gram, cumin and asafoetida for an hour. Grind to a fine paste along with curry leaves and red chillies.

Heat ghee in a 2 quart pot and pop the mustard seeds. Add 1 quart of water and the ground paste. Add palm sugar and salt. Bring to a boil, reduce heat and simmer for 2 minutes. Remove from heat and garnish with coriander leaves.

Lemon Rasam
Elimichampazham Rasam

Tomatoes: 2, cut into small pieces
Split red gram: ½ cup washed and cooked with ¼ tsp turmeric
Black pepper: 1 tsp
Cumin: 1 tsp
Asafoetida: a small piece
Ghee: 1 tsp
Mustard: ½ tsp
Coriander leaves: a handful, shopped
Lemon: 1 or 2, depending on the size of the lemon

My father-in-law took this rasam every day for his diabetes. He controlled the diabetes strictly with his diet. Lemon rasam is mild and is a good choice as an appetizer. It can be eaten with rice.

In a 2 quart pot, add 1 quart of water, tomatoes, salt and asafoetida. Bring to a boil and simmer until the tomatoes are cooked. Puree the cooked red gram and stir them together with other ingredients. Grind black pepper and cumin coarsely and set aside. In a sauté pan, heat ghee and pop the mustard seeds. Then, add the ground black pepper and cumin. Stir for few seconds, then add to the tomatoes and lentils and mix. Bring to a boil and remove from heat.

Garnish with coriander leaves.

Now, add the lemon juice to the rasam. Stir until mixed together.

Lemon Rasam with Ginger

It is stomachic and controls flatulence.

Cook split mung beans in 2 cups of water with ¼ teaspoon turmeric. In a 2 quart pot, add 1 quart water, tomatoes, *rasam* powder, salt and asafoetida. Bring to a boil and simmer until the tomatoes are cooked. Puree the cooked mung and stir them. Heat ghee in a sauté pan and pop the mustard seeds. Add cumin, ginger and green chilli. Sauté for a few seconds and add it to the *rasam*. Stir, bring to a boil, and remove from heat. Add lemon juice and coriander leaves.

Split mung beans: ½ cup
Tomatoes: 2 medium size, chopped fine
Rasam powder: 1 tsp
Asafoetida: a small piece
Ginger: 2-inch cube peeled and chopped
Green chilli: 1 chopped
Mustard: ½ tsp
Cumin: ½ tsp
Ghee: 1 tsp
Rock salt: to taste
Lemon: 1 large or 2 small
Coriander leaves: a handful, washed and chopped

Neem Flower Rasam
Vepampoo Rasam

Neem flowers are an integral part of Ayurvedic medicine. They boost immunity, purify the blood, remove intestinal worms and are full of antioxidants. They are also cooling to the body.

There are many different recipes for this rasam. Here is a traditional recipe that my grandmother very proudly made.

In a 2 quart pot, add ghee and sputter the mustard seeds. Add red chillies, asafoetida and curry leaves. Add a quart of water, tamarind, salt, palm sugar and the soaked red gram. Bring to a boil. Reduce and simmer in low heat for 5 minutes. Remove from heat and add the fried neem flowers. Eat it with rice and ghee in a soup-like consistency. Enjoy!

Split red gram: 2 tsp soaked for an hour
Tamarind: a ball the size of a small lemon
Red chillies: 4 to 6
Asafoetida: a small piece
Palm sugar: 1 tbsp
Rock salt: to taste
Curry leaves: 2 sprigs
Neem flower: ¼ cup fried in ghee or sesame oil until dark brown

Kosamalli Salad

Pachidis & Kosamalli Salads

Pachidi, as it is called in Tamil, is a wholesome and delightful accompaniment to meals often made from raw ingredients. Traditional recipes include a combination of yogurt, lemon, tamarind, palm sugar or jaggery. A typical *pachidi* is yogurt-based, with finely chopped or grated cucumber. Some people add carrots and onions. *Pachidi* dressing consists of mustard seeds, curry leaves, asafoetida, green chilies and ginger sautéed and added to the yogurt with chopped cucumber or tomatoes.

Tomato Pachidi
Thakkali Pachidi

Yogurt: 1 cup
Tomatoes: 3
Green chillies: 2
Asafoetida: 2–3 pinches
Mustard seeds: ½ tsp
Curry leaves: a sprig
Ginger: a small piece, minced
Sesame oil: 1 teaspoon
Rock salt: to taste

Chop tomatoes and chillies into small pieces. In a wok, heat sesame oil, sputter the mustard seeds and add curry leaves, tomato, green chili, ginger and asafoetida. Sauté until the tomatoes are cooked. Add salt. Remove from heat. After it cools, add yogurt and coriander leaves.

Cucumber Pachidi
Velricai Pachidi

Yogurt: 1 cup
Cucumber: 1
Green chillies: 2
Asafoetida: 2 or 3 pinch
Mustard seeds: ½ tsp
Curry leaves: a sprig
Ginger: a small piece
Sesame oil: 1 tsp
Rock salt: to taste

Chop or grate the cucumber, drain the liquid into a pan and drink it or use it later as a face wash. Chop chillies into small pieces and mince ginger. In a wok, heat sesame oil, sputter the mustard seeds and add curry leaves, green chillies, ginger and asafoetida. Sauté. When it cools, add cucumber and thick yogurt. Garnish with coriander leaves. Add salt to taste.

Gooseberry Pachidi
Nellikai Pachidi

Gooseberry: ½ cup
Coconut: 2 tbps, grated
Green chilli: 1 medium
Fresh yogurt: 2 cups
Mustard seeds: ¼ tsp
Curry leaves: 1 sprig
Sesame oil: 1 tsp
Asafoetida: ⅛ tsp

As prepared by my grandma:

Chop and de-seed the gooseberries. Mince the green chillies. Grind the gooseberry and coconut together to form a semi-smooth consistency. Place in a bowl and add green chillies, rock salt and yogurt. Heat sesame oil. Add mustard seeds and as they pop, add curry leaves and asafoetida. Combine with others. Stir and serve.

Stone Apple Pachidi
Vilampazham Pachidi

Vilampazham: 1 big, ripe
Jaggery: ½ cup
Rock salt: ¼ tsp
Mustard seeds: ½ tsp
Green chilli: 2, chopped

Break the fruit open, scoop out the pulp and remove the seeds. Add jaggery and salt and blend to form a jam-like consistency. Heat sesame oil, sputter mustard seeds, add green chillies and garnish the *pachidi*. This rare preparation was eaten to support longevity, because the stone apple takes center stage as a *rasayana* fruit!

Mango Pachidi
Mampazha Pachidi

Tamarind: ½ tsp
Mango: 1 large, ripe
Sambar powder: ½ tsp
Green chilli: 2, chopped
Ginger: 1 inch cube
Asafoetida: ¼ tsp
Fenugreek: ¼ tsp
Curry leaves: 1 sprig
Sesame oil: 1 tbsp
Mustard seeds: ½ tsp

Grandma's favorite.

Dry fry fenugreek to dark brown, grind and set aside. Chop ginger into small pieces. Peel and cut mango into medium-sized pieces. Heat oil in a wok. Add mustard seeds. While they are sputtering, add curry leaves. Add 1 cup of water and tamarind. Bring to a boil and heat for a minute. Add the rest of the ingredients and fenugreek. Sauté until it forms a chutney-like consistency. Season with rock salt to taste.

Kosamalli Salad
Kosamalli

In a traditional south Indian meal, a salad (kosamalli in Tamil) is not served separately at the beginning, but simply as one of several vegetable side dishes. The difference is that the legume used is not cooked, though it may be tempered with mustard seeds or other dressing.

In a classic kosamalli served during weddings, sprouts are combined with chopped cucumber or carrots, lemon juice and rock salt. For this salad, the usual garnish of mustard seeds and asafoetida is used. Kosamalli can be made with arugula, dandelion, onions, tomatoes, cauliflower, broccoli, carrots, bell peppers, sprouted pulses or fruits.

Carrot Cucumber Kosamalli Salad

Split mung: 1 cup
Carrot/ cucumber: 2 cups
Rock salt: to taste
Lemon: 1 juiced
Green Chillies: 2 chopped
Mustard seeds: ½ tsp
Coriander leaves: handful
Asafoetida: 2 pinches
Sesame oil: 1 tsp
Ginger: 1-cube inch

Soak mung beans for 3 hours and then drain the water. Chop or grate carrot or cucumber. Chop ginger into small pieces. In a bowl, mix mung, carrot or cucumber, lemon juice and salt. Heat oil and pop the mustard seeds. To this, add green chillies, ginger and asafoetida. Stir and add to the mung mixture, stir again and serve. Garnish with chopped coriander.

Banana Stem Kosamalli
Vazhai Thandu Kosamalli

Banana stem: 6-inch piece, outer layers removed
Rock salt: to taste
Juice of 1 lemon

Finely chop the banana stalk. Add salt and lemon juice. Mix it well and serve. For a variation, instead of lemon juice, add yogurt and sputter mustard seeds. Soaked split mung can also be added.

Side Dishes

Apart from *pachidis* and salads, a wide variety of cooked side dishes accompany the main entree. Vegetables prepared dry are commonly called *kari* in Tamil. When they are prepared in a gravy, they are called *kootu*. *Usili* is a crumbly sauteed lentil that adds protein and body to an otherwise lightweight vegetable dish. *Thugayal* is a thick preparation that is similar in consistency to hummus. *Keerai* is any kind of greens. *Vadai* is a deep-fried fritter made of lentils and greens.

Black Nightshade Greens
Manathakali Keerai

For stomach ulcers and ailments.

Greens: 1 lb., cut
Onion: 1 medium
Garlic: 6 cloves
Ginger: 1-inch cube, minced
Tomato: 2 medium
Cumin seeds: ½ tsp
Ghee: 2 tsp
Rock salt: to taste

Heat 1 teaspoon of ghee in a wok and sauté chopped onion, garlic and ginger. Add the greens and tomato. Add salt, cover and cook until the greens are soft. Cool and blend. Remove to a serving pot. Heat one teaspoon ghee, pop the cumin seeds and pour it on the greens. Serve with rice. For throat infection and soreness, sauté *manathakali* greens in ghee and eat them slowly, chewing well.

Lentil Usili
Paruppu Usili

Red gram: 1 cup
Bengal gram: ½ cup
Red chillies: 3 medium
Asafoetida: ¼ tsp
Rock salt: to taste
Turmeric: ½ tsp
Mustard seeds: 1 tsp
Sesame oil: 2 tbsp

Wash and soak the legumes for 2 hours. Grind all ingredients except mustard until coarse; adding just enough water and mix to create a batter. Add sesame oil to a wok and pop mustard seeds. Next, add the batter and stir; cook covered. Turn every few minutes until it looks golden and crispy. Add extra oil if needed. Some cooks steam the batter in an *idli* pot first. If you use this method, remove from steam, cool and use a fork to break it into small chunks. Follow the recipe above to sauté.

Banana Flower Usili
Vazhai Poo Usili

Banana flower spike: 1 big
Split red gram: ½ cup, soaked
Onion: 1 medium, chopped
Green chilli: 1 or 2, chopped
Garlic: 8 cloves
Turmeric: ¼ tsp
Red chilli: 1
Rock salt: to taste
Sesame oil: 2 tbsp
Curry leaves: a handful
Mustard seeds: 1 tsp

This usili is said to relieve body aches.

Soak peas for an hour. Preparing the banana flowers takes time. As you remove each large purple bract, you will find a row of small flowers curved like a hand. From each little flower, remove and discard the spoon-shaped cover and stamen. As you get close to the center of the flower spike, the flowers become tiny and you need not remove the stamens. Chop the flowers fine and set aside. Coarsely grind all of the ingredients except the banana flower. In a wok, heat the oil. Sputter mustard seeds. Add the blended mix and the chopped flowers. Sauté and cook covered at medium heat for 5 minutes. Remove the lid and cook further until it gets a bit crispy. *Note:* The traditional recipe does not include onion or garlic.

Banana Stem Kari
Vazhai Thandu Kari

Banana stem: 8-inch piece
Coconut oil: 1 tsp
Mustard seeds: ¼ tsp
Split black gram: 1 tsp
Curry leaves: a few

Removes intestinal worms.

Remove the outer layers of the banana stem and chop into small pieces. Heat oil in a wok. Sputter the mustard seeds. Add black gram, chillies and curry leaves. Add chopped banana stem and sauté until cooked. Use rock salt to taste.

Plantain Kari
Vazhakai Kari

Plantain: 2, peeled & diced
Coconut oil: 1 tbsp
Asafoetida: a pinch
Turmeric: a pinch
Red chilli powder: a pinch

A dish full of minerals and iron, it can be made from raw banana/plantain.

Heat coconut oil in a wok. Add the diced plantain. Sauté for 5 minutes and cover it until cooked. Add the remaining ingredients and sauté briefly, uncovered. Use rock salt to taste.

Snake Gourd Kari
Podlankai Kari

Snake gourd: 2 cups, diced
Cumin: ¼ tsp
Curry leaf: 1 sprig
Green chilli: 1 chopped

Heat 1 teaspoon of ghee or sesame oil, sputter the cumin and curry leaves. Add snake gourd and green chilli and sauté until soft. Instead of cumin, one can also sputter mustard seeds and brown split black beans before adding the snake gourd. It gives a different taste.

Brinjal Kari
Kathrikai Kari

Brinjal: 4 cups, diced, small, round Indian brinjal
Bengal gram: 2 tbsp
Coriander seeds: 2 tbsp
Red chillies: 2 medium
Asafoetida: ⅛ tsp
Mustard seeds: 1 tsp
Sesame oil: 2 tbsp

Roast the Bengal gram until it is golden brown. Add coriander seeds, red chillies and fry a little longer until the coriander turns slightly brown. Grind these into a semi-coarse powder and set aside. In a wok, add the oil and heat. Sputter the mustard seeds and add the chopped brinjal. Add salt and stir fry, covering it once in a while. Once it is soft and cooked, add the ground powder and mix it well. Serve hot.

Jackfruit Kari
Palaakai Kari

Tomatoes: 2
Green chillies: 1 or 2
Cumin: 1 tsp
Turmeric: ½ tsp
Ghee: 1 tbsp
Coconut: ½ cup, grated
Curry leaves: a few
Asafoetida: a few pinches

Clean the jackfruit, remove the hard outer skin and cut the vegetable to 1 inch pieces. Steam them and set aside. The skin is hard to remove. Wear gloves or use coconut oil, as the milk that comes out of the skin is like glue and can be difficult to clean. Heat ghee and add the cumin. When it is browned, add all of the ingredients except coconut. Stir and cook covered at medium heat for 3 minutes. Remove the lid and stir again. Garnish with fresh coconut.

Brinjal Kari

Broad Beans Kari
Avaraikai Kari

Broad beans: 1 lb.
Split black gram: 1 tsp
Mustard: ½ tsp
Red chillies: 2
Asafoetida: a small piece, ground
Sesame oil: 1 tsp
Curry leaves: a sprig

Wash broad beans, remove ends and cut into small pieces. Steam the beans until tender and set aside. In a wok, heat the oil and sputter mustard seeds. Add black gram, red chillies and asafoetida. Once the black gram turns golden brown, add curry leaves and then the steamed beans. Add rock salt to taste. Mix well and remove from heat. This is a basic recipe that can be used for various types of beans. You can add fresh grated coconut as a garnish or stir in some roasted ground Bengal gram and coriander powder.

String Beans Kari
Beans Kari

String beans: 1 lb., destringed
Ghee: 1 tsp
Cumin: ½ tsp

Boil a pound of beans in water for 2 minutes. Drain and set aside. Heat ghee in a wok and brown the cumin seeds. Add the beans and sauté briskly for a minute. Add rock salt to taste. One can also add turmeric powder and red chilli powder for taste.

Sautéed Bitter Gourd Kari
Pavakai Kari

Bitter gourd: 4
Sesame oil: 2 tbsp
Coriander seeds: 2tsp
Bengal gram: 1 tbsp
Tamarind extract: ½ tsp
Asafoetida: a few pinches
Palm sugar: 1 tsp
Turmeric: ¼ tsp
Red chillies: ¼ tsp

Good for diabetics, it balances sugar in the body.

Cut the gourd into thin slices and mix with the turmeric, tamarind, sugar, red chillies and salt. Heat the oil in a wok. Add the bitter gourd pieces and stir. Cook covered for 5 minutes, sprinkling water into it as needed. Remove the cover and sauté until well done. Roast Bengal gram and coriander. Grind until just coarse and add to the gourd. Stir well and remove from heat. Enjoy with rice, millet, or flat bread (*rotis*).

String Beans Kari

Colocasia Kari
Sepakazhangu Kari

Colocasia: 1 lb.
Carom: ¼ tsp
Mustard seeds: ½ tsp
Turmeric: ⅛ tsp
Asafoetida: a pinch
Sambar powder: 1 tsp or red chilli powder ¼ tsp
Rock salt: to taste
Sesame oil: 1 tbsp

Steam colocasia until tender and remove the skin. Dice and set aside. Heat oil in a wok, sputter mustard and add carom. Let it brown. Add asafoetida and turmeric. Add the colocasia pieces, mix well and cook for a couple of minutes. Add salt and *sambar* powder; stir and roast. This makes a delicious side dish or snack.

Ash Gourd Kootu
Pooshnikai Kootu

Ash gourd: 2 lbs.
Mung beans: ½ cup
Bengal gram: 1 tbsp
Coconut: ½ cup grated
Cumin seeds: 1 tsp
Green chillies: 1 or 2
Split black gram: 1 tsp
Mustard seeds; ½ tsp
Rock salt: to taste
Turmeric powder: ¼ tsp
Curry leaves: 1 sprig
Coconut oil: 1 tbsp

Peel and dice ash gourd. In a 3 quart pan, cook Bengal gram and mung in 2 cups of water. Add the ash gourd, salt, turmeric and cook further.

Grind the coconut, cumin and green chillies to a fine paste and add this to the ash gourd. Stir and bring to a boil. Remove from heat.

Heat coconut oil in sputter pan and sputter mustard seeds, add black gram and sauté until it turns golden brown. Add the curry leaves, sauté and stir it in with the ash gourd.

Snake Gourd Kootu
Podlankai Kootu

Snake gourd: 1 lb.
Coconut: ¼ cup
Rock salt: to taste
Split black gram: 1 tsp
Black pepper: ¼ tsp
Red chilli: 1
Asafoetida: 1 pinch
Split mung: ½ cup
Coconut oil: 1 tsp
Mustard seeds: ¼ tsp
Curry leaves: a few

Cook mung and snake gourd together. Heat oil, add half the black gram, black pepper, red chilli and asafoetida and fry them until the black gram is golden. Grind them all with coconut. Add this to the cooked mung and gourd. Add salt and bring to a boil. Sputter mustard, the rest of the black gram and curry leaves in oil and season.

Seven Vegetable Kootu
Ezhukari Kootu

Vegetables: 1 cup each of pumpkin, ash gourd, fava/lima, plantain, sweet potato, broad beans and drumstick
Split red gram: ½ cup
Tamarind: 1 tbsp
Green chillies: 2 or 3
Red chillies: 4 to 6
Coriander seeds: ¼ cup
Bengal gram: 2 tbsp
Grated coconut: 1 cup
Coconut oil: 1 tbsp
Mustard seeds: 1 tsp
Turmeric: ½ tsp
Asafoetida: ½ tsp
Curry leaves: 2 sprigs
Rock salt: to taste

Wash and dice the vegetables, first peeling the banana, ash gourd and pumpkin. Colacasia should be boiled separately like potato and peeled. Wash and cook the red gram with 3 cups of water and turmeric. Set aside.

Fry Bengal gram until slightly brown, add coriander seeds and red chillies, and fry further for a minute in low heat. Fry coconut until golden brown. Grind these with green chillies and water into a paste.

In a large pot, add the cut vegetables, enough water to cover the vegetables, turmeric and salt and cook until the vegetables are half done. Add the tamarind pulp and asafoetida. Simmer until the vegetables are cooked. Add cooked red gram and stir. Add the ground paste to the vegetables and stir until you have a stew consistency. Heat coconut oil in a pan and sputter the mustard seeds, add the curry leaves and season.

Note about tamarind: 1 tablespoon of the concentrate or fresh tamarind the size of a tennis ball, soaked in water and strained to a thick pulp.

Mixed Vegetable Kootu
Aviyal

Vegetables: 1 cup each of pumpkin, ash gourd, lima, plantain, carrots, drumstick, and beans
Coconut: ½ cup, grated
Cumin: ½ tsp
Green chillies: 2 or 3
Rock salt: to taste
Yogurt: 2 cups
Coconut oil: 1 tbsp
Curry leaves: 2 sprigs
Turmeric: ¼ tsp

Aviyal is similar in consistency to a kootu and can be eaten with rice, whole grain bread or adai. It is considered a gourmet dish.

Wash pumpkin, ash gourd, lima and plantain; peel and cut into 2 inch cubes and set aside. Carrots, drumstick and beans can be cut to 2 inch length. Grind coconut, cumin and green chillies to a fine paste and set aside. Steam or cook the vegetables in a little water with turmeric. Add the ground coconut mix and salt. Stir and simmer for a few minutes. Remove from stove, add yogurt and gently mix. Heat coconut oil, sauté the curry leaves and garnish the *aviyal*.

Lime Leaf and Curry Leaf Mix
Veppalai Katti

Curry leaves: 2 cups
Lime leaves: 2 cups
Red chillies: 3 medium
Asafoetida: 1 small piece
Tamarind: ½ tsp
Dates: 3, pitted
Sesame oil: 2 tbsp
Mustard seeds: ½ tsp
Rock salt: to taste

Veppalai means neem leaves, but, since neem is so bitter, this dish is always made with lime leaves and curry leaves for common use in the kitchen. In Ayurveda, the ancient recipe is still followed and only neem is used and a small ball is consumed every day to balance the doshas and keep the heart healthy. However, lime leaf and curry leaf are full of vitamin C, antioxidants and sugar balancing agents.

Heat the oil in a wok. Add mustard seeds. While it is popping, add asafoetida and red chillies. Sauté for a few seconds, and add the curry and lime leaves. Stir at medium heat for a couple of minutes. Cool. In a grinder, grind the leaves with salt, tamarind and dates to a coarse, thick consistency. Remove to a container. Eat with rice or your grain of choice, and ghee or use as a spread in sandwiches with cucumber and tomatoes.

Curry Leaf Chutney
Karuvapilai Thugayal

Curry leaves: 2 cups
Black pepper: ½ tsp
Tamarind: ¼ tsp
Palm sugar: 1 tsp
Cumin seeds: ¼ tsp
Black gram split: 2 tsp
Rice: ½ tsp

Roast black pepper, cumin seeds, black gram and rice until the black gram turns golden. Grind this with all the other ingredients to a coarse consistency. Remove to a serving bowl and garnish with raw sesame oil or olive oil. Season with rock salt to taste. This can be used as a spread in sandwiches or with pita bread or eaten with rice or milllets.

Edible Stemmed Vine Chutney
Perendai Thugayal

Edible stemmed vine: 2 cups
Tamarind: ½ tsp
Split black gram: 2 tsp
Chilli pepper: 2 medium
Asafoetida: 1 small piece
Rock salt: to taste
Sesame oil: 1 tsp
Mustard: ½ tsp
Curry leaves: 1 sprig

Wash and chop edible stemmed vine. Roast black gram, chilli pepper and asafoetida. Set it aside. In a wok, add the oil. Pop mustard seeds, add *perendai* and sauté for several minutes along with curry leaves. Blend all the ingredients to a chutney consistency.

Can be used as spread for sandwiches or eaten with millets or with rice and ghee.

Brinjal Chutney
Kathrikai Thugayal

Brinjal: 1 large
Split black gram: 2 tsp
Tamarind paste: ½ tsp
Palm sugar: 1 tsp
Sesame oil: 1 tsp
Asafoetida: ¼ tsp

Bake, peel and mash the brinjal. Roast black gram until golden brown, add asafoetida. Grind to a coarse consistency. In a blender, mix the black gram powder, palm sugar, brinjal and salt. Remove to a serving bowl. Add a teaspoon of sesame oil on top.

Coconut Chutney
Thengai Thugayal

Coconut: 2 cups grated
Bengal gram: 2 tbsp
Asafoetida: a small piece
Green chillies: 3
Ginger: 1 small piece, cut
Rock salt: to taste
Mustard seeds: ½ tsp
Curry leaves: 1 sprig
Coconut oil: 1 tbsp

Dry fry Bengal gram until golden brown and add asafoetida. Grind coconut, green chillies, ginger, asafoetida and Bengal gram until it is the consistency of chutney, adding a little water to further the process. Heat oil in a sputter pan and pop the mustard seeds. Add curry leaves and garnish the chutney.

This can be eaten with *idli*, *dosai*, sandwiches and with savory snacks.

Tamarind Mint Chutney
Podina Thugayal

Tamarind: ¼ tsp paste
Mint leaves: 2 cups
Cumin: ¼ tsp
Dates: 4, pitted
Red or green chillies: 2
Rock salt: to taste
Asafoetida: 2 pinches
Sesame oil: 1 tbsp

In a blender, grind all the ingredients together to a smooth consistency. Coriander leaves can be substituted for mint. This chutney can be used in sandwiches or as a dip for pita bread or chips.

Bermuda Grass Fritters
Arugampul Vadai

Bengal gram: ½ cup
Black gram split: ½ cup
Bermuda grass: 1 cup, chopped
Red or green chillies: 2
Asafoetida: ¼ tsp
Carom: 1 tsp
Rock salt: to taste
Sesame/coconut oil: 2 cups

Bermuda grass or arugampul makes for a healthy vadai, even though it is deep fried. It contains protein, vitamins and minerals along with antioxidants.

Soak Bengal gram and black gram for 2 hours. Grind coarsely into a thick paste. Add bermuda grass, red or green chillies, asafoetida, carom and salt. Mix them together.

Heat oil in a wok. Make donut-shaped patties about 2 inches round and deep fry until it is golden brown. Serve hot.

Ginger Pickle
Inji Urugai

Ginger: ½ cup, peeled and cut
Rock salt: to taste
Juice of ½ lemon

Ginger pickle promotes digestion. Eat it fresh with yogurt rice.

Peel and cut the ginger into tiny pieces. Add rock salt and lemon juice. Shake and store in a glass container. If you like it spicy, add 3 chopped green chillies to the mix.

Postpartum Recipes

In traditional Indian families, when a woman delivered a baby, she followed a strict diet for 35 days. This is an important time for the growth of the baby, building immunity and strengthening the organs. For the mother, it is an important time to strengthen and promote overall good health. Certain foods used to be taboo at this time, like potatoes that could cause gas or red chillies because they are heat producing. Sour items, such as grapes and sour yogurt, were forbidden. If a lactating mother ate potatoes, the breast milk could give the baby colic. Split red gram and Bengal gram, being *vata* foods, were also not eaten as they promote flatulence.

The recipes detailed here are for drinks and foods that help new mothers produce healthy milk for the baby, rejuvenate the body by purifying the blood and provide nutrients to all parts of the body. The following recipes are mostly prepared for lactating mothers, but they can also be followed by people with digestive problems and as a rejuvenator or simply eaten as a gourmet dish.

Dried Ginger Tea

Dried ginger helps prevent coughs and colds.

Boil a piece of dry ginger in water and drink this tea with honey or palm sugar.

Dried Black Nightshade

Good for ulcers and wound healing.

Fry a tablespoon of dried black nightshade berries in ghee until it turns dark brown. Eat it with whole grain, rice or salad. It is an acquired taste, but the dish is very healthy.

Barley Water

Barley water flushes all toxins from the body. It is diuretic. New mothers should drink barley water once a week.

Boil a tablespoon of barley in 2 quarts of water, simmer for 30 minutes and let it stand for an hour. Strain and drink the water.

Betel Leaf Juice

Betel leaves are rich in calcium and help the digestion. The juice of the betel leaf is given as a tonic. The leaves are also chewed every day after the meal.

Garlic Milk

Garlic milk can be taken daily to improve the production of breast milk.

In a 1 quart pot, heat a ½ teaspoon of ghee and add 4-6 cloves of grated garlic. Stir for few seconds until slightly cooked. Add a ½ cup of water and cook for a couple more minutes. Add 1 cup of milk and 1 teaspoon of palm sugar (or jaggery) and bring to a boil. Remove from stove. Drink it warm or cold. You can use honey instead of jaggery or palm sugar, but do not heat the honey.

Almond Milk

Almond milk provides nutrition and immunity to the mother while her body heals. It helps brain development and memory in newborns, and builds their immunity through the mother's milk.

Soak one ½ cup of almonds in warm water for few hours. Peel the skin and grind to a fine paste with 1 cup water. Add 1 cup milk and 1 cup additional water. Bring to a boil. Remove from heat. Drink warm or cold with palm sugar or honey.

Coconut Water

Coconut water is good for *pitta* and *vata*. It energizes and rejuvenates the body. Fresh young coconut is preferable. However, bottled coconut water is available in markets and can be used too. Note that coconut is cooling—my mother asked us to avoid this drink as this could cause colds.

Black Pepper Stew
Milagu Kuzhambu

Tamarind: 2 tsp
Carom seeds: 1 tsp
Coriander seeds: 2tsp
Sesame oil: 2 tbsp
Asafoetida: ¼ teaspoon
Black pepper: 2 tsp
Mustard seeds: 1 tsp
Split black gram: 4 tsp
Cumin seeds: 1 tsp
Palm sugar: 1 tbsp
Rock salt: to taste
Turmeric: ½ tsp
Fenugreek: ¼ tsp
Curry leaves: 4 sprigs
Garlic: 30 cloves

The milagu rasam recipe given in the Rasam section is good for new mothers. Another dish my mother prepared for postnatal care was milagu kuzhambu. She would give it to the new mother every other day with rice and ghee. This stew is a blood purifier and increases milk production. It rejuvenates the body and helps control colds.

Roast fenugreek till dark brown and set aside. Roast split black gram until golden and set aside. Roast coriander seeds, carom seeds, black pepper, asafoetida and cumin seeds for a minute in medium heat until golden brown. Blend all these ingredients together to a semi-fine powder.

Heat sesame oil. Pop the mustard seeds and add garlic cloves and curry leaves. Slightly brown the garlic. Add 1 quart of water. Mix in the tamarind paste, jaggery, salt and turmeric. Mix in the blended powder. Bring the mix to boil, reduce heat to low and simmer for 20 minutes.

Garlic Rasam
Poondu Rasam

Garlic: 20 cloves
Split red gram: 1 tbsp
Black pepper: 1 tsp
Tamarind: ¾ tsp
Tomato: 2 medium
Cumin: ½ tsp
Red chilli: 1
Asafoetida: a small piece
Palm sugar: ½ tsp
Mustard seeds: ¼ tsp
Ghee: 1 tsp
Rock salt: to taste
Coriander leaves: handful

Used for blood purification and as a galactagogue.

Roast the red gram, black pepper, red chillies and asafoetida until the red gram turns golden brown. Add cumin and remove from heat. Grind and set aside. Heat ghee in a 2 quart pot and pop the mustard. Sauté the garlic for a minute until tender. Add 1 quart of water, tomato and tamarind. Bring to a boil and simmer for 3 minutes. Add the ground-up powder and simmer for a few minutes. Remove from heat and garnish with coriander leaves.

Herb Mix Powder
Angaya Podi

Sundakkai: 1 cup
Bengal gram: ½ cup
Neem flower: 2 tbsp
Curry leaves: 10 sprigs
Coriander seeds: ½ cup
Cumin: 2 tbsp
Dried ginger: 1-inch piece
Red chillies: 2
Black pepper: 1 tbsp
Asafoetida: ½ inch piece, broken into fine pieces
Sesame oil: to fry
Palm sugar: 1 tsp
Rock salt: to taste

Angaya podi is a powder of mixed herbs with prickly nightshade (sundakkai) that heals and strengthens the stomach and uterus. The name is derived from the word Angam, meaning body. The ingredients in this mix rejuvenate, slim, heal and beautify the body.

Fry the *sundakkai* in sesame oil until it is dark brown. Drain and set aside. Roast the Bengal gram until golden brown and set aside. Roast the neem flowers until dark brown and set aside.

Roast coriander, red chillies, black pepper, dry ginger and asafoetida together until slightly brown, add cumin seeds and sauté a few seconds. Add curry leaves, stir and set aside.

Now, grind all the ingredients together to a semi-fine powder and store in an airtight jar. Use it daily or when needed mixed in with hot millets or rice and ghee.

Cumin Powder with Asafoetida
Jeeraga Podi

Curry leaves: 6 cups, washed and dried
Rock salt: to taste
Tamarind: ½ tsp
Asafoetida: small piece, fried and powdered
Ghee: 1 tbsp
Black pepper: ½ tsp

Cumin seeds are healing. They promote digestion and remove gas build-up in the intestines and stomach.

Roast 1 cup cumin seeds with ½ teaspoon asafoetida. Add a little salt. Grind to a coarse powder and store in a jar. Add this powder to vegetables, legumes and rice with ghee and take at least 1 teaspoon every day. Also see the *Cumin Rasam* recipe in the Rasam section.

Post Delivery Tonic
Pillai Pettha Legiyam

Black pepper: 1 cup
Cumin: ½ cup
Coriander seeds: 1 cup
Dried ginger: ¼ cup
Long pepper: 10 pieces
Cardamom: 10 pods
Jaggery: one 2-inch cube
Ghee: ⅛ cup to ¼ cup

Eat a ½ teaspoon every day in the morning for 45 days. It improves digestion, prevents flatulence and purifies the blood.

In a wok, slow roast at low heat black pepper, cumin, coriander, dry ginger, cardamom and long pepper for 3 minutes. Cool and grind to a semi-fine powder and set aside. In the same wok, put a ½ cup of water and jaggery and heat until the jaggery dissolves. Stir in the powder. Mix it well, reduce heat and stir for 5 minutes. Add ghee a little at a time, mix it well and stir until the paste comes together. Remove from heat and cool. Store in a jar. This mixture should be the consistency of paste. It can be used for 6 months.

Garlic Legiyam
Poondu Legiyam

Carom: 2 tsp, ground
Garlic: 50 cloves
Crushed pepper: 1 tsp
Jaggery: 1 tbsp
Asafoetida: ½ tsp
Ghee: 1 tbsp
Rock salt: to taste

It is a blood purifier. But, it is also very tasty and anyone can eat it.

Heat ghee in a pan. Sauté the garlic until soft in medium heat, stir in the carom powder and asafoetida, and then add the jaggery and salt. Mix and stir at low heat until everything comes together. Serve with rice.

Curry Leaf Mix
Karuvepilai Podi

Curry leaves: 6 cups, washed and dried
Rock salt: to taste
Tamarind: ½ tsp
Asafoetida: ¼ tsp
Ghee: 1 tbsp

Nutritious dish for new mothers. It contains iron, calcium and vitamin C.

Sauté the curry leaves in ghee for 2 minutes. Grind all the ingredients with a little ghee. Do not add water. Remove and serve with rice or millet.

Karthikai Festival Prasad

Homam, Offerings to The Sacred Fire

Bibliography

Rig Veda, 107 Healing Plants Hymn: Mandala 10-97, RV X-97

Ayurveda: *Ancient treaties on herbal medicine*. Dastur, J.F. *Everybody's guide to Ayurvedic Medicine*, D. B. Taraporevala Sons & Co. Pvt. Ltd.. Bombay 1978

Dr. R. Thiyagarajan, L.I.M *Gunapadam*-part 1, 2, and 3 (Siddha medicine in Tamil) Thiru.

K. Shanmugavelan, *Siddha Science of Longevity and Kalpa Medicine* (Available at The Directorate of Indian Medicine and Homoeopathy, Arumbakkam, Chennai India.

Jayaram: *Introduction to Hinduism*. Pure life Vision publication July 2012, ISBN-10: 1935760115, ISBN-13: 9781935760115

Chinmaya Mission Trust, publications@chinmaya.org

Hinduism that is Sanatana Dharma: Published 2000, 2007:

Publisher Central Chinmaya Mission Trust. ISBN 81-7597-065-0, Product code: H0007

Georg Feurstein : *A short History of Yoga*, Infinity Foundation The Yoga Tradition: *Its History, Philosophy and Practice*: ISBN 13-9781890772185; Publisher; Hohm Press 2001, Edition 3

Varadarajan Muthusamy: *Traditions and Rituals*, Wisdom tree October 2007, ISBN-10: 8183280714, ISBN-13: 978-8183280716

D. Balasubramaniam; *In search of Sanjeevani plant of Ramayan*a: The Hindu Newspaper: September 10, 2009

Srimad Valmiki Ramayana, 74th chapter, Yuddakanda, Slokas

Case Adams: *Research finds aloe vera may prevent and treat skin cancer* An article in Greenmedinfo.com December 2012

Hildegard, *Healing plants*: From her Medieval Classic *Physica*, Publisher: Beacon Press 2002, ISBN10: 0807021091

Dr. Paul Connett: *The Case Against Fluoride*, Publisher: Chelsea Green Publishing 2010, ISBN 10-1603582878

Notes

Dr. V.R. Rajagopalan: *Pasteurellosis in white Mice and diseases of the cow*, Indian Science Congress 1939, 1949. My father was an eminent scientist, a bacteriologist and a botanist. He was instrumental in developing the serum to cure Hoof and Mouth and Rinderpest diseases of the cows (p. 11).

Charakha and Sushruta Samhita: Oldest written records on Ayurvedic Medicine. Their scholarly work, and the compilation of several writers is practiced in modern day Ayurvedic treatments (p. 17).

Adiyaman was one of the most powerful Tamil kings of the Sangam era. He is known as one of the seven great patrons and lovers of art and literature in ancient Tamizhagam, meaning Tamil kingdom. He was a patron of the poet Avvaiyar who was also of the Sangam period. He wanted her to stay in his court so he gave her the Indian gooseberry as gift to keep her in good health and prolong her life (p. 89).

Adi Shankaracharya was one of the most revered Hindu philosophers and theologians from India who consolidated the doctrine of *Advaita Vedanta*, where he talks about the unity of atman and Nirguna Brahman, Brahman without attributes (p. 89).

Glossary

Abhishekam: Bathing of Deities in temples.

Abortifacient: Causing abortion.

Adai: Hearty, spiced pancake made of lentils, rice and sometimes vegetables.

Anthelmintic: Destroying parasitic worms.

Appalam: Flat, round fritter which is toasted or fried.

Angaya powder: Herb mix for digestion and rejuvenation.

Avial: Vegetable dish with yogurt and coconut.

Carminative: Relieving flatulence.

Demulcent: Relieving inflammation or irritation.

Dosai: Rice and legume batter made into crepes.

Emmenagogue: Stimulating or increasing menstrual flow.

Endorphin: Any of a group of hormones secreted within the brain and nervous system and having a number of physiological functions. They are peptides that activate the body's opiate receptors, causing an analgesic effect.

Expectorant: Promoting secretion of sputum.

Garam masala: A North Indian curry mix.

Idli: A steamed rice and legume dumpling-like dish.

Kadambam: A potpourri of fragrant flowers.

Kashayam: Infusion or extract from herbs and spices.

Kizhangu: A root vegetable.

Kootu: Vegetable side dish in gravy.

Koozhu: Porridge.

Laddu: An Indian sweet made out of chick pea flour in the shape of a ball.

Legiyam: Herbal medicinal paste.

Manditti: A plant belonging to the family Rubiaceae.

Nevedyam: An offering to God.

Milagai podi: A powder mix to accompany Idli and dosai.

Payasam: Sweet pudding made with rice or other grains or legumes.

Postpartum: Period of time following child birth.

Puranas: History of ancient times.

Rasam: Clear soup.

Rasayana: Acting against the effects of aging and promoting longevity.

Sambar: Spiced lentil and vegetable stew served with rice.

Shraradham: Annual ceremony for the deceased and the ancestors.

Siddhar: One who knows and practices Siddha medicine.

Stomachic: Promoting appetite or helping digestion.

Styptic: Stopping the blood flow when applied to wounds.

Tantric: Mystical practices.

Vadai: A fried fritter with legumes

Vastu Shastra: Science of architecture and building based on astrology and the magnetic field of the earth.

Eternal energy flows,
creating, manifesting, building and rebuilding
in the vastness of the universe.

The earth was chosen for such an event
where flowers could bloom,
little children could dance
and sing and avail
of the bounty
from the eternal flow of energy.

I close my eyes,
drawing in with every breath
the abundant life force
that weaves through us all.

With renewed spirit I envision
we are moving closer towards the light.

JAICO PUBLISHING HOUSE
Elevate Your Life. Transform Your World.

ESTABLISHED IN 1946, Jaico Publishing House is home to world-transforming authors such as Sri Sri Paramahansa Yogananda, Osho, The Dalai Lama, Sri Sri Ravi Shankar, Sadhguru, Robin Sharma, Deepak Chopra, Jack Canfield, Eknath Easwaran, Devdutt Pattanaik, Khushwant Singh, John Maxwell, Brian Tracy and Stephen Hawking.

Our late founder Mr. Jaman Shah first established Jaico as a book distribution company. Sensing that independence was around the corner, he aptly named his company Jaico ('Jai' means victory in Hindi). In order to service the significant demand for affordable books in a developing nation, Mr. Shah initiated Jaico's own publications. Jaico was India's first publisher of paperback books in the English language.

While self-help, religion and philosophy, mind/body/spirit, and business titles form the cornerstone of our non-fiction list, we publish an exciting range of travel, current affairs, biography, and popular science books as well. Our renewed focus on popular fiction is evident in our new titles by a host of fresh young talent from India and abroad. Jaico's recently established Translations Division translates selected English content into nine regional languages.

Jaico's Higher Education Division (HED) is recognized for its student-friendly textbooks in Business Management and Engineering which are in use countrywide.

In addition to being a publisher and distributor of its own titles, Jaico is a major national distributor of books of leading international and Indian publishers. With its headquarters in Mumbai, Jaico has branches and sales offices in Ahmedabad, Bangalore, Bhopal, Bhubaneswar, Chennai, Delhi, Hyderabad, Kolkata and Lucknow.

SINCE 1946